Law and the Media

An everyday guide for professionals

Third Edition

TOM CRONE

Focal Press

Focal Press
An imprint of Butterworth-Heinemann Ltd
Linacre House, Jordan Hill, Oxford OX2 8DP

$\mathcal{R}$ A member of the Reed Elsevier plc group

OXFORD   LONDON   BOSTON
MUNICH   NEW DELHI   SINGAPORE   SYDNEY
TOKYO   TORONTO   WELLINGTON

First published 1989
Second edition 1991
Third edition 1995

British Library Cataloguing in Publication Data
Crone, Tom
  Law and the media: an everyday guide
  for professionals – 3rd ed.
  1. Great Britain. Mass media. Law
  I. Title
  070.026

ISBN 0 7506 2008 0

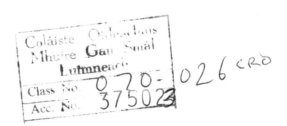
Printed in Great Britain by Clays Ltd, St Ives plc

CONTENTS

ACKNOWLEDGEMENTS

I owe special thanks to F. W. (Freddie) Hodgson, general editor of the media series, both for launching me on this project and encouraging me through it. I would also like to thank Heather Rogers who contributed to the chapters on breach of confidence and copyright. Heather practises at the Bar specializing in libel and media matters. More generally, acknowledgement must go to the friends, colleagues and adversaries who have given me hectic but enjoyable times during the last fifteen years as a media lawyer.

Finally but foremost I thank my wife, Patti, and my sons Rory, Jamie and Jack, for condoning my absence from so many breakfasts while this book was being written. It is dedicated to them.

PREFACE

The 1980s and 1990s will be remembered as the decades in which communications and the media industry were revolutionized. The processing and transmission of information into the homes of ordinary people around the world has become an upto-the-second technology which has given birth to totally new concepts in publishing and reporting.

As we head towards the dawn of a new millennium the rate of technological advance is, if anything, accelerating. While citizens of western cultures grapple to understand the practical implications of 'multimedia' and 'information superhighways', those across broad tracts of Asia and the developing world find themselves suddenly swamped with images of a twentieth century world they hardly knew thanks to satellite airwaves.

While cable and satellite television flourish and computer link-ups allow constant access to both general and specialized news around the world, the old-fashioned medium of newspapers has also undergone a transformation. In the mid-eighties the long overdue introduction of new technology to the process of newspaper production in Britain turned a struggling low-profit industry into a booming business brimming over with opportunity.

The relentless expansion of television and electronic broadcasting may, over the last few years, have taken some of the shine off the long-term future of the print media, but the prospects for the young reporter have never looked better. It is widely predicted that before very long the media will rank among the three largest industries in the world.

However, just as every cloud has a silver lining, the timing of this particular success story was matched perfectly by a disturbing increase in the number and intensity of constraints and dangers which beset the full and free reporting of news and current affairs.

The last ten years has seen a trend towards greater interference in the working of the media from the courts, from the Government and legislators and, at times, from the police. That trend shows few signs of letting up. The rapid development, through the courts, of the law of confidence added greatly to the armoury of those who would apply prior restraints to publications. Dramatic new legislation in the field of copyright, while benefitting the media in some areas, for example the abolition of conversion damages, also created several fresh problems. Further legislation has been passed to widen restrictions upon court reporting and more is threatened in order to introduce a law of privacy.

Perhaps what was most worrying at the end of the 1980s, especially for the small publisher, was the enormously high level of awards in libel cases. Not since William Caxton set up the first printing press had the phrase 'Publish and be damned!' sounded quite so truthful. The dangers of libel have not abated but the realization, brought about by a few high-profile cases, that plaintiffs can lose horrendously, as well as win, has brought some comfort to publishers.

For the young journalist starting a career, there has in recent years been a greater need than ever before to be aware of the framework of laws which impinge on the profession. In ninety-nine out of a hundred cases where the relevant statutory provision or judicial direction is not adhered to it will be no excuse to say you did not know the law.

The purpose of this book, therefore, is to set out in an uncomplicated way the principles upon which every experienced journalist formulates his mental checklist of 'dos and don'ts'. Before embarking on the detailed consideration of each topic, it may be worth giving a brief outline of the changes in some of those areas which most affect the daily working of the media.

Libel is and always has been the legal problem most frequently encountered by the media. Quite rightly, it is a recognized function of the media, both press and broadcasting, to investigate wrongdoing and expose villainy. Society would undoubtedly be the poorer if journalists were to think otherwise.

Between 1987 and 1990, however, there must have been many in the industry who were beginning to wonder whether the risk of losing a libel action was not prohibitively expensive. The trend towards extravagantly high awards started with a little-reported case involving a retired naval commander, Martin Packard, and a Greek newspaper called *Eleftherotypia*. For suggesting that he played a less than honourable role during the regime of the Greek Colonels, a London libel jury awarded him £450,000. This represented about £10,000 for each copy of the journal, which – incidentally is published in the Greek language – sold in Britain.

That award may have been passed unnoticed and not had any marked effect on the minds of future jurors, but it was closely followed, in July 1987, by the case of *Jeffrey Archer v Express Newspapers*. There has rarely in the history of libel actions been greater publicity attaching to a case than there was to that of Mr Archer against *The Star* newspaper. At the end of three weeks the jury awarded him the nicely rounded figure of £500,000 – and this time there was probably not a person in the land who did not know about it.

Not long after Archer's case a former officer of HMS Conqueror won £260,000 from the *Mail on Sunday* although he was not even named in the offending article, and a stationery company was awarded £300,000 against *Stationery Trade News* (circulation 8000) for a suggestion that it sold envelopes under a counterfeited brand name. The nightmare continued with a series of quarter-million pounds plus awards, including £300,000 to Miss Koo Stark for a suggestion in the *Sunday People* that after she married she had 'secret dates' with her former boyfriend, Prince Andrew.

When Sonia Sutcliffe was awarded £600,000 against the satirical magazine, *Private Eye*, in May 1990, there was hardly anyone outside the jury box who did not think it was a ridiculously excessive amount. Certainly, the Court of Appeal did. In the course of overturning the decision, the Appeal Judges ruled that libel judges in future should give juries slightly more guidance in order to avoid excessive awards.

At the end of 1990, Mrs Sutcliffe was back in the libel court, this time against the *News of the World*. After three weeks of highly publicized evidence and argument the jury found for the newspaper. The bruising publicity and £200,000 bill of costs she picked up was likely to deter future libel plaintiffs.

Since 1990, the results of libel cases have certainly been less predictable. In 1991, Janie Allen, a South African journalist lost a sensational case against Channel 4 and picked up a costs bill reputed to be £300,000. Later the same year *Coronation Street* star Bill Roache's failure to beat a protective payment into court of £50,000 made by *The Sun* meant that despite winning the case he ended up sending the newspaper a fat cheque. In January 1994, another television soap star learned the huge risks of libel litigation. Gillian Taylforth of *EastEnders* fame lost a two-week High Court battle, again against *The Sun*, and was faced with financial ruin.

During the same period there have been two awards of £1,500,000: the first to Lord Aldington, who has not seen a penny of it because the defendants (two individuals) simply did not have the money, and the second, during 1994, in favour of a yacht designer and his company after their product was critically reviewed in the magazine *Yachting World*. Although this latter award looks unlikely to survive an appeal, it reminds publishers of the extreme dangers of libel.

In terms of restraint upon a free press, the rapid recent developments in the law governing *breach of confidence* is particularly alarming. While most experienced reporters have always known that injunctions are likely to fly if you make it known that you are about to publish someone's trade secrets or revelations which are in breach of the source's contract of employment, few would have imagined that the legal restrictions in this area would have grown so rapidly.

Throughout 1987 and 1988, the British Government sought to persuade the courts of Britain, Australia, New Zealand and Canada that the media should not be permitted to publish extracts from *Spycatcher*, the memoirs of an ex-MI5 man, because they amounted to a breach of confidence. Meanwhile the book itself was widely available to be read in each of these countries and, of course, almost every other country in the world.

The courts have also ordered that the *News of the World* could not report that there were doctors with AIDS who continued to practise because that information had originally come from medical records. In a number of other cases involving similar facts the court has not only ruled that the story itself should not be published; it has even made stringent secrecy orders concerning the reporting of the case.

The major copyright legislation which passed through Parliament in 1988 is still having a profound impact on the way the media deal with the huge body of freelance reporters and photographers who circulate material throughout the world. Editors and newspaper lawyers will need to watch the developments in this area of law very closely.

Both the independence and the safety of the media were brought sharply into focus by the controversy over the film shot by the BBC and independent television depicting the 1988 murder of two British soldiers in Belfast. The television companies, worried about the security of their staff and about their continuing role as independent news-gatherers in the city, refused to give the film to the police. Special laws applicable to Northern Ireland meant that the police were very quickly able to seize the relevant footage, but the incident raised the important issue of *police powers of search and seizure* and, peripherally, *protection of sources*. There have been a number of instances since the Belfast affair when the police have obtained court orders under the Police and Criminal Evidence Act which compel the media to hand over photographs and footage of riots and violent demonstrations.

Finally, a Law of Privacy has not gone on to the statute books yet, but a large body of opinion (including many in the Government) think it is long overdue. If it comes into being, its effects will be felt acutely in every area of journalism.

It is hoped that this book will go some way to enlightening journalists about these and other areas of law relevant to their work and profession.

1 LIBEL: GENERAL INTRODUCTION

THE PRINCIPLE OF LIBEL

The origins of the laws relating to defamation, of which libel and slander are the twin components, date back as far as King Alfred the Great who, in the ninth century, decreed that slanderers should have their tongues cut out. Although over the years the penalties imposed upon those who transgress this branch of the civil law have become financial rather than physical, the principles have remained virtually unchanged.

Shakespeare's neat summary of those principles in *Othello* has been prayed in aid by many a plaintiff's counsel in libel cases:

Who steals my purse steals trash;
'tis something, nothing; . . .
But he that filches from me my good name
Robs me of that which not enriches him,
and makes me poor indeed.

The legal rationale was expressed less poetically, but with great clarity by Justice Potter Stewart of the American Supreme Court in 1966:

The right of a man to the protection of his own reputation from unjustified invasion and wrongful hurt reflects no more than our basic concept of the essential dignity and worth of every human being – a concept at the root of any decent system of liberty.

LIBEL IN PRACTICE

Talk to the individual whose name has been blackened by a newspaper article and he will tell you that a libel case is a two-year nightmare of massive expense with no prospect of legal aid. The newspaper or television company on the other hand will complain that libel cases are little more than lotteries in which plaintiffs are unduly favoured and damages totally unpredictable. The lawyers who have chosen to specialize in libel would probably agree with both these points of view. If they were being completely frank, however, they would go on to say that, despite their great levels of expertise, the most important quality in any libel litigant is a strong nerve and a deep pocket.

Of all the legal problems which impinge upon the journalist's task of bringing news and information to the public, and there are many, libel is the commonest, and overall the most expensive. The same applies to comment-ators and makers of television documentaries. It follows that any journalist starting out on his career, in whatever medium, is well-advised to learn at an early stage how to recognize stories which are potentially libellous. In fact, it does not require any great amount of special knowledge or skill to identify defamatory statements. Most people know when a statement exposes someone to 'hatred, ridicule or contempt' or lowers him 'in the estimation of right-thinking members of society generally'. The real skill for editors, sub-editors and reporters in relation to libel is in knowing when statements that can be construed in this way may be published with a reasonable degree of safety.

Where an article has been recognized as being defamatory and therefore potentially libellous it normally falls upon one person, usually the editor, to decide whether it should be published. Before reaching that decision he or she is likely in practice to give detailed thought to the following three questions:

- Is the story true?
- Can it be proved to be true? (Or is it covered by one of the other defences to libel?)
- Is the subject of the story likely to sue?

Is the story true?

The editor will consider everything that is known about the story and its subject. That will include on and off the record interviews, information from sources who cannot be publicly identified and an assessment of the personality and previous behaviour of the person being written about. If, having looked at all this material, the editor decides that the story is not true the following two questions are rendered superfluous because the story will be discarded or 'spiked'.

Is it provable?

As far as the law of libel is concerned this is the only question which has any real validity. After all, stories can be true but if the defendant fails to convince the jury of this he or she will lose the case (unless one of the other defences applies). Before an editor can properly answer this question a detailed examination of the *admissible* evidence must take place. Most newspapers, TV stations and publishers have either in-house lawyers or outside legal advice readily available to give an expert opinion on the strength of the evidence. The lawyer will analyse which supporting facts are admissible as evidence and which are not, which of the sources are likely to be useful witnesses and the real legal significance of the matters that are known.

Is the subject going to sue?

As part of the decision-making process surrounding the publication of stories, this question is dangerous in the extreme. Predicting the reaction of persons defamed by television or newspaper reports is a notoriously imprecise science. However, when the answer to the first question above is yes and the answer to the second is no, the likelihood of the relevant person issuing writs is undoubtedly a matter that has to be considered by many editors. A true but unprovable story presents a great temptation to most journalists. Lawyers would, of course, advise that if a potentially dangerous story cannot be proved it should not be published. There are nevertheless times when editors, fortified by their belief in the story's truth and their judgement that no writ will be issued, go ahead and take the risk. In fairness to the rationale behind this practice, experience has shown that certain people are reluctant to run to libel lawyers when they suffer adverse publicity – especially if the publicized matters are true.

There have undoubtedly been cases where a newspaper or other member of the media has published a true story yet lost the resulting libel action. Equally there have been plaintiffs who have sued over untrue stories and emerged from their actions with the right verdict but with an award of derisory damages. In such cases their reputation often suffers greater harm from the libel action than it ever did from the original publication. Their wallets, of course, also take a beating.

LIBEL AND SLANDER

The law recognizes two torts (actionable civil wrongs) which are applicable to the publication of defamatory statements. The more common and more serious is libel. The other, which is sometimes wrongly regarded as of merely academic interest to journalists, is slander.

The primary distinction between the two lies in the way in which the defamatory statement is published. If it is made in writing or some other permanent form, e.g. on a tape recording, the proper course of action is in libel. If, on the other hand the damaging statement is published in a way which is transient, for example simply by word of mouth, the injured party can sue only in slander. Thus, to tell colleagues over lunch that your secretary is a thief would, if untrue, be slanderous. To make the same allegation by way of a statement pinned to the office noticeboard would be actionable as a libel.

Any confusion which may have existed over which of the torts applies to radio and television broadcasts was cleared up by Section 1 of the Defamation Act 1952 which provides that such forms of publication should be regarded as permanent. The appropriate action in such cases is therefore libel. By way of Section 4 of the Theatres Act 1968 libel also applies to defamatory statements made during the public performances of plays.

Actions for slander against newspapers and TV companies are rare. The individual journalist however should always be conscious of the risks he faces in making slanderous statements. This applies particularly to the investigative reporter who is either checking allegations of wrongdoing with third parties or confronting the wrongdoer himself. In either case, if the reporter utters defamatory statements about someone to, or within the hearing of, another person he is liable to be sued for slander.

The main consequence of the distinction between the two forms of action is that in libel the law presumes damage has been suffered and the plaintiff is not required to prove any loss. In slander however the plaintiff will have to satisfy the court that he or she has suffered financial damage arising from the defamatory statement. The exceptions to this rule are slanderous statements which:

1   Impute the commission of a crime punishable by imprisonment.
2   Impute that a person has a contagious or infectious disease.
3   Suggest adultery or unchastity in a woman.
4   Disparage a person in his or her business, calling or profession.

With these four categories of slander the plaintiff will not have to adduce evidence of pecuniary loss.

LIBEL AND MALICIOUS FALSEHOOD

Actions for libel and slander invariably involve statements which are both false and damaging. There is however no truth in the converse. Not every false and damaging statement will enable a person to sue for libel or slander. For such a course of action to arise the plaintiff must be the victim of false words which have a damaging effect on his or her reputation. If those words cause damage but in fact do not have any effect on reputation, e.g. a false assertion that a man has closed down his business, then the person cannot sue in either libel or slander. In such cases the plaintiff may nevertheless have a legal remedy in an action for malicious falsehood.

There are three elements to malicious falsehood. In order to succeed in such an action the plaintiff must establish the following points:

- That the words were false.
- That they were published maliciously, i.e. through spite, dishonesty, (which could include reckless indifference as to the truth), avarice or some other improper motive.
- That they caused the plaintiff financial loss or, in cases where the words are in some permanent form (e.g. writing) or reflect on the plaintiff's office, profession or calling, that they were *likely* to cause financial loss.

In practice, proceedings for malicious falsehood are considerably more difficult for a plaintiff to succeed in than libel or slander. Once a person suing for libel establishes that the words are defamatory (which is usually self-evident) the law will presume that they are false and the defendant is faced with the difficult task of proving their truth. In actions for malicious falsehood the burden is completely reversed – it is for the plaintiff to establish both the falseness of the words and the malice of the defendant. He or she will, of course, also have to show they have lost, or were likely to lose, financially because of the defendant's statement.

While libel and slander actions are invariably decided by a court consisting of a judge and jury, proceedings for malicious falsehood are heard by a judge sitting alone. Who is more likely to benefit by jury trial, i.e. plaintiff or defendant, is perhaps debatable but the weight of opinion among practitioners in the field of libel law favours the view that plaintiffs, if they have the choice, should always opt for trial by jury.

If the burden of proof and mode of trial are perceived as disadvantages for the plaintiff, they are more than balanced by the fact that those who sue for malicious falsehood as opposed to defamation are eligible for legal aid. The two causes of action, moreover, are not always separate and exclusive. There will be occasions when a false statement is both a libel and a malicious falsehood.

In the cases where such an overlap exists the plaintiff who could not normally afford to sue in libel can apply for legal aid to bring his or her action in malicious falsehood.

This window of opportunity for plaintiffs was gratefully seized by former Buckingham Palace maid, Linda Joyce, who sued *Today* newspaper in 1991 for falsely suggesting that she had stolen personel letters belonging to Princess Anne. It was an obvious case for the issue of a libel writ but Ms

Joyce could not fund the litigation. She therefore began a legally-aided action for malicious falsehood. The case went to the Court of Appeal after the newspaper challenged, among other things, her right to 'dress up' a libel claim as something else. The court was not impressed with this argument:

> . . . if a plaintiff establishes that the defendant maliciously made a false statement which has caused him damage . . . the law gives him a remedy. The false statement may also be defamatory or it may not. As already mentioned, it need not be defamatory. Conversely, the fact that the statement is defamatory does not exclude a cause of action for malicious falsehood, although the law will ensure that a plaintiff does not recover damages twice for the same loss.

Joyce v Sengupta (1991)

In the Joyce case the court also hinted heavily that once a plaintiff had proved actual or likely financial loss, he or she could go on to recover damages for emotional distress linked to the financial loss. The principal has yet to be firmly established in law, but, if that is right, such 'parasitic damages' (as they are called by lawyers) could make malicious falsehood every bit as dangerous for the media as libel.

LIBEL: THE PLAINTIFF'S CASE

The balance of advantage in libel

Many of those who have experience of libel cases liken them to games of poker. Between its inception and its conclusion, which can be a period of two or more years, the libel case is a constant test of nerve. On one side is a plaintiff pressured by the enormous expense of a legal battle to clear his name. He is of course ineligible for any form of legal aid – it is not granted in libel actions. On the other side is generally a wealthy media company facing the normal heavy evidential burden of establishing a defence in a case where the lawyers' bills all too frequently overshadow whatever matter of principle happens to be involved.

The plaintiff
Various groups including, not surprisingly, lawyers who lean towards representing plaintiffs, have long argued for legal aid to be made available to those who claim to have been libelled in the same way as it is granted to the victims of other forms of civil wrong. Without it the pursuit of justice in the libel courts tends to be an indulgence of the rich. As we have seen, cases may run for many years. Needless to say the plaintiff's lawyers will wish to be paid as they go along and libel lawyers do not come cheap.

There have been notable examples in recent years of how costs can overshadow the substantive issues in libel actions, for example:

- In *Orme* v *Associated Newspapers Ltd (1981)* the *Daily Mail* spent six months in the high court defending one of its articles which suggested that the Unification Church, i.e. the Moonies, secured converts by methods akin to brainwashing. Over 100 witnesses, many of them Moonies from overseas, were paraded before the jury who eventually found for the newspaper. The total bill for costs was massive – reasonable estimates put it at £750,000.
- In a more recent case Dr Sidney Gee sued the BBC and its presenter, Esther Rantzen, over allegations of professional misconduct made in the course of a *That's Life* programme. This time the case was fought for eighty-seven days before the BBC capitulated. It paid Dr Gee £75,000 in damages and was left holding a bill for an estimated £1,000,000 worth of legal costs.
- Esther Rantzen and the BBC have not enjoyed much luck with libel. In 1992 she sued the *Sunday People* for suggesting that she knew of a working teacher with perverse sexual tendencies but had not exposed him on her TV programme. Her action, which was funded by the BBC, was successful and she was awarded £250,000. The newspaper appealed and the damages were reduced to £110,000. After the plaintiff was ordered to pay the costs of the appeal, Miss Rantzen (or to be more precise, her employers) found themselves out of pocket by over £100,000.

In all of these cases matters of principle were clearly at stake which dictated tactics and overrode financial considerations. It is perhaps ironic then, that the average member of the public who read about the results probably took far more note of the massive financial burden imposed by the legal costs than of any point of principle won by the victors.

There is certainly a case for arguing that the absence of legal aid can lead to injustice. A person of low means who has been falsely defamed in a newspaper or television programme will frequently be denied his remedy in law because of the cost. The media company will naturally have some knowledge of the plaintiff's finances which it may use to advantage in the way its defence is conducted. This is why the plaintiff in libel needs a strong nerve and a deep pocket.

The defendant
The other side of the balance of advantage is that once a plaintiff has established the simple elements of a libel, i.e. that he has been defamed by what was published, the law will presume the falsity of the publication and a heavy burden is placed on the defendant to establish otherwise. This

represents something akin to a reversal of the normal legal presumption that a defendant is innocent until proven guilty. In reality it gives the plaintiff in libel a substantial tactical advantage.

Another factor which distinguishes libel from nearly every other form of civil action is the availability of trial by jury. In practice, almost all libel actions will have a jury rather than a judge deciding the vital questions of liability and the level of damages. There are many who claim that this system is unsatisfactory. Those who spend their time in the libel courts are only too familiar with the unpredictability of juries in such cases. People who work in the media have a feeling that juries are more inclined to find for wounded plaintiffs than for wealthy newspapers or TV stations.

The jury system has, moreover, produced marked inconsistencies in awards of damages. It is hardly surprising, perhaps, when one considers that the jury members probably have no previous experience of libel actions and yet, without any clear direction on amounts, they are asked to assess the damage to the plaintiff's reputation in precise monetary terms.

Thus, one sometimes finds that at the end of broadly similar cases different juries can vary in their awards of compensation by an amount of £20,000 or more. When one also finds that a motorist whose arms and legs are broken by another's reckless driving is awarded significantly less for his injuries than a libel plaintiff gets for his besmirched reputation it is perhaps easy to see why this system of assessing damages is attacked.

Faced with the above considerations and in the sure knowledge that legal costs will rapidly escalate to massive levels, TV and publishing companies frequently bow to the reality of economics and settle at an early stage in the proceedings. The defendant thereby cuts his losses and the plaintiff wins the game of poker.

What the plaintiff must prove

In a libel action the plaintiff has only to demonstrate that a defamatory statement or other matter referring to him was published by the defendant to some third party. Since, as we have seen, there is a presumption at law that the defamatory words about him are false and therefore libellous, the defendant is then faced with the far heavier onus of either proving that the words are true or establishing some other defence recognized by the law of libel.

There are thus three relatively simple elements to the plaintiff's case:

1   *Defamation*:   That the words or other matter are defamatory.
2   *Identification*:   That they are reasonably understood to refer to the plaintiff.
3   *Publication*:   That they were published to some third party by the defendant.

Defamation

What is defamatory? There is no single, comprehensive definition recognized by law. The classic formula devised by Baron Parke in an 1840 case is that a defamatory statement is one which injures someone's reputation 'by exposing him to hatred, contempt or ridicule'.

By the 1920s judges recognized that this definition was too narrow. It was, after all, easy to damage a man's reputation, say in his business dealings, by statements which would provoke neither hatred, contempt nor ridicule. Lord Aitken set out an alternative test in 1924:

> . . . would the words tend to lower the plaintiff in the estimation of right-thinking member of society generally.

Other yardsticks however can, and do, apply. For example, if a statement injures a man in his business, office or employment it is defamatory. So also is it defamatory if it causes others to shun him.

In 1975, the Faulkes Committee on Defamation proposed a single statutory definition:

> Defamation shall consist of the publication to a third party of matter which in all the circumstances would be likely to affect a person adversely in the estimation of reasonable people generally.

The proposal has not been implemented by Parliament but, along with the other definitions, it serves as a useful guide to juries. In different sets of circumstances all of the above tests might be applicable but none is exhaustive.

As society and its morals adapt with the passage of time so also will the proper standard to be applied in judging what amounts to defamation. It is, after all, geared to the thinking of the reasonable man or 'right-thinking member of society'. Thus, what may have been clearly defamatory fifty years ago might not now be regarded as such. Nowhere is this demonstrated better than in society's attitudes towards sexual matters. To say in 1920 that a young lady spent her vacation in a Paris hotel with her boyfriend would certainly have reflected discredit upon her but it is by no means certain that the average person today would think any worse of her for it.

Similarly with our increasingly complex lives, particularly in relation to financial affairs and new technology, there are now classes of defamatory imputation and ways to defame a person which did not exist when our parents were born. Journalists would do well to remember that the categories of statement which can give rise to a libel are never closed.

Many of the categories are obvious. To suggest that a person is a thief, a fraudster or a cheat will always be defamatory. It will similarly be actionable if it is said that someone is incompetent or unqualified in his trade, office or profession. The particular circumstances of the plaintiff will always be highly relevant to this class of statement. For example, it would not normally be defamatory to say of someone that he lacked financial acumen. If, however, the person is a merchant banker or a tax consultant, such a statement is clearly damaging to his professional reputation.

Similarly, while it will not usually incite hatred, ridicule or contempt to suggest that a person has a serious illness, it would certainly be defamatory to state that he has a contagious disease or one which is sexually-transmitted. A court has ruled it is also defamatory to describe a person as having had a mental breakdown (*Bower* v *Sunday Pictorial Pictures (1962)*).

Allegations of immorality are actionable but it must be remembered that the attitude of the 'right-thinking member of society' towards morals is apt to change with the passage of time. In 1959 the celebrated *Daily Mirror* columnist, Cassandra (William Connor), wrote of the American pianist Liberace:

He is the summit of sex, the pinnacle of Masculine, Feminine and Neuter. Everything that He, She and It can ever want . . .

The article went on to liken him to

. . . a . . . deadly, winking, sniggering, chromium-plated, scent-impregnated, luminous, quivering, giggling, fruit-flavoured, mincing, ice-covered heap of mother-love . . .

Liberace claimed the article suggested he was homosexual and sued for libel. At the end of the trial the jury agreed with him and awarded the then substantial sum of £8,000 in damages. Those at the *Daily Mirror* could be forgiven for seeing a certain irony in the fact that Liberace died of AIDS in 1987, some time after his former Californian chauffeur, Scott Thorsen, brought a 'palimony' suit against him.

It is not suggested that a newspaper or TV programme could nowadays successfully plead that calling someone a homosexual does not defame him. The issue was once again aired before a libel jury in 1992.

Jason Donovan, an unmarried Australian singer/actor with a huge following among British teenagers, sued a youth magazine called *The Face* for suggesting that he was homosexual. Since he had previously gone on record to say that he was not gay, he also claimed damages for the implicit suggestion that he was a hypocrite.

The jury's award of £200,000 to the plaintiff produced an uproar from certain sections of society who protested that being thought of as gay is not something which could damage one's reputation. Ironically, Mr Donovan's reaction was to issue a statement which broadly agreed with this viewpoint. He waived the £200,000 damages and proclaimed that his primary motive in suing was to clear his name of the hypocrisy slur.

Finally, the 'right-thinking member of society' is a law-abiding person. It is not therefore defamatory to say that someone informed to the police – even if such a statement causes him to be shunned by his friends.

In the 1937 case of *Byrne* v *Deane* the plaintiff sued over a statement pinned to his golf club noticeboard which said that he told the police about illegal gaming machines in the clubhouse. The notice seemed to cause other club members to turn against him. Lord Justice Slesser stated the law as follows:

> . . . in my view, to say òr to allege of a man . . . that he has reported certain acts, wrongful in law, to the police cannot possibly be said to be defamatory of him in the minds of the general public.

The construction and meaning of words
It has long been recognized that the strict rules of construction which may be appropriate for ascertaining the meaning of words in other areas of law, e.g. contract or tax, will not do for the purposes of libel. As has been seen, the correct standard to apply in assessing the defamatory quality of words is an objective one. The same approach is used in construing the meaning of words, i.e. how would they be understood by the ordinary, reasonable man?

Additionally, however, it is recognized that seemingly innocent statements will convey a defamatory meaning to those who have knowledge of certain facts or circumstances which are extraneous to the offending publication. Thus the law of libel recognizes two distinct types of meaning:

1 The natural and ordinary meaning.
2 The meaning by innuendo.

The natural and ordinary meaning
The natural and ordinary meaning of words will include both the literal meaning and any obvious inference that would be taken from the words. The question for the jury is what would people of ordinary commonsense and worldly knowledge understand the words to mean? It is an objective test.

In this respect, '. . . the ordinary man does not live in an ivory tower . . . so he can and does read between the lines' (Lord Reid). It has been said that the ordinary man is not one who is 'avid for scandal', so that where a statement can be understood in different ways he is unlikely to look for the least probable meaning which happens to be defamatory.

The ordinary man for example would be taken to have a reasonable knowledge of contemporary slang. He would know that words such as 'gay' and 'rip-off' can these days have meanings which are defamatory. He will also look at the context of words rather than viewing them in isolation. He would, for example, be expected to attach particular significance to the fact that a story appears under bold headlines on page one of a newspaper.

Similarly the ordinary man is entitled to say 'no smoke without fire' when he reads that police are 'probing' someone's affairs or that a person denies being a criminal.

It follows that since the construction of the offending words is based upon an objective test, the meaning actually intended by the publisher is irrelevant. What is looked at instead is the effect of the words.

In the 1929 case of *Cassidy* v *Daily Mirror Newspapers* a picture was published of Mr Michael Cassidy with a lady. Acting in good faith on information supplied by Cassidy the newspaper described her as his fiancée. Mrs Cassidy, who lived apart from her husband, sued claiming that the reference to a fiancée in the picture's caption would lead people who knew her to believe that she was not really his wife but only his mistress. She was awarded £500. Lord Justice Russell made it clear that:

> Liability for libel does not depend on the intention of the defamer; but on the fact of defamation.

In the same way as the intention of the publisher is irrelevant so also is the actual interpretation placed upon the words by the person to whom they are published. It follows that neither plaintiff nor defendant may call readers or viewers of the pertinent item to give evidence of what they understood it to mean. To allow otherwise would be to deprive the libel jury of one of its primary functions. Uninfluenced by anyone's opinion but their own, the members of the jury are charged with deciding how the words would be naturally and ordinarily understood. As we have seen, that is a wholly objective test. What this means in reality is that a plaintiff can be libelled even though nobody to whom the defamatory matter was published believed it.

There are, of course, frequent occasions where words can have different meanings, some innocent and some defamatory. In such cases the jury must decide how the ordinary, reasonable person would understand what was published. The judge, however, is empowered to remove the question from the jury if he decides as a matter of law that the words are incapable of the defamatory meaning asserted by the plaintiff. In such cases the plaintiff's claim will be dismissed.

Defamatory meanings can be extracted not only from the actual words used but also by the manner and sense in which they are published. The publication of rumours and denials is therefore extremely dangerous.

In 1982 the *Sunday People* carried a front-page story about footballer Justin Fashanu under the banner headline 'I AM NOT GAY'. The piece revealed that rumours about Mr Fashanu's sexuality had been circulating among his team mates. His denial when asked by the *People* reporter did not legitimize publication of the rumour to millions of newspaper readers who had never heard of it before. The case was settled by payment of substantial damages. (As can happen in such cases the plaintiff admitted years later that he was gay.)

When, in 1993, the *New Statesman* reported rumours circulating around Westminster and Fleet Street that the Prime Minister, John Major, has enjoyed a 'secret affair' with a caterer called Clare Latimer, both subjects of the story issued libel writs against the publishers, printers and distributors. Although the magazine asserted that it had not given the slightest credence to the rumours (which, it accepted, were untrue) and was simply reporting a whispering campaign, the printers and distributors quickly accepted liability and paid damages. In the event, the plaintiffs did not pursue their claim for damages against the *New Statesman*, itself.

Meaning by innuendo

The law recognizes that in certain circumstances words convey suggestions or imputations over and above their natural meaning. This may be because a word or phrase has a technical or slang meaning or it might be because of extrinsic facts known by some people to whom the material is published. In this way seemingly innocuous words can, through innuendo, take on a meaning which is defamatory.

It is not difficult to think of numerous examples of apparently innocent words which convey derogatory imputations in slang. In a 1964 case Lord Reid indicated how the reader's own knowledge of matters not specifically referred to in the published item can produce the defamation:

> . . . to say of a man that he was seen to enter a named house would contain a derogatory implication for anyone who knew that that house was a brothel but not for anyone who did not.

The extraneous matter leading us to defamatory innuendo is thus the knowledge, to some, that the house named was used as a brothel. In *Tolley* v *J. S. Fry & Sons Ltd (1931)* Cyril Tolley, a famous amateur golfer, was depicted in an advertisement with a bar of Fry's chocolate sticking out of his pocket as he swung his club on the golf course. He had not given permission for his likeness to be used in this way. In the subsequent libel action he sued and won on the basis that those who knew him to be an amateur would believe, on seeing the advertisement, that he had abused his amateur status. In itself of course the picture was innocuous. However, it would bear a clear defamatory meaning to those who saw it knowing that he was an amateur and that the rules of amateur golf forbid the commercial endorsing of products.

Similarly, the extraneous matter known to Mrs Cassidy's neighbours in her case against the *Daily Mirror* was that she claimed to be (and indeed *was*) married to the man who, according to the newspaper, was with his 'fiancée' at the races. According to those neighbours, if he had a fiancée he must be free to marry and therefore Mrs Cassidy could only be his mistress and not his wife.

When relying on a defamatory meaning by innuendo the plaintiff must plead those facts and matters which support the innuendo. This means that, unlike in a case where the ordinary interpretation of words is relied upon, he may call witnesses to say what they understood the words to mean. In effect these witnesses will give evidence as to their knowledge of the extraneous fact or facts which give rise to the defamatory innuendo, e.g. that, in the case above referred to by Lord Reid, the house was a brothel.

Identification

The second hurdle which every libel plaintiff must overcome is proving that the defamatory matter would be understood as referring to him or her. In other words the person is identifiable from what has been published and it is his or her reputation which is likely to be damaged. Most plaintiffs will have little trouble with this requirement for the simple reason that they have been named and/or pictured in the newspaper article or TV programme about which they complain. There are, however, frequent occasions when the issue of identity is not quite so clear cut. In such cases the question for the jury is once again an objective one – would the reasonable man understand the defamatory material to refer to the plaintiff?

A journalist may, for example, omit the name of a supposed villain from his report but write in detail of the wrongdoing giving broad hints as to who might be responsible. Such attempts at avoiding or fudging identification are usually made when there is a lack of proof and a fear of being sued. However, there have been numerous cases which show it to be a dangerous practice.

On 9 April 1978, the *Sunday Telegraph* carried a front-page article by its crime correspondent headed 'Two More in Scott Affair'. The report did not name millionaire Jack Hayward but said that the name of 'a wealthy benefactor of the Liberal Party' had been given to the police in connection with the Norman Scott affair. Scott was a homosexual who claimed to have had an affair with the Liberal Party leader, Jeremy Thorpe. The article went on to suggest that the wealthy benefactor had 'arranged for a leading Liberal supporter to be reimbursed £5,000, the same amount Mr Andrew Newton alleges he was paid to murder Mr Scott'.

One week later, on 16 April, the *Sunday Telegraph* ran another story on the Scott affair and this time named Jack Hayward. The court of appeal upheld the jury's finding in favour of Mr Hayward and ruled that they were entitled to look at the 16 April article in order to identify the unnamed benefactor in the 9 April piece – *Hayward* v *Thompson (1982)*.

The journalist who does not name his 'villain' can therefore be in danger of having him identified not only from what he himself has written but also from what has been published elsewhere. There have been many occasions when one newspaper has wisely stopped short of identifying a suspected wrongdoer only to find that a rival newspaper's report of the same story carries both his name and picture. Lawyers will undoubtedly argue over whether identification can be established through publications not connected with the defendant. The decision in *Hayward* v *Thompson* indicates however that the likely answer is yes.

Regardless of what might appear elsewhere the journalist should ensure, if trying not to get sued, that he or she does not identify the potential plaintiff circumstantially. It should be remembered that describing a person's home, car or job might easily lead to identification.

Past cases have produced examples of generalized allegations being published in such a way as to enable individuals to claim they have been libelled. Headmasters and prison governors have successfully sued over damning reports about the institutions in which they presided. A 1985 article which alleged that Peter Sutcliffe, the Yorkshire Ripper, had hoodwinked unnamed prison doctors resulted in two psychiatrists successfully suing the newspaper. They were responsible for Sutcliffe's treatment at the time of the report and were therefore identifiable.

In other cases libel damages have been won where the publisher did not even have the plaintiff in mind. Every editor knows the nightmare of the wrong picture being published with a story. This can happen because the office picture library has supplied photographs of another person with the same name or because the photographer has inadvertently snapped someone else. If the editor is lucky the story will not reflect discredit on the person who was mistakenly identified. However, where the report or the picture caption is defamatory there is unlikely to be any defence. An early and fulsome apology is then usually the best course if one wishes to mitigate the damages.

Another regular pitfall for journalists is where they write a perfectly accurate article about one person only to find someone else with the same name emerges claiming to have been defamed. Since the defamation in such cases is innocent there is a tendency to dismiss them as 'gold-digging' claims. Such an attitude may well be short-sighted for there is ample precedent in favour of this kind of plaintiff.

The well-known case of *Hulton* v *Jones* illustrates the danger. In 1910 the *Sunday Chronicle* published a frivolous feature article about the English habit of crossing the Channel to France to seek enjoyment. The newspaper's portrayal of the merriment at a Dieppe motor festival included the following sentence. 'There is Artemus Jones with a woman who is not his wife, who must be, you know – the other thing.' A barrister of the same name sued and won, despite the newspaper's insistence that they were not even aware of his existence and had certainly never intended to defame him. The court ruled that the intention of the publisher was irrelevant and, as always with libel, what was important was the effect upon the reputation of the plaintiff. Whatever was intended he need only show that the defamatory statements would be understood by some people to refer to him.

In situations where confusion might arise reporters should therefore take care to make the identification of their subject clear. With experience they will know that certain stories are particularly prone to this sort of problem. For example records of holiday firms collapsing (of which there seem to be quite a few each year) inevitably produce a crop of letters from similar sounding holiday companies complaining of the damage they have suffered. It is wise in such cases to publish the firm's address in order to avoid the confusion. Obviously the same applies when the subject of the story is someone with a fairly common name. Especially when reporting court cases the obvious danger of confusion with innocent people is avoided by publishing ages, occupations and addresses.

Similarly, TV and film producers should be careful about portraying innocent people on screen while potentially defamatory words are uttered by the reporter or narrator. In a recent case a London CID officer won £20,000 in libel damages because he happened by chance to be walking out of the police station which a BBC crew was filming in order to illustrate a report on corruption in London's CID. Although the televised report referred only to general allegations, the particular officer was clearly indentifiable from the film.

As will be seen in a later chapter, there is a defence of unintentional defamation recognized by Section 4 of The Defamation Act 1952. The provisions of that section however define the defence so narrowly that it affords scant protection to the unwary publisher.

Defamation of a class

Whether or not a group or class of people can sue over a defamatory statement depends upon the size of the group and the nature of the allegation. The situation arises when a slur is cast, not upon a named individual, but either upon a group as a whole or upon one or more unnamed members of the group. A report may, for example, say that:

the members of the present Cabinet are in the pay of the Russians

or it might say:

a member of the present Cabinet is a traitor

In either case the only identification is by reference to the group and the rule for anyone who wishes to sue is he or she must establish that the defamatory statement would, on its reasonable interpretation, have damaged his or her personal reputation.

Whether, in fact, the plaintiff succeeds in such cases will depend largely on how many are in the group and therefore how closely the individual members of it are associated with the slur.

No action would, for example, be likely to result from the statement that 'all Tory MPs are traitors' or 'one of the Tory MPs is a traitor'. The class is simply too large (at present) for any one member to claim identification. The same allegations made in relation to the Cabinet would however probably enable every individual minister to bring a libel action.

Exactly how large a group or class has to be before identification by reference to it would be safe is impossible to say and would probably depend on the nature of the defamatory allegation being made. Individual jury members, however, have successfully sued over published suggestions that the jury (i.e. twelve persons) on which they sat reached a perverse verdict. *Riches* v *News Group Newspapers* is another case where a group of a dozen or so launched a successful action. In 1978 the *News of the World* published a front-page article under the banner headline 'Siege Man Tells Us Why He Did It'. The story concerned a gunman called David Brain who was holding hostages in order to publicize his deranged belief that one or more officers of the local CID at Banbury had raped and beaten his wife and threatened his son. The newspaper reported his allegations and the siege ended without loss of life. Although no individual officer was named in the article it did identify the group from which the alleged rapist came, i.e. Banbury CID. At the time there were eleven CID men at Banbury. Ten of them sued for libel and won.

There are very few reported cases of identification being established where the group consists of more than twelve people. However, if the defamatory allegation is so specific that the slur attaches itself to every individual there is no reason in law why members of a much larger group should not bring an action.

Who may sue?
No living person is excluded from commencing libel proceedings. Criminals, children, bankrupts and those of unsound mind may all sue to protect their reputation.

In the case of serious criminals there is a tendency among journalists to think that they have no reputation to lose. This will never be the case as a general rule though in relation to specific defamatory allegations it may be so. For example, a man with a long string of convictions for violence and dishonesty could certainly succeed in libel if a newspaper or TV programme wrongly accuses him of a sexual assault. In *Bower* v *Sunday Pictorial (1962)* the newspaper unsuccessfully argued that the plaintiff's conviction for attempted murder so damaged his reputation that an allegation of mental breakdown did it no further harm. It is, however, perfectly conceivable that a person's reputation in respect of one particular form of wrongdoing is so bad that one more allegation concerning similar behaviour would, even if untrue, cause no damage. Every newspaper diarist or gossip columnist will, for example, know of certain 'personalities' whose reputations for drinking, drug-taking or womanizing are so bad that they are unlikely to gain anything (except a large bill from their lawyers) from suing over one more story in that vein. In such circumstances juries might easily find against the plaintiff or make no more than a derisory award – there have been numerous cases in which unmeritorious plaintiffs have left court with a penny or a halfpenny in damages.

The law of libel allows bankrupts to sue on their own behalf and keep any award of damages.

Children may also sue in libel to protect their reputations, though the action must be conducted on behalf of the child by an adult – known in law as his or her 'next friend'.

There is no libel of the dead. Defamatory statements therefore may (and usually are) made with virtual impunity about those who have died. The only risk to the publisher in such cases is that material published may be so inflammatory that it attracts a prosecution for ciminal libel. (See page 57.)

It is also the case that if either plaintiff or defendant dies during the course of libel proceedings the action dies also. The Faulkes Committee on Defamation recommended that when a party to a libel action dies the surviving relatives should be allowed to continue the action. Little enthusiasm has been shown by Parliament for implementing this recommendation.

An incorporated body may sue for libel but only if the defamatory statement refers to its business or trading reputation. The reason for restricting their capacity in this way is simply that although companies are recognized as having legal 'persona' they obviously cannot suffer hurt or injured feelings. The range of defamatory imputation over which a company can sue is therefore much narrower than for an individual. It will include statements about the honesty and efficiency of its business methods and about the strength or otherwise of its financial position. As Lord Reid put it in one case:

> A company cannot be injured in its feelings, it can only be injured in its pocket. Its reputation can be injured by a libel but that injury must sound in money. The injury need not necessarily be confined to loss of income. Its goodwill may be injured.

However when writing in a derogatory fashion about a company journalists would do well to remember that its leading officers, e.g. the managing director or company secretary, will usually be easily identifiable. A defamatory allegation against the company, therefore, can all too easily lead to writs from the individuals who run it.

Prior to 1974 trade unions could, and sometimes did, bring actions for libel. The Trade Union and Labour Relations Act of that year, however, effectively removed that power. This was confirmed in 1980 by Mr Justice O'Connor when he ruled that the electricians union, the EETPU, could not sue Times Newspapers.

The question of whether a local authority can sue in libel was taken all the way up to the House of Lords in 1992. In the end it was ruled (*Derbyshire County Council* v *Times Newspapers*) that local authorities cannot bring such actions – the rationale being that citizens should be free to criticize government, whether national or local, without the fear of litigation. Journalists would do well to remember, however, that any individual councillor who feels he or she has been defamed is perfectly free to take legal action.

Publication

Of the three elements that a plaintiff must prove in order to establish his case, i.e. defamation, identification and publication, it is the last which really triggers actions for libel and slander. A defamatory statement may be thought, spoken or written – it may even be addressed to the person who is defamed – but it does not become actionable until it is published to some third party.

For the purposes of libel and slander, publication takes place whenever there is a communication of the defamatory words to some person other than the plaintiff. The communication to a third party is the very essence of libel for it is at this point that the plaintiff is 'exposed to scandal, odium and contempt' and therefore has a cause of action.

Since it would have no effect on his reputation, communication of defamatory matter solely to the plaintiff is insufficient grounds upon which to commence proceedings. Accordingly, a person may safely write a letter containing any amount of defamatory statements about the addressee providing it remains inside an envelope while in transit.

The position would be quite different if the same statements were made by way of a telegram or postcard. In both such cases the contents are presumed to be transmitted to others between dispatch and arrival and are therefore actionable. As with most other elements of libel it is irrelevant that the defendant did not intend the defamatory words to be communicated to any other person. Providing he is responsible for the relevant publication he is liable to be sued.

At the trial of a libel action the plaintiff must normally call evidence to show that publication of the words has actually taken place. This, however, is usually unnecessary in the case of media defendants, i.e. newspapers, television and radio (also books), because the law presumes that the material has been published to other persons.

If the plaintiff relies on an innuendo meaning, he must still prove that the words were published to those people who would have whatever special knowledge is needed to understand the innuendo.

Since each separate communication to a third party is a separate publication and therefore a separate libel the number of people who may be sued over the same defamatory item can be quite large. As seen above anyone who causes, or is responsible for, a defamatory publication may be liable. Accordingly, where the offending material is in a newspaper interview the plaintiff might conceivably proceed against the journalist, the person interviewed, the editor, the newspaper proprietor, the printer, the distribution wholesaler and the newsagent. If he wished to he might even be able to sue the newspaper delivery boy. Each of these persons has, after all, been responsible for publishing or republishing the defamation.

2 LIBEL: DEFENCES

Like many areas of law, libel is a marriage of conflicting rights and interests. On the one hand is the principle which wholly underlies this particular course of action i.e. that a man's reputation should be protected from wrongful injury. On the other hand there are certain prevailing social interests against which the law decrees that protection of reputation will take second place.

Freedom of expression is the most significant of these dominant interests and a free press is, of course, a fundamental part of that right. The law, however, does not recognize any right to publicize falsehoods. Only the expression of truth is therefore protected. The freedom to voice an honest opinion is seen by the courts to be just as important as the right to publish the truth. Hence fair comment as well as justification is a defence to a claim for libel.

The free and proper administration of justice also takes precedence over the narrow right of the individual in relation to his reputation. It is recognized that judges, witnesses and advocates should be free to conduct their weighty work unhindered by fears of being sued for libel or slander. Similarly, since justice being seen to be done is only marginally less important than justice actually being done, fair and accurate reporting of judicial proceedings is protected against libel claims as well as what goes on in the courtroom itself.

The parliamentarians who make the law and govern the country decided long ago that the work they do is every bit as in need of protection as that done by their legal friends in court. Both the conduct and reporting of parliamentary proceedings is accordingly cloaked in privilege against suits for libel.

The main defences to libel are:

1 Justification.
2 Fair comment.

3   Absolute privilege.
4   Qualified privilege.
5   Leave and licence.
6   Innocent defamation under Section 4 of the Defamation Act 1952.

JUSTIFICATION

Justification will succeed as a defence if the defendant can prove that the defamatory words are true in substance and fact. With one single exception (Section 8 of the Rehabilitation of Offenders Act 1974) truth is a complete defence to an action for libel.

In cases where journalists are sued over factual reports or narrative feature articles, justification will usually be the only plausible defence available. In principle this is not something about which they should complain – journalism is, after all, a profession in which truth and accuracy are supposed to be the bywords.

In practice, of course, the yardstick for success on a plea of justification is not that you have got it right but that you can prove you have got it right. As we have seen, once the plaintiff accomplishes the relatively easy task of establishing that the words are defamatory, the law of libel presumes that they are also false. The defendant has the burden of overcoming this presumption by proving that the words are true. For a number of reasons justifying the offending publication can be a difficult task.

Evidence

On average, a libel action comes to trial between one and two years after the writ is issued. This significant lapse of time often means that memories become hazy and a clear recollection of events is unlikely. Defendants' lawyers may find that some witnesses no longer wish to be involved and others cannot be traced.

The golden rule, especially in the field of investigative journalism, is to have clear and admissable evidence before publication. Sources who have been promised anonymity and notebooks full of nothing but rumour and hearsay are not enough. Moreover, to publish in anticipation of gathering or hardening the evidence to support a plea of justification after the newspaper article or TV programme has appeared is not just dangerous but also frequently disastrous.

What few editors or reporters realize is that the filing of a defence to a libel action is a step governed by formal rules of pleading. Under those rules a defendant is not permitted to plead any point in justification unless he already has evidence to support it. Those who publish in the belief that their story is true but without the supporting evidence are therefore in danger of being left with no defence at all.

Additionally, as many libel defendants have discovered, however hard it is to find witnesses prior to publication it is generally a great deal harder afterwards – especially if a writ has been issued. Experience shows that not many people wish to involve themselves in acrimonious situations and the media, particularly the popular press, is not always identified with the public interest in such matters. While potential witnesses might be willing to help the police solve a crime or describe what they saw of a road traffic accident, they are rarely enthusiastic about siding with a newspaper in defence of a libel action.

The burden and standard of proof

Libel defendants pleading justification must adduce enough evidence to satisfy the jury on the balance of probabilities that the published words are true. This standard of proof is less than that applicable to the prosecutor in criminal cases who must prove his case beyond reasonable doubt. In practice, however, where the published allegations are very serious the defendant's evidence will, in proportion, have to be very convincing. Lord Denning's warning that '. . . as the charge is grave, so the proof must be clear' should be borne in mind by those editors who indulge in exposure journalism.

As with witnesses, it seems that juries sometimes hold a poor view of certain sections of the media. Those who work on tabloid newspapers tend to suspect, possibly with some justification, that the average jury of middle-aged, middle-minded and middle-class people is more prepared to disbelieve them than to disbelieve the apparently aggrieved plaintiff. It may be that the popular press has done much to deserve the low esteem in which many hold them, but if there is anything in their fears concerning the inclinations of some juries it does make the burden of proof that much more onerous.

Aggravation

Ironically, one of the major concerns a defendant frequently has about pleading justification is that the plea itself may exacerbate damages. A plaintiff is perfectly entitled to argue that the newspaper or TV company not only published scurrilous material about him and refused to apologize but it persisted in the damaging and libellous allegations right up to the moment the jury delivered its verdict. In the event of the jury not accepting the plea of justification the very fact that the defendant chose to enter such a defence can operate as an aggravation of the original libel and a reason to award a greater amount in damages than would otherwise be called for.

As we have seen, the existence of justification as a defence to libel is recognition of the fact that the right to free speech takes precedence over the rights which an individual enjoys in relation to his reputation. While it is unarguably correct in a democratic society that truth prevails in such circumstances, this rule may at times have somewhat harsh results. Even those who work in the media would, for example, have trouble finding any genuine public interest in some of the more lurid but true allegations about certain people's private lives which from time to time adorn the pages of our tabloid newspapers.

There are many who argue that the law does not go far enough to protect the individual citizen against unwarranted and damaging publicity. Since, unlike certain other countries, Britain does not have (at the time of writing) a law protecting privacy, the defence of justification effectively means that any person can publish anything about anyone and at any time provided it can be shown to be accurate. A limited protection against the revelation of very old convictions is afforded by the Rehabilitation of Offenders Act 1974 but in general the media are free to drag up and publicize any unsavoury incident, however old, from someone's distant past. Really there is nothing about a person's private life that cannot be published with virtual impunity as long as it is true.

Although there may be moral objections to the licence which is thus enjoyed by the press there has never been any doubt about the legal rationale for such freedom. Mr Justice Littledale succinctly stated the law as long ago as 1829 in the case of *McPherson* v *Daniels*:

'The law will not permit a man to recover damages in respect of an injury to a character which he does not, or ought not to, possess.'

Provided it is provably true it will make no difference that prior to its publication the allegation was not generally known and the plaintiff was held in the highest esteem by all who knew him. For libel purposes a man's reputation is only as good as he is, not as good as he seems.

For this reason, defendants are entitled to rely on matters which occur after the offending publication if they support the generality of the defamatory allegation. Thus, if a newspaper is sued over a January story which suggested the plaintiff was a drunk, it would be entitled in its defence to rely on the fact that the following March he was convicted of being drunk and disorderly and in June he was further convicted of driving while drunk.

On the other hand, relying on fairly old incidents to support an allegation of present misbehaviour will frequently fail. To call someone a thief on the basis that he committed one very minor theft several years before is actionable as a libel and the defendant could well have to pay damages unless he can prove that the person still has dishonest tendencies.

Proving the sting of the libel

Although the defendant, if he is to succeed on a plea of justification, is not required to prove the truth of every minor detail of fact, it is essential that he meets the plaintiff's challenge head-on and establishes as true those allegations which effectively cause the defamation. He must, therefore, prove whatever it is in the publication which has exposed the plaintiff to 'hatred, ridicule or contempt'.

As long ago as 1824 Mr Justice Burrough identified this crucial element as the 'sting' of the libel:

> As much must be justified as meets the sting of the charge, and if anything be contained in the charge which does not add to the sting of it, that need not be justified.

Accordingly, if the published allegation is that the plaintiff robbed the National Westminster bank in Chelsea at 11 a.m. last Thursday, the defendant's plea of justification will not fail if it is established that the plaintiff did indeed rob that bank but in fact did so at 3.30 p.m. last Monday. The sting of the libel is of course the suggestion that the plaintiff robbed the bank and the time and date in this case add nothing to the defamatory content of the published words.

Partial justification

There are many occasions where publications, especially newspaper and TV 'exposures', contain a whole series of allegations against a person. In the event of a writ being issued it may be that the defendant is able to prove the truth of some of those allegations but not of others. In such cases he is entitled to plead partial justification. However, where those parts of the publication which he is unable to justify have a libellous meaning or meanings of their own the defendant is likely to have to pay damages in respect of them.

If these unjustifiable matters do not add significantly to the damage done to the plaintiff's reputation by those matters which can be proved the defendant may have the benefit of a full defence under Section 5 of the Defamation Act 1952:

> In an action for libel or slander in respect of words containing two or more distinct charges against the plaintiff, a defence of justification shall not fail by reason only that the truth of every charge is not proved if the words not proved to be true do not materially injure the plaintiff's reputation having regard to the truth of the remaining charges.

It may be of some help if we consider examples of where Section 5 might be applicable.

- A local newspaper reporting a road traffic accident states that one of the drivers involved had neither insurance nor road tax and was drunk at the time of the crash. Although the newspaper can subsequently prove that he was drunk and had no insurance, it turns out that the man had fully paid his road tax. Since the false allegation does not really add to the imputation of irresponsibility and recklessness proven by the other two matters the newspaper would be entitled to rely on Section 5 to avoid any liability for libel damages.
- A television documentary on the music industry portrays a particular disc jockey as being a regular user of narcotic drugs and a heavy drinker. The first allegation is provable and the second is not. Since the taking of narcotics as opposed to alcohol is both illegal and considered to be far the greater vice, again Section 5 is likely to apply.
- An article is published in the popular press stating that a certain bank manager has been embezzling his employer's money in order to satisfy his lust for prostitutes. It is true that he has stolen from the bank but he has never consorted with a prostitute and is in fact completely faithful to his wife. In this case Section 5 would probably not assist the newspaper. Adultery, especially with a prostitute, is both a serious allegation and one which is materially different from dishonesty.

Reporting rumours and hearsay

Many reporters have trouble understanding why it is that to report a libellous rumour or to repeat an allegation made by someone else is just as dangerous as making the charge yourself. The position under the law of libel as stated by Lord Justice Greer in *Chapman* v *Ellesmere (1932)* is:

> If you report a rumour, you cannot say it is true by saying the rumour existed. You have to prove that the subject matter of the rumour was true.

Reporting criminal convictions

Proving convictions
The existence of criminal convictions on a plaintiff's record frequently appears as the cornerstone to the 'particulars', which must be pleaded in support of a defence of justification. Allegations of criminality, e.g. dishonesty, drug taking or violence, are after all among the commonest categories of libellous statement. There was a time, amazingly, when the fact that a person had been convicted and sentenced for a crime was not, for libel purposes, conclusive proof of his guilt:

- In 1964 Alfred Hinds sued for libel over a Sunday newspaper story headed 'They Called Me the Iron Man'. It was the story of Detective

Superintendent Herbert Sparks, who eleven years earlier had given evidence which led to Hind's conviction and ten-year sentence for robbery. The newspaper reported Mr Sparks's assertion that Hinds was guilty as charged. The criminal trial which led to the conviction lasted for two days. The subsequent libel action took twenty-six days to go over precisely the same issue and produced the opposite result. In the event the jury awarded the plaintiff £1,300.

- In 1967 Douglas Goody, who had been convicted of the Great Train Robbery, brought a similar action against another Sunday newspaper for saying that he had done that for which he was convicted. Like Hinds he won his case. The jury was aware of the fact that his record of convictions went back to 1948 and awarded him the nominal sum of forty shillings in damages.

Influenced, no doubt, by the damage which such absurd results can do to public confidence in the consistency of justice administered through our courts, Parliament changed the law shortly after Goody's victory. By Section 13 of the Civil Evidence Act 1968:

Proof that, at the date when the issue falls to be determined, that person stands convicted of that offence shall be conclusive evidence that he committed that offence, and his conviction thereof shall be admissable in evidence accordingly.

As a result, criminals can no longer secure what amounts to a retrial by bringing a libel action and the media can refer to convictions without having to worry about proving their correctness.

Whatever joy the media may have had from the luxury of uninhibited reference to previous convictions was, however, short-lived. In 1974 Parliament passed the Rehabilitation of Offenders Act 1974.

Spent convictions

Although the 1974 Act concerns a narrow area, i.e. old convictions, it represents a significant departure from one of the basic principles of libel law – that truth is a complete defence.

In essence Section 8 of the Rehabilitation of Offenders Act states that where the publication of a 'spent' conviction is 'made with malice' a defendant to libel proceedings shall not be entitled to rely on a plea of justification. In other words, where malice is proved the plaintiff's crimes will be treated for the purposes of his libel action as if they had never occurred. While there may be good reasons, both logical and moral, why the past sins of a reformed criminal should not be allowed to wreck his rehabilitation, the mental gymnastics called for on the part of the judge and jury who must regard as untrue that which is undoubtedly true are considerable.

The Act provides that convictions may become 'spent' after a period of rehabilitation. The length of these periods depends upon the sentence passed on conviction and once they have elapsed the criminal becomes a 'rehabilitated person'. This means that he must be treated as if he has never been charged, convicted or sentenced for his crime or crimes.

While they are still free, provided they are not motivated by malice, to publish spent convictions, by and large those who work in the media tend to honour the spirit of the Rehabilitation of Offenders Act. In practice journalists and their editors are conscious of its provisions and avoid publicizing the long-past convictions of rehabilitated persons.

In law the term malice has a wider meaning than it is given in common usage. It goes beyond mere spite or ill-will and takes in various other improper motives. The concept of malice is of great importance in the law of libel as its existence has the effect of defeating a number of defences which might otherwise be available to a publisher. Its precise meaning is considered in greater detail in the section on the defence of fair comment (see page 29).

Table 1 shows the rehabilitation periods applicable to the commonest forms of sentence passed by the criminal courts.

Table 1

Sentence	Rehabilitation period
A sentence of imprisonment for a term exceeding six months but not exceeding thirty months	Ten years
A sentence of imprisonment not exceeding six months	Seven years
A fine (In each of the above cases the period is cut by half if the offender is under seventeen years old)	Five years
A sentence of borstal training	Seven years
An order for detention in a detention centre	Three years
A conditional discharge, bind-over or probation order	Either twelve months from conviction or upon the expiry of the discharge, bind-over or probation period whichever is the longer
An absolute discharge	Six months
Any disqualification, disability or prohibition	To the date upon which the disqualification, disability or prohibition ceases to have effect

Sentences of imprisonment for life or for more than thirty months are never spent.

FAIR COMMENT

Just as freedom to tell the truth is fundamental to democracy so also is the freedom to speak one's mind, i.e. to voice an honest opinion. Unfettered rights to express true facts and honest comment are essentials of that most cherished of liberties, free speech. Naturally the law against libel does not encroach upon these principles. The defence of justification protects the first and the defence of fair comment covers the second. The courts have always recognized that society would be all the poorer if people, anxious about receiving libel writs, were afraid to publish true but damning facts or honest but unpalatable opinions. Together, they are the most important and undoubtedly the most commonly used defences available in cases of libel.

The short definition of the defence is that a person may publish fair comment on a matter of public interest providing he does so without malice. Those who make their living by writing or publishing stories about other people will serve their careers well by achieving at least an elementary understanding of this defence. It is certainly not as simple as the above statement suggests. For example, both 'fair' and 'malice' have a legal meaning which goes further than that given to them in ordinary usage.

As with most legal concepts those seeking to understand fair comment should start by learning to identify its principle ingredients. These are:

1 The comment must be on a matter of public interest.
2 The comment must be recognizable as comment.
3 The comment must be based upon facts which are true or privileged.
4 The comment must be fair – as judged objectively.
5 The person making the comment must not be motivated by malice.

Public interest

Only comments on matters of public interest come within the defence of fair comment. It is for the defendant to establish that the matter upon which he or she passed comment was one of public interest and the judge rather than the jury rules on this question if it is at issue. In practice the latitude allowed by the courts in respect of which matters are legitimate areas of public interest is fairly wide. In the words of Lord Denning in the case of *London Artists Ltd* v *Littler (1969)*:

> Whenever a matter is such as to affect people at large, so that they may be legitimately interested in, or concerned at, what is going on, or what may happen to them or others; then it is a matter of public interest on which everyone is entitled to make fair comment.

Obviously public affairs and public occasions are within the definition. Thus national and local government and politics, theatre and television, sporting events, court cases and musical, artistic and literary works are proper subjects upon which fair comment may be made. So, too, are the individuals who appear in these various arenas – provided that the comment is broadly directed at their work or performances rather than at them personally.

Anybody who seeks public attention, e.g. by protesting, by writing open letters to newspapers or by any other form of public demonstration, is a valid subject of comment as also is the conduct of those whose activities affect a significant number of people, e.g. employers and trade union representatives, managers and directors of companies, charities and other institutions – even journalists.

The comment must be comment

The defence of fair comment undoubtedly gives critics and public commentators a wide licence to write or say whatever they think about matters which are in the public eye. One judge has said that:

> A critic is entitled to dip his pen in gall for the purpose of legitimate criticism; and no one need be mealy-mouthed in denouncing what he regards as twaddle, daub or discord.
> *Gardiner* v *Fairfax (1942) NSW*

What critics are not entitled to do, however, is to make derogatory statements of fact in the guise of criticism. Many writers unwittingly (or carelessly) do so and it is a trap which frequently leads to successful libel actions against the media. If what has been written or said is deemed by the court to be a factual statement rather than an expression of opinion then fair comment cannot protect it. In most such cases the only defence which would then be available is justification, i.e. proving that the facts stated are true.

There have been plenty of cases which illustrate this particular danger:

- In 1985 London Weekend Television and Mr Jimmy Greaves, its football commentator, were obliged to apologize and pay damages for 'an unintended slip made in the heat of the moment' by Mr Greaves during his commentary on that year's FA Cup Final. Millions of football fans watching the match on television heard him say that the referee, Mr Peter Willis, had sent off a Manchester United player 'to get his name in history before he retires'. Mr Greaves had undoubtedly intended the remark as no more than a comment but it clearly conveyed an imputation of fact regarding the referee's motive for sending the player off – and that imputation was defamatory.
- Another 1985 case saw the actress Charlotte Cornwell suing the *Sunday People* and its television critic, Nina Myskow, over statements published about Ms Cornwell's portrayal of a rock and roll star in the TV series *No*

Excuses. Apart from candidly remarking that 'her bum's too big' the critic wrote 'She can't act, she can't sing and she has the sort of stage presence that jams lavatories'. The defendants argued strongly that the statements were robust comment on the actress's performance rather than assertions of fact. The jury, however, disagreed and awarded Ms Cornwell £10,000 in damages. In fact the verdict was successfully appealed against (on certain other points of law) and Ms Cornwell then went on to win a retrial – this time picking up £11,500 in damages. It was a classic Pyrrhic victory; her pride was restored but she was left with a huge costs bill for the first trial and the appeal. Reasonable estimates put her about £50,000 out of pocket as a result of the litigation.

Those who seek to criticize in terms which could be construed as lowering the subject in the estimation of right-thinking people should ensure that their statements are clearly recognizable as comment.

> Comment, in order to be justifiable as fair comment, must appear as comment and not be so mixed up with facts that the reader cannot distinguish between what is report and what is comment. Any matter . . . which does not indicate with a reasonable clearness that it purports to be comment and not a statement of fact, cannot be protected by the plea of fair comment.
> Lord Justice Fletcher-Moulton in *Hunt* v *Star Newspapers (1908)*

Prefacing or complementing statements with epithets such as 'in my opinion' or 'it is my view that' will undoubtedly help to identify them as comments though it will not always be conclusive.

The comment must be based on facts which are true or privileged

A defendant is not entitled to plead fair comment in respect of a publication unless:

- He has set out the facts upon which the comment is based or has indicated them with sufficient clarity for them to be gleaned by his readership or audience
  and
- Those facts upon which the comment is based are true or privileged.

The courts take the view that unless the reader is acquainted with the facts upon which criticism is based he cannot know whether the comment is well-founded or even that it is comment rather than an assertion of fact.

In *Kemsley* v *Foot (1952)*, under the headline 'Lower than Kemsley' Michael Foot wrote a piece in the newspaper *Tribune* which savagely attacked the *Evening Standard* for an article it had published during the previous week. Foot described it as 'the foulest piece of journalism perpetrated in this country for many a long year'. Kemsley was a well-known newspaper proprietor but in fact had no connection with the *Evening Standard*. He claimed that the headline suggested his name was a byword for dishonest journalism. The case went as far as the House of Lords which ruled that the headline was a statement of opinion rather than one of fact and that the factual basis for it, i.e. the existence and conduct of Kemsley's newspapers, was sufficiently indicated.

Frequently an issue is so much in the public eye that readers or TV viewers would almost certainly be broadly aware of the facts upon which a piece of comment is based. In such cases the barest indication of what those facts are is likely to be sufficient.

The stated facts upon which the critic has based his comment must be true, or if untrue, must have been published on a privileged occasion. Thus unless privilege applies, the law will not recognize as fair any comment which has a false premise. Where, however, an article has set out a number of facts upon which comment is made and some of the facts are true and others are false the defendant may be able to rely on Section 6 of the Defamation Act 1952 which provides that:

> In an action for libel or slander in respect of words consisting partly of allegations of fact and partly of expression of opinion, a defence of fair comment shall not fail by reason only that the truth of every allegation of fact is not proved if the expression of opinion is fair comment having regard to such of the facts alleged or referred to in the words complained of as are proved.

The occasions upon which statements are privileged against liability for libel and slander are set out in a later section of this chapter. Where privilege applies, fair comment will protect statements of opinion even if the facts upon which they are based turn out to be untrue.

Finally, it is worth noting that the defendant may rely only on existing facts in support of his comment. In pleas of justification the defence may include reference to matters that occur after the publication, but this is not so with fair comment. In *Cohen* v *Daily Telegraph Ltd (1968)* the newspaper commented adversely on the state of a company. In the resulting libel action it attempted unsuccessfully to rely as a basis for its comment on a subsequent resolution which placed the company in the hands of the liquidators. Lord Denning stated:

> In order to make a good plea of fair comment, it must be a comment on fact existing at the time. No man can comment on facts which may happen in the future.

What is fair?

Under existing libel laws the critic is given ample scope for the expression of his true feelings. As we have seen, within fair comment he is allowed to 'dip his pen in gall' and certainly does not need to be mealy-mouthed. The test of what is fair is an objective one and does not require members of a jury to ask whether they themselves agree with the comment.

In the words of Lord Esher:

> The question which the jury must consider is this – would any fair man, however prejudiced he may be, however exaggerated his views, have said that which this criticism has said.

His formulation of the test, or minor variations upon it, has been used again and again in the cases. One such variation, which has the merit of simplicity is that devised by one of the leading libel textbooks *Duncan and Neill on Defamation*:

> Could any fair-minded man honestly express that opinion on the proved facts?

It will not therefore matter that the comment was exaggerated or based upon the general prejudices of the critic. It will not even matter if the critic is an unfair and unreasonable person. As long as the opinion expressed is not such that no fair and honest person knowing the facts could have said the same and as long as the person expressing the opinion is not motivated by malice, fair comment will operate as a defence.

- In *Jameson* v *BBC (1984)*, three-times Fleet Street editor Derek Jameson sued over the BBC's satirical radio show *Week Ending* which described him as the 'archetypal East End boy made bad' and the 'nitty gritty titivation tout from Trafalgar House'. It said that he understood erudite to be a kind of glue and it referred to his editorial policy as being: 'All the nudes fit to print and all the news printed to fit.' Mr Jameson complained that the sketch portrayed him as stupid and illiterate. In turn, the BBC defended on the basis that the words would not be understood as being defamatory and in any event were within the acceptable bounds of fair comment. After being treated to a highly selective examination of the plaintiff's long career in popular journalism the jury gave their verdict to the BBC. Mr Jameson was left holding a bill for legal costs estimated at about £75,000. It is an ironic footnote to this case that since losing the action Derek Jameson has become a hugely successful TV and radio presenter – largely working for the BBC.
- In *Pinder-White* v *Aitken (1985)*, a wealthy Tory lady from Broadstairs, Kent, sued the local Tory MP, Jonathan Aitken, over a piece he had written for the *East Kent Critic* (a newspaper) describing her and her husband as 'dreadful enough' to play JR and Sue Ellen in the TV soap opera *Dallas*. Mrs Pinder-White claimed that she was effectively being compared with a high-class prostitute who was a total alcoholic. She said that the article was 'a dreadful character assassination'. Mr Aitken's counsel told the court that the article had elements of parody and irony

and was not meant to be taken seriously. He also cross-examined the plaintiff about the ten Rolls-Royces owned by her and her husband during their marriage and particularly alleged that they used to travel about in a white one at election time. Again, the jury decided that, though the criticism may have been harsh, it came within the limits of fair comment.

- Another slightly more unusual case was *Lyon* v *Daily Telegraph (1943)* where the newspaper was sued over a reader's letter it had published. The letter criticized the Lyon family's radio shows and was signed 'A. Winslow' of 'The Vicarage, Wallingford Road, Winchester'. It turned out that both the name and address were fictitious. The case went to the Court of Appeal where, applying the objective test, the judges found that the comment came within what was permissable under the defence of fair comment.

Malice

Although the defendant may have set up a plea of fair comment by establishing each of the above ingredients (i.e. it is fair, it is comment, it is on a matter of public interest and it is based on true facts) this defence will nevertheless fail if it is shown that he or she was motivated by malice.

For the purposes of the law of libel, malice is an important concept. Its existence as the primary motive for the offending publication will defeat not only a plea of fair comment, but also a defence of qualified privilege and one of justification in relation to the publication of convictions which are 'spent' under the Rehabilitation of Offenders Act.

The legal meaning attributed to malice in this context is wider than that given to the word in popular usage. While it undoubtedly includes what most people recognize as the constituents of malice, i.e. spite and ill-will, it also encompasses any other improper motive, such as personal advantage or gain, provided it is the dominant motive for the publication. The burden of proving the existence of malice lies with the plaintiff.

The leading case on the subject is *Horrocks* v *Lowe (1975)* which involved a Labour local authority councillor who delivered a stinging rebuke against one of his Tory rivals at a council meeting – a forum in which speakers would normally be entitled to qualified privilege against libel suits. Mr Lowe said of Horrocks: 'His attitude was either brinkmanship, megalomania or childish petulance' and went on to say that he had misled the council committee, his party leader and his political colleagues. The case was fought all the way to the House of Lords on the issue of whether Lowe was malicious and therefore not entitled to claim qualified privilege. The court eventually ruled in favour of the defendant and laid down the following important principles on the question of malice.

1   In situations where fair comment, qualified privilege or justification in relation to spent convictions would normally apply and an allegation of malice is made, the motive with which the defendant made the defamatory statement is crucial. He will be entitled to the protection of his defence 'unless some other dominant and improper motive on his part is proved'.

2   'If it is proved that he did not believe that what he published was true this is generally conclusive evidence of express malice'. The same applies if the defendant published the statement recklessly, i.e. 'Without considering or caring whether it be true or not.'

3   However even where there is honest belief in the truth of what was published (or, in respect of fair comment, an honest expression of opinion) the defendant will still lose the protection of the defence if it is proved that he misused the situation for some improper purpose, e.g. to give vent to personal spite or for the attainment of some personal advantage. The improper motive must be the dominant reason for the publication – where the defendant believed in what he was saying or writing judges and juries should be slow to deprive him of the protection to which he would normally be entitled. Thus, although Lowe was clearly prejudiced and antagonistic towards Horrocks as a Tory, his honest belief in what he was saying sustained the defence.

How malice can be proved
In *Horrocks* v *Lowe* the Lords ruled that: 'The motive with which a person published defamatory matter can only be inferred from what he did, or said, or knew.'

The matters which plaintiffs usually rely on to substantiate their allegation of malice are:

1   *Style, manner and prominence of publication*:   With media publications the prominence and choice of headline can be taken as an indication of malice. A comparatively trivial matter blown up into a front-page story and set under screaming banner-headlines could suggest an improper motive. The strength of language used might also, in extreme cases, be evidence that the defendant was malicious.

2   *Personal grudges or ill-will between the parties*:   Plaintiff's who allege malice can, in support of their plea, adduce as evidence any history of ill-feeling between the parties. Anything which might indicate that the defamatory publication was an act of revenge or part of a vindictive campaign is strong evidence of malice. In *Horrocks* v *Lowe* the plaintiff predictably made much of the defendant's political antagonism.

3   *Refusal to retract or apologize*:   The refusal by the defendant to correct and apologize for the offending publication can be used against him as

evidence of malice. Logically this should only apply in cases where the defendant persisted in his refusal to retract after he was clearly shown to be in the wrong. After all, refusing to apologize can just as properly be interpreted as a continuing honest belief in what was originally published.

Liability for the malice of others
Although the law makes an employer liable for the malice of his employees, fortunately for the media it does not generally make the publisher responsible for the malice of independent third-parties. Thus, newspapers and television stations may be answerable for the malicious motives of their own reporters but they will not be infected by those of other people, e.g. interviewees or letter-writers who appear genuine but are in fact vindictive.

The legal principle governing such situations was expounded by Lord Denning in the 1965 case of *Eggar* v *Viscount Chelmsford* which involved an allegation of malice against the secretary and ten members of the Kennel Club who had written a letter critical of the plaintiif. The court held that although the letter was jointly published by all defendants the malice of some of them did not infect the others. Lord Denning said:

> If the plaintiff relies on malice to aggravate damages, or to rebut a defence of qualified privilege, or to cause a comment, otherwise fair, to become unfair, then he must prove malice against each person whom he charges with it. A defendant is only affected by express malice if he, himself, was actuated by it; or if his servant or agent concerned in the publication was actuated by malice in the course of his employment.

PRIVILEGE

In respect of media publications there are only three major defences to libel. The first two are, of course, justification and fair comment. The third and only other category of defence upon which the media relies on a daily basis for protection from libel is *privilege*. The privilege from defamation actions which is bestowed by law comes in two forms, that which is *absolute* and that which is *qualified*. Both are the result of public policy considerations which recognize that statements and publications made on certain occasions should have immunity from civil proceedings even if they are untrue and damaging.

Where absolute privilege applies, no action for libel or slander may succeed irrespective of the honesty or motive of the speaker or writer. Qualified privilege is a lesser protection which is defeated if the plaintiff establishes that the maker of the relevant statement was motivated by malice.

Absolute privilege

Absolute privilege is undoubtedly the strongest defence available to libel defendants. In situations where it is applicable it will succeed however false and defamatory the statement and however malicious the speaker or writer. Predictably the occasions where privilege is absolute are few in number and narrowly defined.

The categories of absolute privilege which are likely to affect the media are:

1   Statements made in, or as part of, parliamentary proceedings.
2   Statements made in the course of judicial proceedings.
3   Fair, accurate and contemporaneous reports of judicial proceedings.

Parliamentary statements

The origin of the privilege attaching to statements made in, or originating from, parliamentary proceedings lies in the Bill of Rights, 1688, which states that:

> . . . the freedom of speech and debates or proceedings in Parliament ought not to be impeached or questioned in any court or place out of Parliament.

Absolute privilege will cover anything which is said in the course of proceedings in either the House of Commons or the House of Lords. It will also protect statements made during hearings of committees set up by either House. A Member of Parliament or a witness before a parliamentary committee may say whatever he chooses in the sure knowledge that he will not be answerable under the law of libel.

On numerous occasions over the years MPs have used the absolute protection afforded to them to make allegations which, if publicly uttered outside the chamber of the House of Commons, would probably see them on the receiving end of a writ for libel. For the most part these MPs have been performing what they saw as a public service, e.g. naming a villian who, for some reason, was likely to escape the normal process of justice. There has, however, in recent years been a tendency for one or two MPs to use the safety of absolute privilege to make unprovable but headline-grabbing accusations from the floor of the House.

Journalists, whether on newspapers, radio or TV, should take care over reporting such accusations. The original statement inside Parliament is protected by absolute privilege; any report or repetition of it in the media, even though it is contemporaneous and accurate, attracts only qualified privilege.

The Parliamentary Papers Act 1840, extended the protection of absolute privilege to all reports, orders and other papers published under the authority of either House of Parliament. Thus, proceedings for libel will not succeed in respect of any statement recorded in Hansard's parliamentary reports or in other official parliamentary documents, e.g. Government white papers.

Statements made in court

The rationale for attaching absolute privilege to statements made during the course of judicial proceedings is identical to that which applies in respect of parliamentary proceedings. Public policy dictates that those involved in the administration of justice, like those who administer Government, should be free to speak openly and honestly without fear of being dragged into actions for defamation. In fact, the protection afforded them by absolute privilege extends to statements which are neither honest nor true. The courts have nevertheless always held, quite rightly, that the proper process of justice cannot, and should not, be conducted alongside the threat of vexatious civil litigation against those who participate. The possibility that witnesses and lawyers might be deflected from their duty by the fear of such consequences is seen as a greater danger to the public good than the occasional abuse of absolute privilege by dishonest or malicious persons.

Accordingly, the defence covers statements made in the course of judicial proceedings by judges, counsel, witnesses and parties. It will also protect the contents of documents produced for, or during, such proceedings, e.g. pleadings, affidavits and proofs of evidence.

The proceedings to which absolute privilege attaches obviously include all courts of law, both criminal and civil. It also applies to coroners' courts and tribunals which exercise judicial functions, e.g. industrial tribunals and others which operate on principles and procedures which are close to those applying in courts of law.

Fair, accurate and contemporaneous court reporting

This is undoubtedly the most important category of absolute privilege as far as the press is concerned. Almost every issue of every newspaper carries at least one court report, as do daily news bulletins on radio and television. The scope of the protection afforded to these reports is set out in Section 3 of the Law of Libel Amendment Act 1888:

> A fair and accurate report in any newspaper of proceedings publicly heard before any court exercising judicial authority shall, if published contemporaneously with such proceedings, be privileged; provided that nothing in this section shall authorise the publication of any blasphemous or indecent matter.

This defence was enlarged to cover broadcasting by the Defamation Act 1952. As one can see, Parliament chose not to define this privilege as being absolute. The few cases which have been before the courts on the meaning of Section 3, however, seem to indicate that the privilege bestowed is indeed absolute rather than qualified. Certainly the overwhelming weight of legal opinion supports that interpretation.

The constituent parts of the section should be memorized by every trainee journalist.

'A fair and accurate report'

- *Fair*: In order to be fair, court reports should be sufficiently balanced that the reader or listener is not likely to be misled. Absolute privilege will be lost if the report of the case is one-sided or lacks impartiality. For example, a report which details prosecution counsel's opening speech but omits to mention that the defendant denies the charge would not be regarded as fair and would therefore lose its privilege. Reporters ought, accordingly, to take great care to present an even-handed account of the proceedings. Rebuttals should be reported, as well as the allegations to which they refer; statements should be attributed to the maker, whether counsel or witness, rather than presented as straight fact.
- *Accurate*: Accuracy is, of course, of paramount importance. While some latitude is allowed for minor discrepancies any material mis-reporting is likely to deprive the publisher of his privilege. Thus, wrongly to describe a defendant as facing a charge more serious than that which is actually before the court is a libel for which there is probably no defence.

The failure by a reporter to clearly particularize the facts of the court case he is covering can also lead to libel problems – even if what he has written is ostensibly accurate. By far the greatest danger occurs where the defendant is not fully and properly identified in the published report.

The famous case of *Newstead* v *Express Newspapers Ltd (1940)* is a prime example. Harold Newstead, an unmarried hairdresser who lived in Camberwell successfully sued for libel over a *Daily Express* report about another Camberwell man of the same name who had been convicted of bigamy. The newspaper described the villain simply as 'Harold Newstead, a Camberwell man' and omitted to give his age, address or occupation.

The lesson to be learned from Newstead's case is not confined to court reporting. Whenever a story which reflects discredit on an individual is published or broadcast, care should be taken to ensure that no room is left for innocent namesakes of that person to step forward claiming to have been libelled.

'Published contemporaneously'

If the report of a case is not published as soon as reasonably practicable, given the particular type of publication, it will not be protected by absolute privilege. Daily newspapers should therefore be reporting the court proceedings of the previous day and the weeklies may summarize cases heard during the previous seven days. Radio and television stations, assuming they broadcast every day, will obviously satisfy the contemporaneous requirement by reporting on the same day as the case is heard but it is unlikely that they would lose their absolute protection for reporting the case the following morning.

It should be noted that where, under the Contempt of Court Act 1981, an order is made which postpones the reporting of a particular case, the requirement for contemporaneity will be met if the report is published 'as soon as practicable after that order expires'.

If a court report is not published contemporaneously the publisher will still be entitled, provided malice is not established against him, to rely on the defence of qualified privilege.

'In any newspaper'

By Section 1 of the Newspaper and Libel Registration Act 1881 only newspapers which are printed for sale and at intervals not exceeding twenty-six days qualify for the defence of absolute privilege in respect of court reporting. *Monthly magazines and free newspapers accordingly are not protected.*

In the case of monthlies this is perhaps understandable since such publications, because of their production timescale, would frequently be far from contemporaneous in their coverage. For freesheets, however, one has to say that the law has not caught up with recent developments in the media. Giveaway papers, especially at a local level, are a primary source of news to the reading public. A significant part of their content is bound to be devoted to coverage of the courts and to treat such reports differently in law simply because they appear in a product for which the public is not asked to pay seems both illogical and unjust. As with non-contemporaneous court reports, those that appear in free newspapers will enjoy the benefit of qualified privilege.

'Proceedings publicly heard'

- *Proceedings*:   Anything said in open court by judge, counsel, solicitors, officials or by witnesses in their evidence can be safely reported. Interruptions from the public gallery are unlikely to be regarded as part of the proceedings but there is authority to the effect that outbursts from parties to the case or from witnesses who have left the witness box will be. As regards documents in a case, their contents only become privileged if they are read out in court. Reporters who simply file the information contained on a charge sheet are not therefore completely safe unless that information is made public during the actual proceedings.

- *Publicly heard*: Only reports of cases held in open court attract absolute privilege. The defence is not therefore available in respect of proceedings which are heard 'in camera', i.e. behind closed doors. It also does not apply to cases heard in foreign courts.

Other areas of absolute privilege

Perhaps of less immediate importance to those who work in the media, but worth noting nevertheless, the other areas to which absolute privilege applies are:

1 Communications between lawyers and their clients.
2 The contents of reports by the Monopolies Commission and the Director General of Fair Trading.
3 Communications between officers of state (i.e. government officers and senior ranking civil servants and possibly members of the armed forces) in the course of their duty.

Qualified privilege

Qualified privilege is capable of covering a wide variety of statements and communications. Certain occasions to which it attaches are defined with reasonable particularity. Others rely simply on the existence of some duty or interest in the making of a statement which, provided he or she is acting honestly, will protect the maker against writs for libel or slander – even if the statement is inaccurate and defamatory. The defence has been developed over the years to encourage and protect open and honest communications, both of a public and private nature, which are recognized as being 'in the general interest of society'. (*Whiteley* v *Adams (1863)*.)

What distinguishes qualified privilege from absolute privilege is that the defence fails if the plaintiff can prove that the defendant was motivated by malice. Unlike those situations where the privilege is absolute, e.g. in the course of legal or parliamentary proceedings, a person who abuses an occasion of qualified privilege will be liable to pay the normal penalty for libel or slander.

Categories

The categories of statement to which qualified privilege will apply are as follows.

1 Statements made where there is a moral, legal or social duty or interest in communicating the relevant information.
2 Fair and accurate reports of parliamentary proceedings and extracts from parliamentary papers.
3 Fair and accurate reports of judicial proceedings whenever, and however, made.

4   Statements made on those occasions specified in Section 7 and the schedule to the Defamation Act 1952.

1   Statements made from a legal, moral or social duty
The situations which might come under this heading of qualified privilege are potentially endless. Over the years the courts have developed the defence to protect the many instances in everyday commercial, public and private life where information is passed on either from a sense of duty or in protection of some valid interest of the informant. In order to merit protection the duty or interest must be shared between the maker and recipient of the statement. In other words, the court must recognize both that the publisher was acting properly in passing on the information and that the publishee was the valid person to receive it.

The principle was defined with some authority by Lord Chief Justice Campbell in 1856:

> A communication made bona fide upon any subject matter in which the party communicating has an interest, or in reference to which he has a duty, is privileged, if made to a person having a corresponding interest or duty, although it contain criminatory matter which, without this privilege, would be slanderous and actionable
>
> *Harrison* v *Bush (1856)*

Examples of such communications include the reporting of suspected crimes to the police, neighbours who pass information about child welfare to the social services, character references by ex-employers, credit assessments provided by banks and a host of similar instances where information is transmitted for proper and responsible reasons. If, in circumstances like these, damaging statements are made which turn out to be inaccurate the person making them will be safe providing he has not acted from malice.

Unfortunately, however noble their motives, this particular category of qualified privilege is rarely available as a realistic defence to members of the media. The reason is that even though it may be socially, legally or morally proper to divulge or reveal certain information it is extremely unlikely that the general public, via the mass media, will be considered by the court to be the appropriate and proper recipient of such a communication. If a person can validly claim that he has a duty to state certain facts, say about wrongdoing, his statements will undoubtedly be cloaked in the protection of qualified privilege if they are made to the police. It is highly unlikely that they would be entitled to come within this defence if they are relayed to newspaper readers or television viewers.

2   Fair and accurate parliamentary reports
Providing the simple requirements of fairness and accuracy are satisfied the

media is given a good deal of latitude in the reporting of Parliament, safe from the threat of libel lawyers. As long as the reporting itself is accurate and honest the publisher will not be liable if the original statement which is the subject of the report is incorrect.

Not only parliamentary debates but also committee hearings and the contents of parliamentary papers and orders may be safely reported. Through a mixture of the defences of qualified privilege and fair comment parliamentary sketches, in which some lobby journalists specialize, and discussion pieces, however colourful or critical, will usually be acceptable.

3   Fair and accurate court reports

Reports of court cases which are not contemporaneous, not published in newspapers (as required by Section 3 of the Law of Libel Amendment Act 1888) and, in certain circumstances, not relating to the courts of this country are covered by qualified privilege even though they do not meet the requirements of absolute privilege. Such reports do, of course, still need to be fair and accurate accounts of the proceedings and the publisher should be free of malice.

Foreign court cases may be reported under this defence provided they are heard in public and the subject matter is of legitimate interest to the readers or viewers of whatever British newspaper or television station happens to be carrying the report.

4   Statements protected by Section 7 of the Defamation Act 1952

Qualified privilege is bestowed by statute on reports published in news-papers or broadcast by television or radio of those matters referred to in Section 7 of the Defamation Act 1952 and set out in detail in the Schedule to this Act.

The Schedule, in fact, creates two categories of statutory protection. Statements which come under Part 1 are privileged without explanation or contradiction. Those under Part 2 will not be entitled to the protection of the defence:

> . . . if it is proved that the defendant has been requested by the plaintiff to publish in the newspaper (or, for broadcasting, in the manner) in which the original publication was made a reasonable letter or statement by way of explanation or contradiction, and has refused or neglected to do so, or has done so in a manner not adequate or not reasonable having regard to all the circumstances.

Section 7 also stipulates that privilege will not apply to:

1   The publication of any matter prohibited by law.
2   Any matter which is not of public concern and the publication of which is not for the public benefit.

The full Schedule to the Act reads as follows:

Part 1: Statements privileged without explanation or contradiction

1   A fair and accurate report of any proceedings in public of the legislature of any part of Her Majesty's dominions outside Great Britain.
2   A fair and accurate report of any proceedings in public of an international organisation of which the United Kingdom or Her Majesty's Government in the United Kingdom is a member, or of any international conference to which that government sends a representative.
3   A fair and accurate report of any proceedings of an international court.
4   A fair and accurate report of any proceedings before a court exercising jurisdiction throughout any part of Her Majesty's dominions outside the United Kingdom, or of any proceedings of a court-martial held outside the United Kingdom under the Naval Discipline Act, the Army Act or the Air Force Act.
5   A fair and accurate report of any proceedings in public of a body or person appointed to hold a public inquiry by the government or legislature of any part of Her Majesty's dominions outside the United Kingdom.
6   A fair and accurate report of, or extract from, any register kept in pursuance of any Act of Parliament which is open to inspection by the public, or of any other document which is required by the law of any part of the United Kingdom to be open to inspection by the public.
7   A notice or advertisement published by, or on the authority of, any court within the United Kingdom or any judge or officer of such a court.

Part 2   Statements privileged subject to explanation or contradiction

8   A fair and accurate report of the findings or decision of any of the following associations, or of any committee·or governing body thereof, that is to say:
    (a)   An association formed in the United Kingdom for the purpose of promoting or encouraging the exercise of, or interest in, any art, science, religion or learning, and empowered by its constitution to exercise control over, or adjudicate upon, matters of interest or concern to the association, or the actions or conduct of any persons subject to such control or adjudication.
    (b)   An association formed in the United Kingdom for the purpose of promoting or safeguarding the interests of any trade, business, industry or profession, or of the persons carrying on or engaged in any trade, business, industry or profession, and empowered by its constitution to exercise control over, or adjudicate upon, matters connected with the trade, business, industry or profession, or the actions or conduct of those persons.
    (c)   An association formed in the United Kingdom for the purpose of promoting or safeguarding any game, sport or pastime to the playing or exercise of which members of the public are invited or admitted, and empowered by its constitution to exercise control over, or adjudicate upon, persons connected with, or taking part in, the game, sport or

pastime; being a finding or decision relating to a person who is a member of, or is subject by, virtue of any contract, to the control of the association.

9   A fair and accurate report of the proceedings of any public meeting held in the United Kingdom, that is to say, a meeting bona fide and lawfully held for a lawful purpose and for the furtherance or discussion of any matter of public concern, whether the admission to the meeting is general or restricted.

10   A fair and accurate report of the proceedings at any meeting or sitting in any part of the United Kingdom of:
   (a)   Any local authority or committee of a local authority or local authorities.
   (b)   Any justice or justices of the peace acting otherwise than as a court exercising judicial authority.
   (c)   Any commission, tribunal, committee or person appointed for the purposes of any inquiry by Act of Parliament, by Her Majesty or by a Minister of the Crown.
   (d)   Any person appointed by a local authority to hold a local inquiry in pursuance of any Act of Parliament.
   (e)   Any other tribunal, board, committee or body constituted by, or under, and exercising functions under, an Act of Parliament; not being a meeting or sitting, admission to which is denied to representatives of newspapers and other members of the public.

11   A fair and accurate report of the proceedings at a general meeting of any company or association constituted, registered or certified by, or under, any Act of Parliament or incorporated by Royal Charter, not being a private company within the meaning of the Companies Act 1948.

12   A copy or fair and accurate report or summary of any notice or other matter for the information of the public by, or on behalf of, any Government department, officer of state, local authority or chief officer of police.

OTHER DEFENCES

Offer of amends under Section 4 of the Defamation Act 1952

A brand new defence to libel was created by Section 4 of the Defamation Act 1952. It was introduced to protect innocent publishers against some of the harsher aspects of the libel laws – as instanced by the famous case of the fictional Artemus Jones who happened in real life to have a somewhat litigious namesake. The defence is aimed at protecting those publications which, through unforeseen accident and no lack of care, turn out to be actionably defamatory.

The defendant has the burden of establishing this defence and is required to prove:

1   That the words were published innocently in relation to the plaintiff.

2   That he has made a suitable offer of amends including a 'suitable correction' and a 'sufficient apology'.
3   That the offer was refused by the plaintiff but is still available up to the time of trial.

The test of innocence in relation to the publication is strictly defined. The words will be treated as published innocently of another person 'if and only if':

1   The publisher did not intend to publish them of, and concerning, another person, and did not know of circumstances under which they might be understood to refer to him.

or   2   The words were not defamatory on the face of them and the publisher did not know of circumstances by virtue of which they might be understood to be defamatory of that other person.

and   3   In either case, the publisher exercised all reasonable care in relation to the publication.

In practice the Section 4 defence is hardly ever used by the media. Accidental libels in newspapers or TV and radio programmes very rarely fit the narrow requirements of innocence as defined in the act.

Leave and licence

As one would logically expect, if a person consents to the publication of certain statements he or she is not then entitled to libel damages because of that publication.

The evidence of consent, however, should be clear and unequivocal. Whatever authorization the plaintiif is said to have given should be seen to refer to the publication of the libellous matter. If someone is approached by a reporter and asked about a particular defamatory statement concerning himself he will not, by indignantly denying it, be taken to have authorized the publication of the slur in the form of the denial. Similarly, if during the course of an acrimonious conversation one person challenges another to repeat what he has said in front of witnesses this will rarely amount to consent for the publication of slander.

The situation where this defence is most likely to arise is where the plaintiff has sold his or her story to a newspaper. The publisher would be entitled to rely on consent in relation to defamatory statements about the plaintiff which had come from the plaintiff's own mouth.

Innocent dissemination

Libel proceedings may be commenced against the original publisher of the offending statements and against anyone who thereafter republishes it. Thus in the case of libel in a newspaper liability may attach not only to the journalist, his editor and the proprietor but also against everyone down the line of printing and distribution. This could include the printers themselves, the wholesalers, the newsagents and even the newspaper delivery boy. The potentially disastrous effects of such wide liability are mitigated however by the defence of innocent dissemination.

A mere distributor of defamatory material may avail himself of this defence, i.e. innocent dissemination, if he can establish both of the following:

- That he was unaware the particular publication contained, or was likely to contain, libellous matter.
- That his lack of such knowledge was not due to his own negligence.

The defence is aimed at protecting those who deal in the publication as a product but have nothing to do with its content, e.g. wholesalers, retailers and libraries.

3 LIBEL: PROCEDURE, INJUNCTIONS AND DAMAGES

PROCEDURE

Since most libel actions are fought on issues of fact they should be no more complicated than the average criminal trial which simply decides who did what, to whom, when and where. Unfortunately for the litigants involved, proceedings in this particular area of law are nothing like so straightforward.

Between the issuing of the writ and the hearing of the action some nine to eighteen months will generally elapse in which professionally drafted pleadings are exchanged between the parties, all relevant documents are disclosed for inspection and hearings in chambers (rooms in the High Court) take place to decide preliminary or procedural points.

The procedure prior to trial usually takes the following pattern:

- The plaintiff commences his action by having a writ issued out of the High Court and served on the defendant. Either with the writ or shortly after it he will serve the Statement of Claim which must set out the actual words he alleges are libellous and the defamatory meanings he attaches to them.
- If he intends to fight the action the defendant is required to file a Defence with the High Court and serve it in turn on the plaintiff. The purpose of the Defence is to respond paragraph by paragraph to those matters alleged in the Statement of Claim and to plead whatever legitimate defence, e.g. justification or fair comment, relied upon by the defendant. All fact and matters in support of the plea must be particularized in the Defence.
- The plaintiff may then, if he wishes, serve a Reply dealing with any fresh matter raised by the Defence.
- During the exchange of pleadings both sides are likely to serve Requests for Further and Better Particulars which are designed to clarify, and extract more detail about, what is alleged by the other side.

- At the close of this procedure Discovery of Documents takes place. This is a formal exchange of lists setting out the documents relevant to the action which are, or have been, in the possession of each side. The parties are under a strict duty to disclose all documents which are relevant.
- Finally, the parties, or more usually their lawyers, attend a hearing in chambers at which directions for trial are given. This hearing is aimed at deciding the place of trial, whether it will be heard by judge alone or judge and jury, when the matter can be set down in the list of pending actions, and any outstanding matter relating to the pleadings.

The procedure at trial is not so different from other sorts of civil action except that the plaintiff has the last word and a jury is present to decide the major issues. The trial generally commences with the evidence called in support of the plaintiff's case. The evidence for the defence follows and after that there are speeches, first by counsel for the defendant and then by counsel for the plaintiff. The final address to the jury comes from the judge whose function at this stage of the trial is to sum up the evidence and give whatever directions are necessary on points of law. The members of the jury then retire to consider their verdict. If they decide for the plaintiff they must also assess the appropriate amount of damages.

LIMITATION PERIOD

Anyone wishing to sue for libel must issue a writ within three years of the publication which gave offence. An action begun after the three-year limitation period will be struck out by the court.

Although it will rarely debar them from proceeding, plaintiffs should remember that long delays either in notifying the original complaint or in advancing the libel action towards trial, can count against them. Juries are likely to suspect that an injured party who did not even bother to complain for, say, one year cannot have felt particularly distressed.

INJUNCTIONS

As every reporter knows, before publishing a story in which a person might claim to be defamed it is proper journalistic practice to confront the individual concerned and seek his or her reaction to the allegations. Human nature being what it is, the initial reaction of the person confronted is to try to work out what can be done to stop the story appearing. With that in mind it is not surprising that such people frequently prefer speaking to their lawyers than the reporter on their doorstep. The first thought that goes through the mind of a lawyer confronted with such a situation is whether it is possible to get a court injunction to restrain publication.

The injunction is undoubtedly the strongest weapon in the plaintiff's armoury. On the principle that prevention is better than cure it has far more practical effect than a writ being issued after the damage has been done. Fortunately for the media, courts are generally unwilling to grant injunctions preventing intended publications where the defendant claims that he has a defence to the alleged libel.

Applications for injunctions against the media to restrain the publication of a story are fairly commonplace and usually matters of some urgency. If a person discovers on a Saturday morning that one of the Sunday newspapers is planning to run a damaging article about him that weekend he has every right to regard his plight as an emergency. In such situations, if his lawyers act quickly enough, it may be possible to obtain an injunction from a judge out of court hours. If it is a genuine emergency the restraining order might even be granted without giving the media defendant time to organize representation.

To obtain an *ex parte* injunction of this nature the plaintiff would need to establish both of the following:

1   A *prima facie* case that the intended publication is libellous.
2   That damages awarded after the event would be an inadequate remedy.

In addition, the plaintiff would be required to undertake to the judge that he will issue a writ as soon as possible and that in the event of his action ultimately failing he will pay for whatever loss or damage the defendant has suffered as a result of the injunction.

The recipient of an *ex parte* injunction has the right to apply for its discharge almost immediately. He will succeed on such an application if he gives sworn evidence that he can justify the relevant statements or that he comes within some other recognized defence to libel. Similarly, if the publisher manages to attend the plaintiff's initial application for the injunction and makes such a plea, the restraining order is most unlikely to be made.

The legal principles which govern prior restraint of the press have not changed since the end of the last century. In a 1969 case they were summarized by Lord Denning as follows:

> The court will not restrain the publication of an article, even though it is defamatory, when the defendant says he intends to justify it or to make comment on a matter of public interest.

The primary reason for this is:

> . . . the importance in the public interest that the truth should come out. As the court said . . . (in *Bonnard* v *Perryman* – an 1891 case on the same legal point) . . .

'The right of free speech is one which it is for the public interest that the public should possess, and, indeed, that they should exercise without impediment so long as no wrongful act is done.' There is no wrong done if it is true, or if it is fair comment on a matter of public interest. The court will not prejudice the issue by granting an injunction in advance of publication.

Fraser v *Evans (1969)*

DAMAGES

Of all the unsatisfactory elements in the law of libel the one which has perhaps attracted most criticism is the manner of awarding compensation. The assessment of damages is solely a matter for the jury. They are not told how much other libel plaintiffs have won in the past nor are they given specific guidance on what might be an appropriate figure or even what range of figures they should be considering. It is hardly surprising that marked inconsistencies exist between awards and outrageously high sums have been given for comparatively trivial libels.

When the award of £34,000 to the actor Telly Savalas for unkind things said in a *Daily Mail* article came under attack in 1976, the foreman of the jury wrote a letter in his defence to *The Times*. In it he stated that at the time of the trial he and his fellow jurors had '. . . not the remotest idea what compensation is paid for anything . . . Apparently that is why we were asked. If that is so, the court had the outcome it deserved from the appointed procedure.' (*The Times*, 22 June 1976.)

It is difficult not to both agree and sympathize with the foreman's conclusion. If seemingly excessive or inconsistent awards emerge from the libel courts the fault lies with the system which dictates that assessment of damages is a subjective process performed by jurors without any real guidance.

There have certainly been some odd results. On 3 June 1987 Royal Naval intelligence officer, Martin Packard, was awarded £450,000 for three articles which appeared four years earlier in the Greek daily newspaper, *Elefthero-typia*. Only fifty or so copies of this newspaper are circulated in the United Kingdom and all of them, not surprisingly, are printed in the Greek language. The award was, at the time, the largest ever by a British libel court – it represented about £10,000 for each person in Britain to whom the libel was published.

However, Mr Packard's record stood for barely one month. At the end of July 1987, the famous author and erstwhile politician, Jeffrey Archer, was awarded £500,000 in libel damages against the *Daily Star* newspaper for an article suggesting that he had slept with a prostitute. The newspaper did not appeal.

These two cases, particularly Archer's, which was fought for three full weeks amidst enormous newspaper and television publicity, started a trend of massive awards in libel cases. Three months after Archer's victory another plaintiff, Narendra Sethia, was awarded £260,000 against the *Mail on Sunday* for an article in which he was not even named. The newspaper suggested that the logbook of the submarine *Conqueror* had been stolen by one of its former officers who then went to live on the island of St Lucia. Sethia satisfied the jury that, although not named, he was identifiable.

In early 1988 another libel jury awarded £300,000 to a company which manufactured stationery for the suggestion in a low-circulation trade magazine that the company sold cheap copies under the guise of respectable brand names. Since the plaintiff company did not claim for any loss of profits and obviously could not claim for the distress and injured feelings which individual plaintiffs always make so much of, the award does seem unreasonably high.

In the event, neither award was paid. After appeals were filed both dependants agreed to settle for a greatly reduced sum.

Categories of damages

Damages for libel can fall under three possible headings:

1 Compensatory damages
2 Aggravated damages
3 Exemplary damages

The first two are broadly concerned with compensation and the third is aimed at punishing the defendant.

Compensatory damages

The purpose of compensatory damages is to provide the plaintiff with *restitutio in integrum*, i.e. to restore him to the position he would have been in had the defamatory material never been published. Under this heading of damages he will therefore be entitled to recover the monetary equivalent of everything he has lost and suffered as a result of the libel.

There are two components to the compensatory award:

- *Special damages*:   These will amount to a sum equal to the actual financial or material loss suffered. Thus if the plaintiff can establish, for example, that the publication of the libel caused him to lose his job or caused his customers or clients to withdraw their business, he would be entitled to claim the full amount of his lost income as special damages.
- *Damages for the plaintiff's distress and the injury to his reputation*:   This element of the award is undoubtedly the more difficult to calculate. In most areas of civil law damages are limited to identifiable material loss

and are therefore calculable with some precision. By contrast, in libel the court is required to place a figure on the extent to which the feelings and good name of a plaintiff are hurt. Quantifying such intangible losses in monetary terms is particularly difficult. The only parallel in other areas of the law can be seen in personal injuries litigation where damages are awarded for the pain and suffering experienced by the physically injured plaintiff. There, however, the level of damages is assessed solely by a judge whose expert knowledge of previous cases ensures a large degree of fairness and consistency.

The critical difference in libel actions is that the jurors, rather than the judge, are the sole arbiters of damages. Ironically, the very quality for which they are chosen, i.e. open-mindedness uncluttered by legal professionalism, is the very factor most likely to produce marked inconsistencies and apparent unfairness in libel awards. In other words, to quote the foreman of the jury in the Savalas case, most juries have 'not the remotest idea what compensation is paid for anything'.

Because the system of assessing damages for libel allows for such a large subjective element it is, not surprisingly, quite difficult for a losing defendant to appeal against the award of damages with any real hope of success.

In *Cassell & Co* v *Broome (1972)* Lord Reid identified why it is so difficult for the Appeal Court to rule, however extravagant an award, that it is one which no reasonable jury would give. Contrasting those cases where the plaintiff 'has been held up to hatred, ridicule and contempt' with the normal civil case about strictly material loss, he said of libel cases:

> Not only is it impossible to ascertain how far other people's minds have been affected, it is almost impossible to equate the damage to a sum of money. Any one person trying to fix a sum as compensation will probably find in his mind a wide bracket within which a sum could be regarded by him as not unreasonable – and different people will come to different conclusions. So, in the end, there will probably be a wide gap between the sum which on an objective view could be regarded as the least, and the sum which could be regarded as the most, to which the plaintiff is entitled as compensation.

Factors bound to be considered by the jury in deciding on compensatory damages are such things as the seriousness of the libel and the extent of the publication. Thus, publishing an accusation of murder will normally result in higher damages than suggesting that a person does not pay his bills on time. Similarly, damages are likely to be higher in respect of a defamatory statement published in the *News of the World*, which has a circulation of several million, than for the same allegation published in a small local newspaper.

Where the Court of Appeal finds that the damages are excessive (i.e., greater than any reasonable jury would award) it can substitute its own figure if both parties agree to this course. One such recent case was *Esther Rantzen* v *Sunday People (1992)* where the appeal judges reduced the jury's award of £250,000 to £110,000.

If one or both parties object to the Appeal Court substituting its own figure, a successful appeal simply results in the case being sent back to the High Court for a fresh trial on the question of damages alone.

Aggravated damages

Aggravated damages are awarded where the behaviour of the defendant has somehow added to the hurt and injury to the plaintiff which resulted from the mere publication of the defamatory words. In *Cassell* v *Broome*, by way of generalized example, Lord Reid said that any 'high-handed, malicious, insulting or oppressive' behaviour by the defendant could give cause for aggravated damages.

Various factors may give rise to an award under this category of damages. Anything that looks like a campaign of vilification, even if many of the derogatory things said about the plaintiff are true, might certainly qualify, as would repetition of the libel after the original complaint is made. Failing to publish the plaintiff's denial or explanation, or making no attempt to check the defamatory allegations with him could also be said to aggravate the injury. Similarly, failing to apologize and persisting in a plea of justification are normally put forward with some success as arguments for awarding aggravated damages.

Exemplary damages

In certain circumstances the jury in a libel action may decide that the defendant should be liable not only to compensate the plaintiff for the wrong committed but also to suffer punishment for the way he has behaved. The appropriate course in such cases is to make an award of exemplary damages. They are a purely punitive measure which will only apply where the jury are satisfied that the defendant showed a cynical disregard for the feelings of the plaintiff by knowingly publishing the libel in the hope of profiting from it.

To establish an entitlement to exemplary damages the plaintiff must therefore establish both:

1 That the defendant knew, or was reckless as to whether, the defamatory statement was true or false.
2 That the defendant published the libel in the hope that the material advantage gained from his wrongdoing would exceed whatever penalty he might have to pay for it.

Plaintiffs have in the past found to their advantage that a finding in their favour on the question of exemplary damages can be very profitable. In the 1986 action brought by millionaire publisher Robert Maxwell against the satirical magazine *Private Eye* over allegations of improper political funding the jury decided that the appropriate sum in compensatory damages was a modest £5,000. It then went on however to award Mr Maxwell exemplary damages of £50,000.

Again, in *Riches* v *News Group Newspapers (1984)* the ten officers of Banbury CID received a paltry £300 each at the end of their libel action against the *News of the World*. Those in court at the time were stunned when the foreman of the jury went on to announce that each of the plaintiffs would also receive £25,000 in exemplary damages. The total of £253,000 made it, at the time, the largest sum of damages ever awarded in an English libel action. Fortunately for common sense the newspaper successfully appealed and the case was settled before the retrial for a small fraction of that sum.

In mitigation of damages the defendant is, of course, entitled to rely on his own honourable or innocent behaviour, e.g. an apology published promptly or a genuine mistake in the original publication. He may also, where appropriate, adduce evidence of the generally bad reputation of the plaintiff. It is, after all, reasonable that a habitual bank robber should receive less in damages than a completely honest man if he happens to have been wrongly accused by the media of a particular theft.

COSTS

Having to pay damages is, of course, not the only financial penalty which an unsuccessful defendant has to bear. He or she will usually also have to pay the entire costs of the action, including those of the other side. Although the awarding of costs is entirely a matter for the discretion of the judge it is invariable practice that the loser in civil litigation must meet the legal costs incurred by the winner. A losing plaintiff, therefore, would be similarly penalized.

More and more in libel actions the question of costs is tending to become the consideration which overrides all others when deciding whether or not to fight a case to its bitter end in court. Recent examples have provided glaring examples of the dangers.

- *Gee* v *The BBC (1985)* was settled on the eighty-seventh day in the High Court when the BBC agreed to pay Dr Sidney Gee £75,000 damages for allegations of malpractice relating to slimming drugs. The total costs bill faced by the Corporation was estimated at a staggering £1,200,000.

- Archer *v* Express Newspapers Ltd (1987) – an action against the *Daily Star* newspaper went onto the record books for producing the largest award of libel damages made by a British court, i.e. £500,000. The sum awarded was undoubtedly a blow to the *Star*. It was comfortably exceeded however by the bill for costs which according to reports amounted to about £750,000. The trial lasted exactly three weeks.
- *Orme* v *Associated Newspapers (1981)* was a case where the plaintiffs, a religious sect known as the Moonies, paid the price for taking the case all the way and losing. On this occasion the liability for costs was reported to be in excess of £500,000.

Payments into court

In libel, and indeed in all civil cases, there is a way in which a defendant can seek to protect himself against the frequently horrendous expense involved in being ordered to pay the costs of the trial. A defendant who recognizes that he may lose the action may pay the sum to which he thinks the plaintiff is entitled into court. The plaintiff then has a choice between accepting that payment in settlement of his claim or proceeding to trial in the hope that the jury will ultimately award a greater sum in damages.

This procedure, like many aspects of libel litigation, calls for the sort of steady nerves and cool judgement expected of poker-players. For if the amount paid into court equals, or exceeds, that which is awarded by the jury the plaintiff will be ordered to pay all the legal costs incurred *after* the date of the payment. Conversely, if the jury's award is greater than the 'payment in' (as it is known by lawyers) then the defendant will be burdened with the costs of the action from start to finish.

The payment in must be made before the actual trial of the action commences. Since by far the largest part of the legal costs are run up by the trial itself, this means that an enormous amount rests on pitching the size of the payment correctly.

It should be big enough either to persuade the plaintiff that it is worth taking the money rather than risking a lower award from the jury or, if the plaintiff is not tempted into taking it, to equal or exceed the damages which are ultimately awarded.

One recent plaintiff who gambled against a defendant's payment into court and lost was *Coronation Street* actor, William Roache. In 1991 he sued *The Sun* for an article which labelled him smug and boring. Several weeks before trial the newspaper paid £50,000 into court. Mr Roache declined to take the money out. In the event, the jury (who of course had no knowledge of the payment in) found that he had indeed been libelled but gave him exactly the same amount, i.e., £50,000.

Because he failed to beat the newspaper's payment, Mr Roache was ordered to meet *The Sun*'s costs from the date it lodged the money. At the end of the case he was severely out of pocket.

4 CRIMINAL LIBEL

Every journalist and publisher knows the risk of attracting a High Court writ for libel. Not many, however, realize or fully appreciate that the publication of a libel can also land them in jail. For as well as being a popular and fertile area for the institution of proceedings in the civil courts, libellous publications can, if they are sufficiently serious, lead to criminal prosecutions.

There are many who consider that criminal libel has no place in modern law. In 1975 the Faulkes Committee on Defamation considered whether it should be abolished but concluded that it provided a useful extra remedy in certain special categories of libel and in any case there was nothing better with which to replace it. Since then various judges have commented on its shortcomings and the Law Commission has, at different times, recommended either that it should be drastically amended or that it should be abolished and replaced with a statutory offence of criminal defamation.

The origin of criminal libel appears to lie in the thirteenth century public offence of *Scandalum Magnatum*. The objective of this law was to prevent the uttering and dissemination of stories which tended to arouse the people against their masters or cause a breach of the peace.

In later years this element of scandalizing the mighty is a recurrent feature of criminal libel cases.

- In 1789 the editor of *The Times*, John Walter, was sent to prison for sixteen months after his newspaper published an article which suggested that the Prince of Wales and the Duke of York might not have been genuinely happy when their father, George III recovered from an illness.
- Exactly 100 years later Adolfus Rosenburg, who edited *Town Talk*, was given eighteen months imprisonment for implying that the then Prince of Wales, who was to become Edward VII, was having an affair with the actress Lillie Langtry.

These days, criminal proceedings for libel are rare. That is not to say editors should be dismissive about the risk for it might often suit a plaintiff to pursue his case in the criminal courts instead of, or, if he or she wishes, as well as, the civil courts.

Actually, there are certain advantages in choosing such a course. The one which is likely to occur first to the victim of a serious libel is that the penalties imposed for criminal libel are harsher than those which might be imposed in the civil courts. An embittered plaintiff may get far more satisfaction out of trying to send the individual reporter or editor to jail than from an action for damages against their employer.

The real tactical advantage for a plaintiff, however, is that criminal libel is in some ways more difficult to defend successfully than its civil counterpart. For example, while truth is in almost all cases a complete answer to a civil action for libel it is not in itself a defence to a charge of criminal libel.

WHAT IS CRIMINAL LIBEL?

In one of the comparatively few recent cases Mr Justice Comyn directed the Old Bailey jury that a criminal libel is: 'A written statement so serious in itself, and so greatly affecting a person's character and reputation as to justify invoking criminal punishment instead of, or as well as, the civil law and damages.'

Probably because of its public order origins it was at one time thought that a tendency to provoke a breach of the peace was an essential ingredient of criminal libel. More recent cases have shown, however, that for a libel to amount to a criminal offence it must simply be *serious* as opposed to *trivial*. Any remaining doubt about a breach of the peace element in criminal libel was cleared up by the House of Lords' judgement in the case of *Gleaves v Deakin (1980)*:

> A criminal libel must be a serious libel. If the libel is of such a character as to be likely to disturb the peace of the community or to provoke a breach of the peace, then it is not to be regarded as trivial. But to hold . . . that the existence of such a tendency tends to show that the libel is a serious one, is a very different thing from saying that proof of its existence is necessary to establish guilt of the offence.

Viscount Dilhorne

Lord Scarman's judgement in the same case also suggested that a criminal libel might be identified by a comparison between what is deemed to be serious and what would be regarded as trivial:

> It is, however, not every libel that warrants a criminal prosecution. To warrant prosecution the libel must be sufficiently serious to require the intervention of the

Crown in the public interest. . . . The libel must be more than of a trivial character: it must be such as to provoke anger or cause resentment.

In this particular case, Roger Gleaves, also known as the Bishop of Medway, prosecuted the authors and publishers of the book *Johnny Go Home*. Gleaves, who had once been described by a judge as 'a cruel and wicked man with an evil influence on others' had a string of convictions for violence and homosexual offences involving teenagers. In 1975 he was sentenced to four years at the Old Bailey for wounding and homosexual offences against homeless boys. Not surprisingly his activities provoked widespread public outrage which was reflected in a number of articles both in the press and on TV. This wholly justifiable media interest culminated in a documentary production by Yorkshire Television entitled *Johnny Go Home*. The book of the same name was the subject of the criminal libel proceedings. Eventually, after a two-week trial (again at the Old Bailey) the authors were acquitted by the jury.

DISTINCTIONS BETWEEN CIVIL AND CRIMINAL LIBEL

Apart from the place and mode of trial criminal libel differs from civil libel in a number of important respects.

- Except where convictions deemed to be spent under the Rehabilitation of Offenders Act 1974 are published, truth is a complete defence to civil actions for libel. Perhaps because the original objective of bringing libel within the criminal law was related to preserving the peace, the accuracy or truth of a statement will not necessarily protect its maker from punishment. 'The greater the truth the greater the libel' is a phrase which is rooted in this branch of the law and it has always been recognized that the awful truth is often more likely to arouse fury than an obvious falsehood. Unlike the civil version those accused of criminal libel must establish not only that the words were true but also that they were published for the public benefit.
- In civil actions the plaintiff must prove that the defamatory statement was published to a third party. For the purposes of criminal libel publication to other people is not essential and it would be sufficient to show that the defendant published the words to the plaintiff alone. Again, in the historic context of preventing a breach of the peace this is quite logical.
- It is a basic principle of civil libel that publications about a person or persons who have died are not actionable. If, however, the libellous statement is sufficiently serious the fact that it refers to a dead person will not prevent the institution of criminal proceedings.

- Section 1 of The Defamation Act, 1952, which brings defamatory statements made on television and radio within the ambit of libel (as opposed to simply being slander) does not apply to criminal libel. Proceedings in the criminal courts can therefore be instituted over such transmissions only if the words are read from a written text.

CRIMINAL LIBEL IN NEWSPAPERS

Despite the harshness and severity of this small area of the law there is some comfort for those who run newspapers. By The Law of Libel Amendment Act 1888, Section 8, no criminal prosecution for libel may be commenced against 'any proprietor, publisher, editor or any person responsible for the publication of a newspaper' without the consent of a judge in chambers. This, in effect, means that anyone who wishes to pursue a newspaper or its editor must obtain the leave of a High Court judge.

In this context a 'newspaper' includes periodicals providing there are not more than twenty-eight days between regular issues.

As recent cases have demonstrated, this filtering process provides significant protection to newspapers. In deciding whether to permit prosecutions against them, judges have a wide discretion to consider all the circumstances in each case. In practice it seems that the plaintiff has to show a strong *prima facie* case of serious libel for which the public interest requires a criminal prosecution.

A clear indication of how judges will treat such applications to prosecute newspapers was given by Mr Justice Wien in *Goldsmith v Pressdram Ltd (1977)*. On 12 December 1975 the satirical fortnightly periodical *Private Eye* published an article headed 'All's Well That Ends Elwes' which was illustrated with a picture of Sir James Goldsmith. The piece suggested that friends of Lord Lucan led by Goldsmith had conspired to obstruct police investigations into the death of Sandra Rivett, the Lucan family nanny. According to *Private Eye* the conspiracy was hatched at a lunch given on the day after the nanny's death by another of Lord Lucan's friends, John Aspinall. Goldsmith was said to have sent Dominic Elwes to visit Lady Lucan in hospital in order to discover what she had told the police. The article also implied that he had persuaded a witness not to appear at the coroner's inquest into Miss Rivett's death. It turned out that *Private Eye* had its facts monumentally wrong. At the time of Aspinall's lunch Goldsmith was out of the country. There was, in any case, no evidence to support the allegation of a conspiracy. When *Private Eye* published two more libellous articles about him in its next issues it proved more than Goldsmith could bear. His lawyers issued over eighty writs and gave notice that they intended to institute proceedings for criminal libel. There was no doubt that the articles were seriously libellous. There was also little dispute that they were false. This was acknowledged in part at least when, on 5 April 1976, some four months after the first article *Private Eye*'s solicitors admitted in a letter to Goldsmith's lawyers that he was not at the relevant lunch and was no part of any conspiracy. They offered to publicly withdraw the allegation and apologize. Goldsmith decided nevertheless to press on and his application for leave to prosecute came before Mr Justice Wien on 13 April 1976. In granting permission for Goldsmith to proceed the judge set out the principles which will normally apply in such cases.

> First, before a discretion can be exercised in favour of an applicant who wishes to institute criminal libel proceedings in respect of a libel . . . there must be a case to go before a criminal court that is so clear at first sight that it is beyond argument that there is a case to answer. Secondly, the libel must be a serious one – so serious that it is proper for the criminal law to be invoked. . . . Thirdly, the question of public interest needs to be taken into account, so that the judge has to ask himself the question, 'Does the public interest require the institution of criminal proceedings?'

The same three criteria were used by Mr Justice Taylor to produce the opposite result in the 1982 case of *Desmond* v *Thorne*. The *Sunday People* had published an article about Paul Desmond headlined, 'Bully Boasts, I Beat Up Tragic Deb'. The piece described him as 'a habitually violent, drunken bully'. There was evidence before the court that Desmond himself had tried to sell the same newspaper a story about his relationship with the deceased debutante and that he had admitted mistreating her. Taking these matters into account the judge was far from satisfied that a sufficiently clear *prima facie* case of serious libel had been made out. On the other hand, he was satisfied that this was not a case: 'In which the public interest requires the institution of criminal proceedings.'

Where the alleged criminal libel appears other than in newspapers, e.g. in books, correspondence, public notices, etc. no special leave is required to institute proceedings and the action commences like any criminal case. Prosecutions are normally brought and conducted by the individual who claims to have been libelled but they may be handled by the Director of Public Prosecutions or the usual prosecuting authority.

DEFENDING CRIMINAL LIBEL ACTIONS

There are two defences to criminal libel which are clearly recognized by the courts and one more about which there is some doubt.

- By Section 6 of the Libel Act 1843 the defendant will have a good defence if he establishes that the words complained of were true and were published 'for the public benefit'.

- The defendant will also have a good defence if the words were published under absolute or qualified privilege. The occasions to which privilege will apply are generally the same for criminal libel as for civil libel.
- In the absence of recent authoritative cases on the point there is a degree of doubt as to whether fair comment can be successfully pleaded in answer to a criminal libel charge. Leading textbook writers, however, suggest that it would be accepted as a good defence.

Although it seems both unfair and illogical it is, in fact, considerably more difficult successfully to defend an action for criminal libel than one for civil libel.

It is a normal principle of justice in criminal cases, especially those where the liberty of an individual is at stake, that the primary burden of proof rests on the prosecutor. It is also normal in terms of justice that the standard of proof which the prosecutor must satisfy is greater than that required to prove a civil case.

In both respects the opposite applies in actions for criminal libel. Although the prosecutor must prove the mechanics of the offence, i.e. that the words were published and they constitute a very serious slur, it falls upon the defendant to prove the matters of real evidential substance. He must convince the jury that the words were true and that they were published in the public interest. If there is any serious doubt about either matter the benefit of that doubt must be given to the prosecutor and not, as in nearly all other criminal cases, to the defendant.

The balance is tipped even further in favour of the prosecutor by the absence, in criminal libel proceedings, of any necessity to prove a guilty mind or intent. It will not avail a publisher or editor in the slightest on the issue of liability that he honestly and genuinely believed the words to be true if he cannot prove that they were, in fact, both true and for the public benefit.

PENALTIES

The punishment for criminal libel is provided for in Sections 4 and 5 of the Libel Act 1843. Under Section 4 a person who publishes such a libel knowing it to be false may be sentenced to a maximum of two years in prison. Section 5 applies where the publisher did not know that the libel was false and provides a maximum sentence of one year. In either case the fine is unlimited.

THE FAULKES COMMITTEE

Since the mid-seventies there have been barely half a dozen criminal prosecutions for libel each year. In 1975 the Faulkes Committee on Defamation actually considered its abolition. It was concluded, however, that the offence should be preserved – particularly as a worthwhile sanction against those instances where 'the libellous matter may be gross and persistent and the conduct of the defendant very bad indeed.'

5 BLASPHEMOUS LIBEL AND SEDITIOUS LIBEL

BLASPHEMOUS LIBEL

The law of blasphemous libel, which many considered to have been long forgotten as a basis for criminal prosecution, enjoyed something of a revival in the mid-seventies. The successful private prosecution launched in 1977 by campaigning moralist, Mary Whitehouse, against *Gay News* taught contemporary writers and journalists something about which their forebears in the last century would have been well aware, i.e. blasphemy can be a crime as well as a sin.

The common law offence of blasphemous libel is traditionally defined, according to Archbold, in *The Criminal Practitioner's Handbook*, as:

> . . . to speak, or otherwise publish, any matter blaspheming God, e.g. by denying his existence or providence, or contumeliously reproaching Jesus Christ, or vilifying or bringing into disbelief or contempt or ridicule Christianity in general or any doctrine of the Christian religion or the Bible.

The essence of blasphemy is the use of language which tends to vilify Christ or some aspect of Christianity in a way which is likely to arouse resentment. It is clear that the manner and context of the publication is as important as its content in assessing whether the law against blasphemy has been contravened. A responsible debate or an honest and serious publication in which attacks are made upon Christian beliefs will not constitute the offence. However, where those attacks amount to a scurrilous and public vilification of Christ or Christianity the criminal law may intervene.

The *Gay News* case established that the intention of the publisher is irrelevant and once the fact of publication by the accused is proved, the jury needs only to consider the meaning and effect of the words.

Whitehouse v *Gay News and Lemon (1977)* was the first prosecution for blasphemous libel since 1922. The Particulars of Offence which were put to the jury at the Old Bailey alleged that the magazine and its editor

'. . . unlawfully and wickedly published . . . a blasphemous libel concerning the Christian religion, namely an obscene poem and illustration vilifying Christ in His life and His crucifixion.' The poem, which was written by Professor James Kirkup, contained explicit references to Christ having indulged in homosexual acts with a number of men. It was intended, according to the defendants, to be a serious expression of the all-encompassing nature of God's love. The jury found by a majority that it amounted to blasphemous libel. On appeal, the House of Lords (again by a majority) confirmed that it was not necessary for the prosecution to prove an intent to attack the Christian religion. If a person deliberately publishes that which 'crossed the line which divided the blasphemous from the non-blasphemous he cannot thereafter be heard to say he did not know or realise or intend.'

In the event *Gay News* was fined £1,000 and the editor was sentenced to a suspended term of nine months imprisonment and a fine of £500 (the nine months was successfully appealed).

As with criminal libel, leave must be sought from a judge in chambers before a prosecution for blasphemy may be commenced against a newspaper.

There have been various lobbies for the abolition of blasphemy as a crime. It was, perhaps, noteworthy in terms of official attitudes towards this branch of the law that at no time during the privately-funded prosecution of *Gay News* did the Director of Public Prosecutions suggest that his office would take over from Mrs Whitehouse in bringing the case to court. The fact that it protects Christianity and no other religion certainly places it out of step with general attitudes about the role of criminal law in a multicultured society.

SEDITIOUS LIBEL

The third of the old forms of libel to which the sanction of the criminal law attaches is seditious libel. It consists of words or statements which do any of the following:

1 Promote ill-will, discontent or dissatisfaction between the sovereign's subjects.
2 Incite or encourage the use of unlawful means, particularly physical force, over any public issue.
3 Bring the Government, the law or the Sovereign into hatred or ridicule.

In many ways the law against sedition, like that relating to blasphemy and criminal liable, is a hangover from less tolerant days. The essence of the crime was the encouragement of active discontent through attacks on the established order.

Though the last prosecution for seditious libel took place over fifty years ago, the offence still exists and there is no reason why, like blasphemy and criminal libel, it should not enjoy a revival given appropriate circumstances (e.g. an enthusiastic private prosecutor).

According to the leading textbook (Archbold) seditious libel:

> . . . does not prevent candid, full and free discussion of any public matter, which is the right of every citizen, unless the discussion takes place in circumstances calculated or intended to incite tumult . . . or the statements made are an appeal to the passions of the hearers and an incitement to violence or outrage.

Once again, therefore, it is the likely *effect* of the published statements as much as their content which constitutes the offence. The law does not inhibit serious and honest criticism of the law, the Government or the Sovereign, even where the words used are forceful or extreme. It may, however, intervene if such attacks are malicious as well as extreme and if the effect is 'an incitement to violence or outrage'.

In *R.* v *Aldred (1909)*, the defendant had published statements aimed at Indian students which preached the message that political assassination in the cause of Indian independence was not murder. The publication hailed one Indian student who had murdered Sir Curzon Wyllie as a martyr. It was held to be a seditious libel.

It seems likely, according to the authorities, that providing the accused was responsible for the publication and understood what was being published, the fact that he did not intend it to have any of the effects set out in points 1, 2 and 3 above is no defence.

Similarly, it is no defence that the words were true or that they were published as a matter of fair comment, though this may amount to strong mitigation.

The accused will, however, avoid conviction if he is able to prove that although technically responsible for the publication, e.g. as a printer or distributor, he was unaware that the contents were seditious and had no reason to suspect it.

Newspaper reports of parliamentary proceedings and judicial proceedings are privileged against prosecution providing they are fair and accurate.

6 THE LEGAL SYSTEM

Every journalist should have a sound knowledge of his country's legal system. An understanding of how the courts run, the people who run them and the basis for their authority is essential for anyone who wishes to work in the media.

It is, after all, virtually impossible to present the daily news, either local or national, without referring in some measure to events at the law courts. Covering the nearest Magistrates or Crown Court a few days each week is part of basic training for reporters. Simply attending court and observing the cases dealt with is of limited use, however, without a reasonable understanding of the legal procedures involved. Reporters should be familiar with the criminal process from arrest to sentencing and with the civil process from issue of writ to judgement. They should be able to recognize the functions of, and distinctions between, the officers and agents of the courts and have a fair knowledge about the system of appeals.

This chapter attempts to introduce the reporter to the legal system and its personnel and procedures.

WHAT IS THE LAW?

The law is one of the major influences on the life of every person in the country. It is a controller, a protector and a regulator. In one sense it is simply a body of dos and don'ts representing the minimum standards of conduct which every member of society is obliged to follow. In another, it is an immensely sophisticated set of rules and regulations for administering the complex relationships between fellow individuals and between the individual and the state. Since, in general, the law reflects the standards of society it does, albeit very slowly, move with the times.

For most people, not surprisingly, the law, the courts and lawyers are subjects which tend to cause some anxiety. What is certain, however, is that whichever time or society one lives in, without law there is chaos.

THE SOURCES OF LAW

Unlike many countries where the law originates with a single code or a set of codes, English law is found in an untidy mix of ancient custom and relatively recent parliamentary legislation.

The primary sources are the common law and statute.

Common law

The old common law dates from the twelfth century when the King's judges were entrusted with the task of setting up a system of laws which would apply throughout the realm. No such thing had existed before this time and the people of the country had been subject, for the most part, only to local law and custom as enforced by whatever nobleman owned the land upon which they lived.

In execution of the King's wishes the judges set about first finding and then administering, as a single unified system, those old customary laws which were common throughout the realm. In order to become part of the common law a custom had to date from 'time immemorial', had to be accepted as binding by the people and had to be capable of precise definition.

It was the first system of national law to exist in Britain and, not surprisingly, relied for its interpretation and development on the very judges who had set it up. Although it may have had its origins in binding customs which date from time immemorial the common law, in its present form, is effectively a set of laws made by judges.

Over the last few decades there has been a slow but sure process, undertaken by Parliament and the legal profession, of rationalizing and codifying the old common law through statutes.

Statute

Statutory legislation, which is the other main source of law, also relies heavily on the judiciary for its interpretation as well as its application. Statute law comes in the form of written Acts of Parliament which receive the assent of the Sovereign after being passed by both the House of Commons and the House of Lords. Unfortunately what is passed as law by both Houses of Parliament is not always clear to those who might be subject to the particular piece of legislation. The precise meaning of many statutes has therefore to be determined by the courts. Every year there is a fresh crop of test cases aimed at settling the actual meaning and effect of recent legislation.

The Contempt of Court Act 1981 is one of the more significant pieces of recent legislation affecting the media. It enlarged upon the common law crime of contempt by adding a statutory offence which was defined in terms of creating a 'serious risk of substantial prejudice'. After a particularly stormy passage through Parliament it was perhaps inevitable that the final draft of the Act which received the royal assent (thereby officially becoming law) would be much in need of clarification.

During the parliamentary debates Lord Hailsham, the Lord Chancellor, had promised the media, at whom the new act was primarily aimed, that it would be a liberalizing measure. How this was possible when Parliament seemed to be creating a new 'strict liability' offence *in addition to* the old crime rather than in place of it was far from clear. Since the definition of the new offence rested largely on the meaning of the somewhat flexible qualifications, 'serious' and 'substantial', there were many who suspected that the new Act would turn out to represent a hardening of the old law rather than a more liberal approach.

Fortunately for the media, a series of cases since the Contempt of Court Act became law have shown that judges are inclined to interpret the new legislation so as to allow greater freedom than was thought possible under the old common law. Certainly it is a prime example of how the judiciary can choose in which direction the law should develop. Here, they opted for greater freedom than was previously permitted.

In other areas of the law judges have displayed a marked preference for taking the law in the opposite direction.

The *Spycatcher* case is probably the best example, to date, of how judicial views can change drastically from court to court. The issue concerned the Government's attempts to restrain publication of the memoirs of former British MI5 (i.e. security) man, Peter Wright. Within a two-year period (1986–88) the case was twice taken right through the civil court system of appeals up to the House of Lords. Although there was some disagreement in their ranks the judges first time round interpreted the law against publication of the book and in so doing set out principles which represented a considerable hardening of the law of confidentiality.

During the second batch of hearings, however, the judicial attitude swung markedly against restraint and towards freedom of speech.

The *Spycatcher* case is also a good example of the power judges have to state the law (and therefore effectively to change it). At the same time, because of the lack of consistency between one set of judges and the next, it is a bad example of how that power should be exercised. The case is discussed more fully in Chapter 7.

Although judges would always say that their function is merely to *state* the existing law, it is frequently said, with some justification, (and cases like *Spycatcher* demonstrate it) that judicial precedent is itself a source of law.

After all, when a higher court, say the Court of Appeal, reaches a decision on a point of law all courts at the same level of seniority or below (e.g. the High Court) are bound to follow the precedent. If a lower court is faced with arguments on the same legal point in a later case it would look to the Court of Appeal's decision in order to ascertain the law. In this respect precedents set by the judges are themselves a source of the law.

Under this system, whereby judicial precedent is binding, only the House of Lords, which is the supreme court in Britain, has the power to overrule its own previous decisions.

DIVISIONS OF THE LAW

The English legal system, like many others, consists of two main divisions – civil law and criminal law.

Civil law

Civil law is concerned primarily with the rights and duties which exist between individual members of society. The courts which administer the civil law exist to enforce those rights and duties and to provide redress when they are breached or infringed.

Each division of the legal system has its own hierarchy of courts. In relation to civil matters the lowest level of litigation takes place in the County Court. More weighty matters (generally those involving claims greater than £50,000) commence in the High Court. Appeals go to the Court of Appeal (civil division) and from there to the House of Lords.

For the most part civil cases involve disputes between private parties. Such parties may be individuals, companies, associations (e.g. trade unions) or even government departments seeking to enforce some civil entitlement. The party bringing the action is known as the plaintiff and the party against whom it is brought is the defendant.

Criminal law

Criminal law is perhaps better understood by the ordinary person. Whereas many people would be utterly confused by the finer points of civil law there are probably very few who are not familiar with the meaning of crime. Since honest and peaceable behaviour is, by and large, the norm in society, the average person knows that serious deviation from such standards is contrary to the criminal law.

The police exist to enforce the provisions of the criminal law and there is a separate system of courts to deal with those who offend against it. Unlike under the civil law where proceedings are instituted by individual litigants, criminal cases are brought by the Crown as represented by the Crown Prosecution Service.

At the bottom of the criminal court system is the Magistrates Court above which is the Crown Court, the Court of Appeal (criminal division) and finally the House of Lords. In certain circumstances appeals on points of law may be heard by a special division of the High Court.

THE LEGAL PROFESSION, JUDGES AND LAW OFFICERS

The legal profession

Most countries have a legal system in which one class of professional lawyer conducts all legal work from litigation to wills. In Britain and various Commonwealth countries, however, there is a split profession comprising two classes of lawyer, the barrister and the solicitor.

The reason for the split can be traced back to the evolution, in the Middle Ages, of a class of professional advocates or barristers who were permitted, by the old common law courts, to argue cases. Solicitors emerged to form a separate branch of the legal profession at a later date and were responsible for most forms of legal work outside that of advocacy. Although today there is a far greater overlap of roles played by each branch of the profession, the broad distinction still remains.

Barristers

Barristers specialize, for the most part, in advocacy and the drafting of pleadings in civil cases. Until very recently they enjoyed a virtual monopoly over rights of audience (the right to be heard) in the senior courts, i.e. Crown Court, High Court and above. For proceedings held in open court, other than in Magistrates Courts, barristers wear wigs and gowns and are referred to as counsel.

All barristers are self-employed and must belong as a member to one of the Inns of Court, i.e. Gray's Inn, Lincoln's Inn, the Inner Temple or Middle Temple. They must also practise from *chambers* which is an association of several barristers (anything up to about forty) sharing common offices and clerks. The profession is governed by the Bar Council.

Barristers are not permitted to deal directly with the public. They may be 'instructed' only by solicitors who in turn receive their instructions straight from the lay client. Effectively their work falls into three categories. Either they will be instructed to appear in court on behalf of the lay client, to draft the necessary written pleadings which must be filed with the court in civil actions or to give specialist advice on pending cases or particular points of law. In each instance the instructions from the solicitor are normally in writing and are described as counsel's 'brief'.

In order to qualify as a barrister or be 'called to the Bar' as it is known, a person must join one of the Inns of Court, pass the professional Bar Examinations and serve a full year in pupillage. That year is a form of apprenticeship in which the pupil is attached to a practising barrister of some years' experience and accompanies him both in chambers and in court.

When he has achieved a certain seniority (at least ten years) a barrister may apply to become a Queen's Counsel, known as a QC or 'silk' because he is then entitled to wear a gown made of silk. The applications are made to the Lord Chancellor who is the official head of the legal profession in this country. All barristers who do not 'take silk' are described as juniors. A QC generally conducts the more difficult or complicated cases and is normally assisted in the preparation by a junior. About 10 per cent of the practising Bar are QCs.

Solicitors

All solicitors are required to belong to the Law Society which administers the profession, lays down rules of conduct and disciplines those who transgress. When a person qualifies as a solicitor he is entered on the Rolls of the Supreme Court and becomes an officer of that court. For serious misconduct he may be struck off the rolls with the result that he would be unable to practise.

In the main, solicitors practise in partnerships and, unlike barristers, are consulted and paid directly by the public. They may conduct every kind of legal work. The workload for an average partnership would consist of conveyancing (property transfers), probate (drafting and administering wills), matrimonial (divorces etc.), some commercial matters and litigation.

The rights of audience enjoyed by solicitors were traditionally limited to the Magistrates Courts, the County Courts, and minor matters heard in the Crown Court and the High Court. From early 1994, however, the restrictions upon them appearing in and addressing the upper courts have been removed. Providing solicitors satisfy certain basic standards on an Advocacy Training Course run by the Lord Chancellor's Department, they may conduct any sort of case in the Crown Court, High Court or the Appeal Courts.

They may also appear at Coroner's Courts and at various legal tribunals, e.g. in relation to employment or immigration matters. In those courts where robes are *de rigeur*, i.e. Crown Court, and above, solicitors wear a gown alone as opposed to the barristers' wig and gown.

In order to qualify as a solicitor one must pass the professional examinations set by the Law Society and serve the required period under

Articles of Clerkship. The articled clerk must sign up with a principal, who must be a practising and experienced solicitor, for a set number of years – usually about four for non-law graduates and two and a half for those with a law degree.

As of July 1993, there were 68,600 practising lawyers in England and Wales, comprising 7271 barristers and 61,329 solicitors. In terms of the population as a whole this amounts to one lawyer per 900 people. (In the USA the figure is more like one per 600).

Over recent years, particularly in the mid-seventies, there has been a considerable lobby in favour of fusion of the two branches of the legal profession. The debate came to a head at the time of the Royal Commission on Legal Services. The opposing arguments were long and complicated but very broadly centred around the saving of cost to the public which the pro-fusion lobby claimed would result from abolishing the distinction between barristers and solicitors as against the loss of quality in legal services which was predicted by those who preferred the status quo. After giving the matter massively detailed consideration the Royal Commission concluded that at the present time no pressing public interest would be served by fusion.

Judges

The appointment of judges in Britain is effectively controlled by the legal profession. Unlike the practice of some other countries it is an entirely non-political process. The Settlement Act 1700, which provided a statutory basis for the creation of a judiciary, decreed that judges should hold office *quamdiu se bene gesserint* – as long as they are of good behaviour. More recent legislation has regularized the length of their tenure by introducing retirement ages. Judges sitting at the level of High Court and above should retire at seventy-five and those below that level should go at the age of seventy-two. The latter category, i.e. circuit judges and recorders, may now also be removed by the Lord Chancellor for misconduct or misbehaviour.

All judges are appointed by the Queen on the recommendation of the Lord Chancellor. Starting at the bottom the judicial hierarchy is broadly as follows.

Recorders

Recorders are part-time judges who sit at the Crown Court. They are required to perform judicial duties for a certain number of days each year, the rest of their working time being spent as ordinary private practitioners. In order to be appointed a recorder one must be a barrister or solicitor of at least ten years. A recorder who has held office for five or more years may be selected to become a full-time judge of the Supreme Court (i.e. Crown Court or High Court).

Circuit judges
Circuit judges hear cases in the Crown Court and the County Court. They comprise the largest section of the judiciary numbering around 500 (exactly 503 as at February 1994) and are appointed from the ranks of barristers who have practised for at least ten years. In their official capacity they are individually referred to as 'His Honour Judge . . .'(or 'Her Honour' as the case may be) and addressed as 'Your Honour'. Outside court they are simply referred to and addressed as 'Judge . . .'.

High Court judges
There are currently 98 judges of the High Court. All are based at the Supreme Courts of Judicature (the Strand Law Courts) in London and have been appointed from the ranks of practising lawyers of a least ten years seniority or circuit judges or recorders who have held office for five or more years. In most cases appointments to the High Court bench come from extremely experienced and successful barristers.

Each judge is allocated to one of the three divisions of the High Court. The Queen's Bench division is the largest with 64 judges; the Chancery division has 18 judges and the Family division has a complement of 16.

High Court judges are knighted upon appointment. In court they are referred to as 'Mr Justice . . .' and addressed as 'My Lord'.

Lord Justices of Appeal
The Lord Justices of Appeal man the Court of Appeal and are appointed from the ranks of the High Court judges. They are presently 30 in number and hear both civil and criminal appeals. The civil division of the Court of Appeal is presided over by the Master of the Rolls. The leading judge in the criminal division is the Lord Chief Justice, who also presides over the divisional court of the High Court which specializes in appeals based solely on points of law.

Lords of Appeal in Ordinary
These most senior judges sit in the House of Lords which is the highest court in the country for both civil and criminal matters. They are appointed from the Court of Appeal judges and are commonly referred to as the Law Lords.

The law officers

The senior law officers in the English legal system are the Lord Chancellor, the Attorney General and the Director of Public Prosecutions. The first two are political appointments effectively made by the Prime Minister; the third is non-political.

The Lord Chancellor

The office of Lord Chancellor is unique in the British constitution in that it overlaps all three traditional institutions of state power: the judiciary, the executive and the legislative. As a former incumbent, Lord Elwyn-Jones, described it, the Lord Chancellor is a 'universal joint in the machinery'. He infringes the normal constitutional concept of the separation of powers by being, at one and the same time, the head of the judiciary, a member of the Cabinet and the Speaker of the House of Lords.

Although he is, *ex officio*, a Law Lord and is entitled to sit as a judge in the House of Lords, few of the more recent Lord Chancellors have taken any sort of active judicial role. The notable exception was Lord Hailsham who held the office from 1970–4 and again from 1979–87.

Perhaps the greatest area of influence over which the Lord Chancellor exercises control is the appointment of the judiciary. Nearly all judges are selected and recommended for appointment by the Chancellor or his office. At the lowest level of the legal system his power is even greater in that Justices of the Peace are appointed by him directly. The names of prospective candidates are submitted to his office with recommendations by local advisory committees around the country.

The Attorney General

Unlike the Lord Chancellor, the Attorney General is not a member of the Cabinet. He does, however, come from the same mould as the Chancellor in that he is a career politician and is usually, at the time of appointment, a member of the House of Commons.

The Attorney General is the government's chief legal adviser and represents the Crown in both civil and criminal litigation where there is a strong public, political or national interest involved. On such occasions the Attorney may personally appear in court, as in some of the major spy cases or murder trials (e.g. that of Peter Sutcliffe, the 'Yorkshire Ripper'), or he may be represented by one of a select group of barristers known as Treasury Counsel who specialize in matters of this sort for the Crown.

Prosecutions under some criminal law statutes may be commenced only after the Attorney General has given his consent. This applies, for instance, to certain prosecutions under the Official Secrets Acts 1911 and 1989, the Public Order Act 1936 and the Race Relations Act 1965. For the purposes of this book the most significant cases requiring the Attorney's consent are prosecutions brought for contempt under the Contempt of Court Act 1981, and for breach of the restrictions on court reporting, notably under Section 8 of the Magistrates Courts Act 1980 (in respect of committal proceedings).

It is a normal part of the Attorney General's function to institute proceedings himself where he considers the public interest requires it. In 1986, for example, he went to court in order to obtain an injunction against the *News of the World* preventing the newspaper from publishing certain detailed allegations against the test cricketer, Ian Botham, on the grounds that the proposed article constituted a contempt. The same allegations were at the centre of a libel action being brought by the cricketer against the *Mail on Sunday* which had already been set down in the court list for a hearing. After losing at first instance, the newspaper took the matter to the Court of Appeal and won the right to publish. Although on this occasion the Attorney General failed it was a good example of how he can act, not only to enforce the law against past transgressors, but also to prevent future wrongdoing.

Among the other powers which the Attorney General alone has is the authority to halt proceedings for an indictable offence. He achieves this by entering what is properly known as a *nolle prosequi* (meaning 'do not prosecute'). This power has been exercised to halt private prosecutions which the Attorney considers not to be in the public interest. One such intervention which caused some controversy occurred in 1982 when he stepped in to put an end to Mary Whitehouse's prosecution of those responsible for the play, *Romans in Britain*, under the Sexual Offences Act 1956.

The Attorney General's deputy is the *Solicitor General* who, surprisingly in view of his title, is a barrister and like the former is usually a member of the House of Commons. In the absence of the Attorney General he is empowered to exercise the same authority and functions.

The Director of Public Prosecutions

The Director of Public Prosecutions (DPP) is not a political appointment although he is answerable to, and subject to, the directions of the Attorney General.

The office of Director was created over 100 years ago by the Prosecution of Offences Act 1879, which stated:

> It shall be the duty of the Director of Public Prosecutions, under the superintendence of the Attorney General, to institute . . . such criminal proceedings . . . as may be . . . prescribed by regulations . . . or may be directed in a special case by the Attorney General.

Most serious crime is referred to the office of the Director. He is required by statutory regulations to be involved in any criminal matter of importance or difficulty or which for any reason justifies his intervention. Obviously criminal investigations which involve considerations of public policy or national security will be referred to his office, as will a large number of specified offences, e.g. homicide, treason, perjury, perverting the course of justice, kidnapping, robbery with firearms, serious cases of arson and, of course, criminal libel.

In many of such cases the Director will exercise his discretion as to whether a prosecution should be brought. Exactly how that discretion is exercised in practice was explained by a recent Director, Sir Thomas Hetherington, when he gave evidence in 1978 to the Royal Commission on Criminal Procedure.

> The test normally used in the Department in deciding whether evidence is sufficient to justify proceedings is whether or not there is a reasonable prospect of a conviction; whether, in other words, it seems rather more likely that there will be a conviction than an acquittal.

Where the evidence passes the first test, i.e. there seems to be at least a 51 per cent chance of securing a conviction, the DPP, according to Sir Thomas, will go on to consider whether a prosecution would be in the public interest.

The manner in which the Director is entitled to exercise his discretion was thrown sharply into focus by two contrasting cases in 1986:

- In the first, apparently because of evidential weaknesses he decided not to prosecute in the case of nineteen-year-old John Williams who had collapsed and died after being injected with the drug Palfium by a man called Gary Austin. Incensed by that decision the dead teenager's mother launched a private prosecution against Austin on a charge of manslaughter. After the committal stage the DPP relented and took over the prosecution in order, he said, to save Mrs Williams 'further time, trouble and expense'. Austin was eventually convicted as charged.
- Spurred on to some extent by the result in that case another mother tried to pursue the same course of action a few weeks later. Mrs M. had been informed that the DPP would not prosecute the alleged rapist of her nine-year-old daughter. Medical evidence seemed to confirm that she had indeed been raped and the girl named an Essex doctor as her assailant. However, because of the evidential difficulties of proving the uncorroborated account of a minor, the Director took the decision that a conviction was unlikely and therefore did not proceed. With the financial backing of *The Sun* newspaper the mother brought a private prosecution. At the committal proceedings the magistrate accepted that there was a *prima facie* case against the doctor and sent him to Chelmsford Crown Court to face trial on a charge of rape.

On this occasion the DPP stood firm and did not take over the prosecution. In the event his refusal was to some extent vindicated by the jury's verdict of not guilty. The trial judge nevertheless considered that it was a proper case for the costs of the prosecution to be met out of central funds.

In 1986 the Crown Prosecution Service (CPS) was created to give England and Wales its first unified and national system for prosecuting criminal cases. The CPS employs over 2300 lawyers in a network of offices up and down the country. Each office prepares and runs the prosecutions brought before the courts in its own area. Working on the initial material provided by the police (i.e., statements, charge sheets, interviews with the accused, etc.), the CPS lawyers decide whether to proceed with a prosecution. They themselves conduct nearly all Magistrates Court cases and minor matters in the Crown Court. It is usual for outside counsel to be instructed by the CPS on more serious Crown Court prosecutions. The Director of Public Prosecutions is, of course, at the head of that system.

THE COURTS

Within the system of courts in this country there is a broad division between those that administer the criminal law and those that administer the civil law. The courts 'of first instance', i.e. where the trials actually take place, in relation to criminal matters are the Magistrates Court and the Crown Court. On the civil side their equivalents are the County Court and the High Court.

The functions and powers of those courts are as follows.

The criminal courts

The Magistrates Court
The Magistrates Court is the most junior and the most numerous of all the courts in the legal system. There are about 1000 such courts throughout England and Wales and more than 25,000 magistrates, also known as justices of the peace, to man them. Of the latter, all but about fifty, who sit at the frantically busy metropolitan Magistrates Courts, are lay persons who have no legal qualifications. They are appointed by the Lord Chancellor upon the recommendation of area committees and devote on average one day every two weeks to court work.

Metropolitan magistrates, on the other hand, are experienced lawyers who sit full time at the courts. Unlike their lay colleagues who are paid only subsistence allowances, they receive salaries – because of this they are known as Stipendiary Magistrates. Stipendiaries generally sit alone on the Bench whereas their lay colleagues will always sit as a Bench of at least three.

All criminal cases commence in the Magistrates Court and about 95 per cent are concluded there. Most of the cases which they hear through to a conclusion involve summary offences, i.e. those which may be tried only by magistrates.

Each year half of the cases dealt with involve motoring violations. The remainder of the cases concluded at this level are in respect of indictable offences which may be heard with either at the Magistrates Court or the Crown Court. Both prosecution and defence have various rights of election as to where the matter is tried. The more serious indictable offences must be tried at the Crown Court.

For a case to go to the Crown Court it has first to be *committed* there by the Magistrates Court. In this context the role of the justices is to examine the prosecution evidence during the course of Committal Proceedings in order to ascertain that there is a *prima facie* case to be tried (i.e. there is a case to answer).

The sentencing powers of magistrates are limited. They may impose fines of generally no more than £5,000 and pass sentences of imprisonment limited to six months for any single offence and a total of twelve months for two or more offences. Where more than one sentence of imprisonment is imposed against a convicted person the relevant court must stipulate whether they are to run concurrently or consecutively.

Every Magistrates Court has a clerk of the court who is usually legally qualified. It is the function of the clerk to organize the business of the court and to advise lay magistrates on points of law. The enormous importance of magistrates in terms of the successful day-to-day working of the legal system should never be underestimated. Apart from their vast workload of criminal cases they deal with large amounts of domestic or family litigation and, as licensing justices, administer and monitor the granting of liquor and gaming licences nationwide.

There are two avenues of appeal available to persons convicted at the Magistrates Court.

If the appellant's only contention is that a point of law was wrongly decided or that there was some material defect in the procedure at trial he may appeal by way of 'case stated' to the Divisional Court of the Queens Bench which is part of the High Court. Such an appeal normally consists solely of legal argument.

Alternatively, appeals from the Magistrates Court against either conviction or sentence may be heard at the Crown Court. Where the appeal is against conviction it takes the form of a retrial; if it is against sentence only, the Crown Court simply re-hears the plea in mitigation plus any points the appellant may have as to why the sentence was wrong in principle (e.g. he was fined a large sum which he patently cannot afford to pay).

The Crown Court

The Crown Courts were introduced by the Courts Act 1971, in order to replace the very old and relatively inefficient system of Assizes and Quarter Sessions. The Act meant that from 1972 onwards the Crown Court was the only senior court able to hear criminal trials and that along with the High Court and the Court of Appeal it constituted what is known as the Supreme Court.

The Crown Court has three functions:

1   To try indictable offences; in the event of a not guilty plea such trials are conducted by means of a judge and jury.
2   To sentence offenders who have already pleaded or been found guilty in the Magistrates Court and have been sent to the higher court because the magistrates regarded their sentencing powers as inadequate; this function of the Crown Court is usually conducted by a judge sitting with one or two lay magistrates.
3   To hear the appeals from the Magistrates Court; again, it is usual for such appeals to be heard by a judge sitting with up to two lay magistrates.

There are three different sorts of judge who may preside over the Crown Court.

- *High Court judges*:   The judges of the Queen's Bench Division spend some of their time travelling the Crown Court circuits hearing the more serious criminal cases. Such a senior judge is immediately distinguishable in this role from his more lowly colleagues by the colour of his robes – he is referred to colloquially as 'the Red Judge'.
- *Circuit judges*:   There are around 500 circuit judges, so named because they belong to one of the six circuits which cover England and Wales.
- *Recorders*:   As discussed above these are part-time judges who give up a certain number of days each year from their private practices in order to perform judicial duties.

The cases which are heard at Crown Court are themselves categorized into four classes. Class 1 offences such as murder and treason must be dealt with by a High Court judge. Class 2 covers slightly less serious crimes, e.g. rape or manslaughter, and again would normally involve a High Court judge. Class 3 offences, e.g. grievous bodily harm, may come before any sort of judge and Class 4, which covers the more minor indictable offences, is the realm of any but the senior judges.

Appeals from the Crown Court, whether against conviction or sentence, are usually heard by the criminal division of the Court of Appeal.

Under Section 2 of the Criminal Appeal Act 1968, The Court of Appeal should allow any appeal against conviction if they decide any of the following:

1   That the conviction should be set aside on the grounds that under all the circumstances of the case it is unsafe or unsatisfactory.
2   That the judgement of the court of trial should be set aside on the grounds of a wrong decision on any question of law.

3   That there was a material irregularity in the course of the trial.

In every other case they should dismiss the appeal. There is, however, a crucially important proviso to Section 2. Despite being satisfied of 1, 2 or 3 above, the Appeal Court may still dismiss the appeal if it considers that no miscarriage of justice has actually occurred. The proviso is aimed at preventing obviously guilty defendants escaping their just desserts because of a technicality.

A convicted person has an absolute right of appeal if his or her plea is based on a point of law, such as a misdirection by the judge to the jury or the jury being permitted to hear inadmissable evidence.

If the defendant wishes to appeal against findings of fact then he or she may do so only with the leave of the trial judge or the Court of Appeal itself. The same applies where the appeal is solely on the question of sentence. Applications for leave to appeal are initially made to a single Appeal Court judge, though in the event of refusal it may be possible to repeat the application for leave before the full court.

Just as one can from the Magistrates Court, it is possible to appeal also by way of 'case stated' from the Crown Court to the Divisional Court of Queen's Bench if the issue is purely a question of law.

In the event that either prosecution or defence wish to take their case beyond the Court of Appeal a final appeal may be made to the House of Lords provided the following two points are satisfied:

1   Either the Court of Appeal or the House of Lords gives leave to appeal.
2   The Court of Appeal certifies that a point of law of general public importance is involved.

Civil courts

The County Court
The County courts are the junior civil courts. They were established by the County Courts Act 1846, as a cheap, speedy and accessible tribunal through which to settle or decide private legal disputes. Their jurisdiction has always been limited by the size of claims upon which they are entitled to adjudicate. Despite this the County Court is responsible for dealing with the vast majority (said to be in the region of 90 per cent) of civil litigation throughout the country.

In terms of subject-matter as opposed to size of claim the County Court's jurisdiction is enormous. Its normal business encompasses not only all the traditional areas of civil dispute, e.g. contract, tort and debt, but also includes the overwhelming bulk of divorce and ancillary matrimonial litigation as well as adoption, landlord and tenant disputes and certain bankruptcy matters.

Cases at the County Court are decided by a circuit judge sitting alone or, in the area of small claims, by a district judge (formerly known as a registrar). The district judge is essential to the smooth running of every County Court. He is a solicitor of a least seven years standing who not only adjudicates on the smaller claims (generally up to £1000 and, in certain circumstances, up to £5000) but also handles the administrative business of the court. The latter involves hearing pre-trial applications, setting dates and giving directions for trials before the judge and the 'taxing' (assessing) of the costs which should be reimbursed to the winning litigant.

The financial limits of the County Court's jurisdiction may be varied from time to time by the Lord Chancellor in order to accommodate changing economic values. The current limit is £50,000. Claims for more than £50,000 should be brought in the High Court.

The High Court

The High Court is the senior court of trial for civil litigation. It has a jurisdiction which encompasses practically every area of civil law and imposes no limit to the size of claims.

Most of its work is conducted at The Strand law courts in London though it also sits in the main metropolitan areas around the country. There are just under 100 High Court judges; they are generally appointed from the most senior and talented members of the Bar.

Since the Administration of Justice Act 1970, both the caseload and the judges of the High Court have been organized in three divisions – Queen's Bench, Chancery and Family. Each division has jurisdiction over its own areas of civil law although there is considerable overlap among the three.

The work of the High Court is broadly divided as follows:

Queen's Bench Division

This is by far the largest and busiest division of the High Court with about three times more judges assigned to it than either the Chancery or Family Divisions. It has jurisdiction over both civil and criminal matters.

Most of the common areas of civil dispute are heard by the courts of Queen's Bench. Actions in contract, negligence and nuisance come before them, as do defamation and copyright claims. Trespass on land and trespass to the person also fall within their sphere. Separate sections of the Queen's Bench Division deal with company and commercial cases and admiralty (i.e. shipping) matters.

The Queen's Bench Division also performs two valuable and important functions in the criminal law system. The first is its involvement on the Crown Court circuits. Each Queen's Bench judge spends a good deal of his time travelling around the circuit presiding over the more serious cases. As already discussed, in this role the judge is known as the 'Red Judge' (the robes are red as opposed to those of circuit judges which are black). Queen's Bench judges deal primarily with Class 1 and 2 offences (see above).

The other function of the Queen's Bench's criminal jurisdiction is exercised through its Divisional Court, which has both appellate and supervisory powers over lower courts and tribunals. The Divisional Court hears appeals by way of 'case stated' against decisions on points of law or procedure made by the Magistrates Court or the Crown Court. Significantly for the media, it is also the court which deals with cases of contempt brought by the Attorney General. In recent years practically all such cases have been against newspapers. It was the Divisional Court of Queen's Bench, for example, which heard the Attorney's application in 1982 to have five national newspapers punished for contempt of court over their pre-trial coverage of the Buckingham Palace break-in by Michael Fagan (who has gone down in history as the 'Palace Intruder').

More recently it was again the Divisional Court in *Attorney General* v *News Group Newspapers* (1988) which found *The Sun* newspaper to be in breach of the old common law of contempt for stories about an Essex doctor who was subsequently charged with raping a nine-year-old girl. It fined News Group Newspapers £75,000) The same court dealt with a similar case against *The Sport* in 1991. On that occasion the newspaper was cleared.

Unlike the rest of the High Court, where cases are presided over by a single judge, the Divisional Court consists of at least two, and more usually three, judges. The head of the court, and of the whole of the Queen's Bench Division, is the Lord Chief Justice.

Chancery Division
While traditionally the Queen's Bench exercised most of its jurisdictional powers in areas of the common law, Chancery concerned itself with the laws of equity. Although there are considerable areas of overlap these days between the work of the two Divisions, the Chancery Courts are still widely known as the Courts of Equity. In practical terms this means that Chancery deals with areas such as the ownership and administration of land and trusts, various aspects of company and partnership law, revenue and tax problems and disputes over wills.

There are currently 18 judges attached to the Chancery Division. Their nominal head is the Lord Chancellor though in reality the senior judge is the Vice Chancellor.

A large proportion of barristers specialize in Chancery matters and rarely go near either the criminal courts or the rest of the High Court.

Family Division

The Family Division of the High Court did not exist before the Administration of Justice Act 1970. As the name implies, it has a jurisdiction over all matters arising from matrimonial and guardianship disputes.

The judges of the Family Courts thus spend most of their time dealing with divorce and matrimonial property, custody and adoption of children, wardship proceedings and the various other forms of dispute which can arise from family affairs.

Like the Queen's Bench, it also has a Divisional court which hears appeals from matrimonial and domestic cases heard in the County and Magistrates Courts.

The judge in charge of the Family Courts is known as the President of the Family Division. There are currently 15 other Family judges.

The Court of Appeal

Before 1966 there were two separate Courts of Appeal, one dealing with civil cases and the other hearing criminal appeals. Under the Criminal Appeals Act of that year they were consolidated to form a single court comprising two divisions. It is empowered to hear appeals from the Crown Court on the criminal side and from the County Court and the High Court on the civil side. The Master of the Rolls heads the Civil Division and the Lord Chief Justice is in charge of the Criminal Division. Apart from *ex-officio* members (i.e. the present and former Lord Chancellors, the Law Lords, the Vice Chancellor and the President of the Family Division) There are 30 Lord Justices of Appeal. Like the Divisional Court of Queen's Bench, the Court of Appeal sits with at least two and usually three judges.

The House of Lords

The final court for appeals is the House of Lords – more precisely known as the Appellate Committee of the Upper House of Parliament. Members of the Upper House who have held high judicial office are entitled to be on this committee, as are the Lord Chancellor and former Lord Chancellors. In practice, however, the work of the House of Lords is undertaken by the eleven life peers who are appointed as Lords of Appeal in Ordinary (commonly referred to as Law Lords). Two Law Lords are always appointed from Scotland.

It is unusual for a case to be taken as far as the House of Lords unless a major point of law is involved. Indeed in criminal cases it is generally a requirement for the granting of leave to appeal to the Lords that the case entails a point of law 'of general public importance'.

A minimum of three judges sit to decide cases, although the usual number is five. Strangely, in view of the fact that it is the supreme court, the procedure in the House of Lords is extremely informal. Neither judges nor counsel are wigged or robed and the judgements are not read aloud – they are simply handed over in written form.

Like the Court of Appeal the House of Lords resolves its cases by a majority verdict. Given that by the time a dispute gets to this stage both sides in the litigation will have spent vast sums on legal costs, it is perhaps ironic that the ultimate decision might depend on a slender three to two vote. Many historic and important legal precedents have however been set by just such a margin. The most recent example is the *Spycatcher* appeal where the emphatic judgements of two Law Lords against granting injunctions restraining newspaper publication of extracts from the memoirs of Peter Wright, the ex-MI5 man, on the grounds that it would make the law look ridiculous were overruled by the contrary decisions of their three brethren.

7 BREACH OF CONFIDENCE

The idea of *confidence* is a familiar one to any journalist. A journalist will always preserve the confidentiality of a source. Information provided 'off the record' will not be published.

But the law of confidence is a boom area in the law. Originally devised to protect secret processes or inventions or trade secrets, its boundaries are being pushed back. It is being used more and more often to prevent publication of information in the media.

For a private person, an action in breach of confidence will avoid the rule that injunctions will not be granted if a defendant intends to justify what will be published. The truth of the allegations will not matter – an injunction in breach of confidence may still be granted.

For the government, an action for breach of confidence is frequently a more effective alternative to a prosecution under the Official Secrets Act. There is no jury in an action for breach of confidence. The interests of the state and of the public are weighed by a judge.

Injunctions to restrain publication may be obtained easily. The cost of taking an action to trial frequently deters defendants from further resistence and means that the information never sees the light of day. The action for breach of confidence is becoming the most significant fetter on a free press.

There are three elements to a breach of confidence claim:

1 Information which has the necessary quality of confidence.
2 Information which is imparted in circumstances imposing an obligation of confidence.
3 Unauthorized use (or threatened use) of the information to the detriment of the owner of the information.

OBLIGATIONS OF CONFIDENCE

An obligation of confidence can be imposed by the terms of an agreement – whether as one of the terms in a written agreement or in an oral agreement. The obligation can arise also by virtue of the nature of the relationship between 'confider' and 'confidant'.

MARRIAGE

The law will not permit the revelation of anything confided by one spouse to the other during a marriage. This protection of matrimonial secrets is based on the sanctity of marriage.

In *Argyll* v *Argyll (1967)* the Duke of Argyll intended to reveal to the press secrets of his marriage to the Duchess. The marriage had ended in divorce, because of the adultery of the Duchess. She had already published allegations of drug-taking against him but still succeeded in stopping him by injunction. The court said that: 'There could hardly be anything more intimate or confidential than is involved in that relationship, or than in the mutual trust and confidences which are shared between husband and wife. The confidential nature of the relationship is of its very essence.'

Even matrimonial secrets may be published if the confidence of the whole marriage has been destroyed. In *Lennon* v *News Group (1978)* John Lennon applied for an injunction to prevent his first wife, Cynthia, from selling stories about the marriage to the *News of the World*. The court decided that their relationship had ceased to be their private affair. Each had written a number of articles about the marriage in the past (presumably for reward) making allegations about the other. The marriage had been put into the public domain.

Confidences exchanged during an affair do not receive this absolute protection. 'Kiss-and-tell' revelations – particularly concerning a married person in an adulterous relationship – are unlikely to be stopped for breach of confidence. In *M and N* v *News Group (1988)*, a male barrister tried to prevent publication in *The Sun* of letters he had written to his male lover. The judge held that there was no confidentiality in a 'transient homosexual relationship'.

The same principle would deprive transient heterosexual relationships of the protection of the law of confidence.

However, the law in this field is developing rapidly. Two months after the M and N decision a different judge doubted whether only marriage could cloak sexual relationships in confidence. In *Stephens* v *Avery (1988)*, a woman sued for damages for breach of confidence after the *Mail on Sunday* published details of her sexual relationship with another woman, the victim of a sensational murder. The judge held that there was no reason why information relating to sexual matters should not be the subject of an enforceable duty of confidence. Details of their sex lives were high on the list of matters regarded as confidential by most people. The decision was made at a preliminary legal skirmish in Mrs Stephens's case which was brought after the material had been published.

EMPLOYMENT

A contract of employment may contain terms which expressly prevent an employee from disclosing information learned in the course of their employment. A contractual term explicitly imposing a duty of confidence is more likely if the employee has access to secret information – whether about technology or trade practices.

Even if their contracts do not contain a confidentiality clause, all employees owe a duty of 'fidelity' to their employers. This will include an obligation not to disclose employers' trade secrets or confidential inform-ation. Originally this was used to prevent employees from setting up in competition with their ex-employer, making use of lists of customers or other information taken from the employer. It can also be used to stop employees leaking information about the employer to the media, or 'blowing the whistle' on what is going on.

The duty of confidence would apply to any journalist who took a job in order to find out from the inside how a particular business worked – to investigate high pressure sales techniques, or training methods, for example.

The employee's duty of confidence obviously lasts for the whole period of employment. But even after the end of employment, the obligation of confidence lingers on. It covers all information learned in the course of employment. For example in *Woodward* v *Hutchins (1977)* Chris Hutchins, formerly employed as PR to pop stars Tom Jones, Engelbert Humperdinck and others, exposed their secrets in a newspaper. He was bound by a duty of confidence but, in the particular circumstances of this case, the court refused an injunction and allowed him to publish the truth. The stars had courted publicity and tried to create a particular image. It was in the public interest that the record be set straight, if that image was false.

Those who live by publicity will be left by the courts to die by publicity.

The courts draw a distinction between ex-employees disclosing details which reveal the truth about a false image, and those who simply reveal private secrets. Palace employees who attempt to reveal private details about the Royal Family may be stopped by injunction. When one newspaper published details of 'Koo's Sex Romps at Palace' as revealed by a Palace servant it ended up paying £4,000 to charity for the acknowledged breach of confidence.

Other famous employers have been swift to resort to the courts to preserve their privacy. Television presenter Anne Diamond obtained an injunction to prevent her ex-nanny's story from appearing on the front page of *The Sun*. Publisher Robert Maxwell attempted to stop publication of a biography after one of his former secretaries gave an interview to its author.

Employees of the Government who give information about their work to the press may be liable for breach of confidence. Injunctions will be granted where the employee had access to secret information. The Government is especially keen to preserve a blanket silence about the security and intelligence services. It obtained injunctions against former GCHQ employee Jock Kane, who wanted to make allegations of inefficiency and wasted money at GCHQ in Hong Kong. Dennis Mitchell, another ex-employee of GCHQ was also enjoined when he revealed his intention to go public. The Government obtained an injunction against Joan Miller's book *One Girl's War*, which gave details of her work as an MI5 agent. Peter Wright, former senior MI5 officer, whose book *Spycatcher* led to legal proceedings in Australia, New Zealand, Hong Kong and the UK to restrain publication, showed the lengths to which the Government will go to keep its employees' work secret.

The action for breach of confidence can be used by the Government not only to protect genuinely secret information, but also to suppress embarrassing or politically sensitive facts. In theory criminal sanctions apply to any leak of any official information by a Government servant. The 1985 acquittal of Clive Ponting, which again discredited use of Section 2 of the Official Secrets Act, showed that the Government cannot trust a jury to convict unless genuine national secrets are put at risk. Civil actions in confidence are more likely to be effective in keeping official information from, and out of, the media.

Civil servants and members of the armed forces and secret services do not have written contracts of employment but they do owe a duty of confidence.

OTHER CONFIDENTIAL RELATIONSHIPS

What clients tell their lawyers is confidential. The law will always protect the privilege of these communications. What a penitent tells a priest is also confidential, as is what patients tell their doctors. It is in the public interest that communications between these people can be made in confidence and kept secret. The courts recently emphasized the public interest in preserving the confidentiality of medical records. In *X* v *Y (1987)* a newspaper wished to identify two doctors who had contracted AIDS but continued in practice. The information about the doctors had come from an employee at the hospital which was treating the doctors concerned. After a trial held entirely in camera, a permanent injunction was granted.

The judge ruled that discussion of the issues of public importance was permissable – i.e., whether there was any danger to patients who were treated by a doctor with AIDS – but the doctors, and their places of work could not be identified.

If people who thought that they might have AIDS decided not to get medical help because they feared that their condition might be made public, that would be detrimental to the public interest. Medical confidentiality does prevent a doctor from revealing that a patient has AIDS even to another member of the patient's family who might be affected. The issue of whether what a child tells a doctor should be kept confidential from a parent was discussed in the case recently brought by Mrs Victoria Gillick. The issue was whether a doctor must tell a parent if a daughter under sixteen asked for contraceptive advice? It is open to question whether what a child tells a teacher is subject to an obligation of confidence – or whether reporters can try to obtain private information from teachers about the offspring of the famous.

A member of the Cabinet owes a duty of confidence to other members of the Government. In *AG* v *Jonathan Cape (1974)* the Government applied to prevent publication of *The Crossman Diaries*, records of the career of former Cabinet Minister Richard Crossman, mainly on public interest grounds. Publication would deter Cabinet discussions from having the frankness they needed for the effective running of government. The court refused an injunction – the information was several years old.

Whether or not a relationship is confidential depends on all the circumstances. Written or oral agreements that certain material will be dealt with confidentially are the most obvious cases – for example, the sending of a manuscript to potential buyers of the serialization or film rights in confidence, or the circulation of a memo marked 'confidential'. But even if nothing is said about confidentiality, it may be so obviously intended by the nature of the transaction that a duty of confidence will be imposed.

In November 1993, the High Court granted the Princess of Wales an injunction against the owner of a gymnasium who secretly photographed her as she exercised on his fitness machines. Although her membership of the gym was complimentary, there had been an express assurance by the owner that 'every aspect of Her Royal Highness's involvement. . . will be treated with the utmost confidentiality.' The court was prepared to enforce that assurance and banned further publication of the offending pictures.

JOURNALISTS

Journalists should be aware of the circumstances regarded by the courts as creating confidential relationships, because the obligation of confidence extends beyond the original parties involved to any third person who receives the information knowing of the breach of confidence.

If someone says 'I shouldn't tell you this, but . . .' that is easily enough to put someone on notice of a potential breach of confidence. But the danger is that the courts will say that the third party, e.g., the enquiring journalists, should have realized, simply by considering the type of information revealed, that confidence was being broken. This applies particularly to information provided by current or former employees about their employers, and to information concerning someone's medical history.

It is a defence to be a completely innocent third party – but complete innocence is a difficult state to prove.

WHAT IS CONFIDENTIAL?

Any type of information, whether conveyed orally or preserved in writing, can be confidential. An idea can be secret. In *Fraser* v *Thames TV (1981)* a writer gave a television company an idea for a TV series in confidence. The company later made a similar series, *Rock Follies*, but without involving that writer. He won damages for breach of confidence for the unauthorized use of his idea.

Care should be taken in discussing ideas for articles or programmes – it can be difficult to show that the idea had been independently and originally devised.

It may seem obvious to say that to be confidential information must be secret since that is the whole idea of confidence. But the courts do not always see this as a simple issue. In some circumstances a plaintiff can obtain an injunction for breach of confidence to restrain publication of information available to the public. In *Schering Chemicals* v *Falkman (1981)* a TV executive who's job was to train employees of a chemical company in television techniques had the idea of making a programme about one of the company's products. The drug, Primados, had been the subject of some controversy when allegations were made that it had caused defects in children whose mothers had taken the drug while pregnant. The executive had been given confidential information by the company as part of the training course. In preparation of the programme a researcher gathered all of the relevant information from public sources. The Court of Appeal ordered that the programme should not be shown. The executive had abused his position of trust, and could not be allowed to profit from that.

One member of the court thought that it was ridiculous to issue an injunction when the material was public but the majority saw no such difficulty.

Whether, and at what point, the publication of once-secret information, destroys its confidentiality creates problems. The English court is faced with difficulties if asked to stop publication of material which has been published abroad. The English law of confidence is very different to the law of other countries, notably the USA, where prior restraint of publication in the media is forbidden. The history of the *Spycatcher* litigation shows what a fiasco the law of confidence can produce. In *Attorney General* v *Observer, Guardian (1988)* injunctions were originally ordered in June 1986 preventing newspapers from publishing allegations made by former senior MI5 officer, Peter Wright, in his memoirs, *Spycatcher*. In June 1987 the House of Lords, by a three to two majority, ordered the continuation of those injunctions, although by that time the whole *Spycatcher* book had been published in the USA, and the major allegations in the book had been reported by the UK press and television, and the media worldwide. By the time the case reached trial *Spycatcher* was being published in America (where it had topped the bestseller list for ten weeks), Canada, Australia and Ireland, and was available throughout Europe. It could be imported freely into the UK. Both the trial judge (in November 1987) and the Court of Appeal (in January 1988) decided that an injunction should not be ordered against the newspapers, largely because of the book's widespread distribution. When the case reached the House of Lords on this second occasion the Law Lords recognized reality – no injunction was granted.

The Government in the *Spycatcher* case continued to argue strongly for injunctions on the grounds of confidence to prevent the British media from reporting information, even after it had been published worldwide and *Spycatcher* had sold more than a million copies. Despite the final outcome of the case the law of confidence had suppressed the information for two years, and involved two national newspapers in a very expensive piece of litigation.

The English courts can control only what happens in England and Wales. They ordered an injunction preventing publication of Joan Miller's MI5 memoirs *One Girl's War*. But anyone could obtain a copy of the book by taking a trip to Dublin. The Irish courts had refused to grant an injunction to the Government, because of the free speech provision of the Irish Constitution. Anomalies can arise even across the Scottish border. English newspapers cannot publish certain parts of the autobiography written by former MI6 officer, Anthony Cavendish. The Scottish newspapers are free to publish that material as a result of a ruling from the Scottish court. The ease with which information can be communicated across borders can make nonsense of an English court injunction on confidential material.

In February 1992, Mr Paddy Ashdown, leader of the Liberal-Democratic Party, discovered that injunctions do not always work in suppressing guilty secrets. Knowing the *News of the World* was about to publish the fact that he had a brief affair with his secretary some years before, he was able to get a gagging injunction on the grounds that the newspaper's information had been obtained from a confidential memo prepared by his solicitor. As is normal in such cases, the court order not only prevented publication of the confidential information but also of the fact that Mr Ashdown had taken legal action, i.e., a blanket ban on all facts and all names. In order to ensure universal compliance every other newspaper was served a copy of the order. Media reaction ranged from extreme concern to total outrage at the extent of the legal censorship. Within one week, *The Scotsman* published the full story. Being a wholly Scottish newspaper it was not subject to the orders of the High Court in London.

Secrecy is the English obsession, with documents routinely being overclassified as confidential. Even documents which have been read out in open court have been treated as if they were still protected from public view.

DEFENCES

Various defences are available to an action for breach of confidence:

1   That the information is not 'confidential', that it is in the public domain.
2   That the owner of the information has permitted its publication.
3   That the information discloses iniquity.
4   That the public interest requires publication.

Public domain

The first of these defences has been discussed above – it is not enough (necessarily) to show that the information is available in some form to the public. Because information has been published in an obscure journal does not mean that it can be published on nationwide television.

If information is publicly available in some general form, then it is much less likely that an action will be brought. This is certainly truer of private secrets, than of Government information. There, the fact that information has been published in a small circulation newsletter abroad has not in the past prevented the Attorney General from starting proceedings in the English courts.

Consent

If the owner of the information consents to its publication, he cannot later try to restrain its disclosure. It is important to get consent from the right person – the fact that a lawyer is happy to reveal the sordid secrets of a client is not enough, because the information belongs to the client. Any consent must be given by the owner or 'confider'.

Once the owner of information has consented to its going into the public domain, any rights in confidence are lost.

Iniquity

The defence of iniquity is the most important for an investigative reporter. There is no confidence in iniquity – information which reveals iniquity cannot be 'confidential'.

There is no exact meaning for iniquity. It clearly covers crimes and serious misconduct but how far the concept extends to lesser wrongs, inefficiency or waste for example, is not clear. In *Cork v McVicar (1984)* a journalist tape recorded an interview with a former Metropolitan Police officer about police corruption. Unknown to the former officer, the journalist had a concealed tape recorder which he used to record 'off the record' parts of the conversation. Despite the breach of confidence, the courts would not prevent publication of a story based on the secret tapes. The information clearly revealed allegations of police corruption and miscarriages of justice.

This was the plainest case of iniquity. But it may be impossible for a defendant to show that the information is true, and that there is actual iniquity. In some cases a defendant will be able to obtain evidence at the 'discovery' stage of an action. For example, if a newspaper has alleged financial malpractice in a company, it will be entitled to the relevant accounts and records. However, where the Government is the plaintiff, the court will not order the handing over of certain types of documents, which may be vital. In *Attorney General v Observer, Guardian (1988)* the newspapers wanted to publish allegations about the activities of MI5, which had come from Peter Wright, a former senior officer. The Court of Appeal held that some of the allegations clearly revealed iniquity (namely, that the former Director General of MI5 had been a Soviet agent, and that MI5 officers had conspired to overthrow the government of Harold Wilson). They were not unanimous about whether every 'bugging and burglary' would amount to iniquity. The majority held that the newspapers were not required to *prove* that the allegations were true, but that they should, before publication:

1   Assess the authenticity of the source.

2 Carry out any possible investigations to corroborate the allegations.
3 Give due weight to the findings of any investigations which had already taken place into the allegations.

Editors must act 'responsibly', and must consider the possible harm that will be done if confidence is broken.

These guidelines relieve the media of the need to be able to prove the truth of their publications by legally admissible evidence. They are helpful to investigative reporting.

There is a limitation on the defence of iniquity which affects the media. The courts often say that what the information discloses does justify a breach of confidence, but only to the extent that the information may be handed to the appropriate authority – the employer, the police, or some other authority. For example in *Francome* v *Mirror Group (1984)* a newspaper was given transcripts of the telephone conversations of a leading jockey. The newspaper claimed that these showed misconduct on his part. Despite the enormous interest of the public in horseracing and bookmaking, the court held that the newspaper could not publish articles based on the transcripts. The material should be handed to the Jockey Club or to the police, but it could not be published to the public at large. The court was influenced by the fact that the tapes had been obtained by committing a criminal offence (under the Wireless Telegraphy Act). If the conversations had been overheard on a crossed line, they could have been published. Anyone talking on the telephone takes the risk that they may be overheard accidentally. There would be no breach of confidence.

The intention to prove iniquity will not be a good defence to an application for an injunction. Anyone intending to publish a story obtained in breach of confidence must consider the nature of the iniquity defence in advance. What is the nature of the misconduct revealed? (Can the misconduct be proved conclusively? Is the source credible, or, for example, an embittered ex-employee? Is any independent evidence available?) Has the misconduct been investigated by anyone else? (With what result? Why should the finding be disbelieved?) Is there a need to publish the information to the public at large (beyond giving them a good story) rather than to some 'responsible authority'? Consideration of such factors will help to assess the likelihood of a successful defence to any legal action.

Public interest

Sometimes the iniquity defence is referred to as the public interest defence. But there is also a separate defence that publication of the information is in the public interest, even if there is no iniquity. In *Lion Laboratories* v *Evans (1984)* an employee gave information to the press about defects in his employers' 'Lion Intoximeter', a machine used to test drivers' breath for alcohol in the police station. The accuracy of the machine was important as the lives and liberties of members of the public who were tested on it were affected. There was no inquity; no one in the company had lied or been guilty of misconduct or inefficiency. But the court allowed the newspaper to publish. It was clearly information which the public ought to know.

Publication to the public at large was allowed because the responsible authority, the Home Office, had thrown its support behind the machine and was not in a position to examine its accuracy impartially.

There are many types of information which, arguably, it is in the public interest – as distinct from being merely interesting to the public – to publish. The Scientologists have failed on several occasions to prevent publication of their documents or information about their internal affairs. The court has found that the public ought to know about activities of the Scientologists.

In 1993, the court similarly decided that it was in the public interest for the views of former Prime Minister, Baroness Thatcher, about current government ministers to be published. The *Daily Mirror* had obtained an early copy of Margaret Thatcher's autobiography and began running selected extracts before the book was officially released and before the commencement of its 'exclusive' serialisation in the *Sunday Times*. The book's publishers, Harper Collins, and the *Sunday Times* tried and failed to injunct the Mirror. Although not all of the book came within the defence, both the original judge and the Court of Appeal ruled that the former Prime Minister's opinion of her successor and his colleagues was clearly a matter of public interest.

The questions to ask before publication are similar to those on iniquity – how grave is the matter revealed? How likely to be true is the information and ought the information to be published to the public at large?

Difficulties exist, but the courts occasionally pay more than just lip service to the benefits of the investigative journalist.

PROCEDURE

It is not difficult to obtain an injunction in order to restrain publication of confidential material. The procedure is the same as that described for libel (see Chapter 3). Truth, however, is no defence to an injunction in confidence.

Even the fact that a defendant intends to prove iniquity will not automatically prevent an injunction. The court weighs two conflicting public interests – one in publication (i.e. the exercise of free speech) and the other in confidentiality, which is said to be necessary for the efficient running of Government, of companies and of private relationships.

Once information is published by the media its confidentiality is gone for ever. Confidential information is like an ice cube; it melts and is lost, say the courts. No damages can properly compensate its former owner. The courts are ready to defer publication pending a full trial. The interests of the publisher take second place.

Very few actions in fact go to full trial. Grant or refusal of an interlocutory injunction is decisive. If an injunction is granted it is seldom economically worthwhile for the media to go for a trial just to publish a story. In *X* v *Y*, the AIDS doctors case, the full trial (which took place extremely quickly) cost more than £200,000. The costs of the *Spycatcher* trials around the world have run into millions. Conversely, if a plaintiff fails to get an injunction, the action is likely quietly to go away. Victory at the injunction stage is important, which is why evidence and arguments should be ready at the earliest possible moment.

In urgent cases a plaintiff seeking an injunction can apply *ex parte* without giving any notice to the publisher. The first a defendant may know is a telephone call warning that an injunction has been issued preventing publication of a particular story. A simple telephone call to the duty judge at the High Court can mean that an injunction is granted as the presses are rolling, or shortly before a broadcast. Anne Diamond obtained the injunction to prevent her ex-nanny's story from appearing on the front page of *The Sun* in precisely this way.

The dilemma for a publisher with confidential information is very difficult. On the one hand you may want to confirm the authenticity of the information with its owner, whether for editorial or legal reasons or to satisfy the IBA. But if you do attempt to check, that will put the owner on notice and might lead to an injunction.

There is no easy answer. Failure to check may lead to an incorrect story and expensive libel action. But at least the problem can be addressed properly.

If an *ex parte* injunction is granted, the defendant may apply to discharge it at an *inter-partes* hearing – both sides are present and can call evidence and argue about the situation. But evidence is produced in affidavit (sworn written statement) form, and the difficulties about balancing interests until the full facts can be investigated thoroughly can weight the balance against defendants as the *Spycatcher* saga illustrates. The more evidence a defendant has about previous publications, or the truth of any allegations, the better the chances.

The plaintiff is usually more interested in an injunction than any other remedy. But other available remedies are:

- *Damages*: In most breach of confidence actions, for trade secrets or business information, the market value of the information is recovered by the plaintiff. This is not applicable to most media cases, where no amount of money can compensate for the revelation to the public of confidential matters. The amount of damages will be decided by a judge (unlike libel damages). To date there are no useful guidelines to assess the likely awards for loss of non-commercial confidences.

- *Account of profits*:   This is most relevant to book publishers. The plaintiff can recover all profits made by the defendant by use of its secrets. All profits from a whistleblower's book could be lost in this way. Where a newspaper contains one story in breach of confidence, or a television company broadcasts one offending story, the difficulties of apportioning part of the profits to the breach of confidence will be considerable.
- *Delivery up*:   The plaintiff can get back all of his confidential documents. Any defendant handing material back should bear in mind Section 10 of the Contempt of Court Act, which protects the identity of sources.

The interlocutory stage is the most important in breach of confidence cases. With a growing number of successful applications for injunctions by private persons and by the Government, the constraints on the press are tighter.

8 COPYRIGHT

The law of intellectual property protects things which are created by people's skill, labour, and investment of time and money. Patents protect scientific developments, and Trade Marks prevent unfair advantage being taken of the goodwill of established businesses. The law of copyright protects two kinds of investment. It protects authors' labours by copyright in books, scripts, articles and so on. It also protects the investors who provide the technology necessary to produce broadcasts, films and records. Copyright is the exclusive right to use material in certain ways.

The law of copyright is important to journalists because it determines to what extent they can quote or use the work of third parties in their reports and articles. It has a further importance in establishing what rights a journalist, newspaper or television company, have to exploit their own work, and prevent others from taking the benefit of it. It is true that there is no copyright in ideas, nor is there copyright in news. But the law does protect information which is expressed in a particular way. Anyone can report the fact that the SAS killed an IRA bomb squad. But one newspaper cannot use another's report verbatim, and a television company cannot lift another's footage of the event.

The law of copyright is extremely complex. At one time it was all based on the Copyright Act 1956. A major reform, after a series of piecemeal reforms, Government Committee reports and Green and White Papers took place in the late 1980s. The result was the Copyright, Designs and Patents Act which received the Royal Assent in November 1988. The new Act is intended to consolidate and modernize the law. It also introduces new principles into English law, for example the author's 'moral right'.

It is unlikely that many working journalists will ever master (or want to master) the present copyright law in all its intricacy. A reasonable acquaintance with the four primary areas of the subject is, however, highly recommended.

1   What is a copyright work?
2   Who owns copyright?
3   What is an infringement of copyright?
4   What remedies are available for breach of copyright?

COPYRIGHT WORKS

Copyright does not protect ideas or information from being copied. It protects the material form, or manner of expression, of information. If a particular joke is recorded in a cartoon, copyright will protect that cartoon, so that others cannot reproduce it without permission. However, anyone is free to use the same joke in a different way. The same news event may be reported in many different forms. The law strikes a balance between the right of authors to benefit from their work and the public's need for a free flow of information.

There are two main classes of copyright works. The first is original literary, dramatic, musical or artistic works. The second consists of sound recordings, films, television and sound broadcasts and cable programmes. The first class, with its requirement that the work be *original* protects the author's rights, the second those of the investor.

Literary work

Literary work includes newspaper articles or features, books, plays, songs and poems, in fact almost any words written down or recorded will qualify. There is no requirement of literary merit. Letters are subject to copyright, but where a letter is sent to a newspaper the writer permits publication of it in the newspaper on at least one occasion.

The 1988 Act makes no attempt at a precise definition of literary work. It is described simply as 'any work, other than a dramatic or musical work, which is written, spoken or sung'. Specifically included are 'tables or compilations'. Thus railway timetables and logarithmic tables are both literary works. Football fixture lists and pools coupons also qualify for copyright protection. This enables the Football League which owns copyright to permit football clubs to reproduce the fixtures in their programmes without charge, while charging football pools promoters to do so.

Television listings are copyright works. Considerable skill and labour goes into devising weekly schedules. Copyright is owned by the BBC and by the independent television companies. They used to regulate publication of the listings strictly. However, the Broadcasting Act which went through Parliament in 1990 now stipulates that TV companies must make full seven-day listings available to publishers at least two weeks in advance. For this service they are entitled to charge a 'nominal' fee.

Despite the fact that the Broadcasting Act has broken the TV companies' monopoly on listings it may not be all good news for publishers. In the past they received up to two days of listings for nothing. Now they get more, but they have to pay.

Some things may be too short to be protected by copyright. Although much time, money, skill and effort may go into devising a name for a new product or company, copyright cannot exist in a word. Exxon, the huge American industrial corporation, sued to prevent the use of its made-up name by an insurance company on copyright grounds. It failed. Only the law of Trade Marks or passing-off could prevent imitators from trading on its name and goodwill.

Since 1985 computer programs have been included in the definition of literary works for copyright purposes. This settled a legal debate about whether the old law could be stretched to protect new technology. A great deal of new ideas, skill and effort can go into devising a program, which can all too easily be stolen. Programs are now protected by copyright.

Dramatic works

Plays are the conventional dramatic works, but choreographed work and mimes are also included. The scenarios and scripts for films may also be protected.

Musical works

Copyright exists in musical works once they are written down. If music is recorded without ever being written down, it may be protected only as a sound recording, for example, if a record is made of a jazz quartet improvising. Another complication is that where a song is written, the tune and the lyrics have separate copyrights. One person may own the words and want to use the song in a particular way, while the owner of the music could refuse. Difficulties in ownership of the music may also occur if one person writes the basic theme while another adds an improvised and highly significant part to the finished piece. There is great potential for difficulties where members of a band write or record material together without deciding who is to own copyright, as a number of actions involving well-known artistes have shown.

Artistic works

Artistic works include paintings, sculptures, drawings, engravings and photographs, irrespective of any artistic quality. Cartoons and photographs for newspapers and television are covered by this definition. Buildings and models for buildings, and other works of artistic craftmanship are also artistic works. Like literary works, skill and labour must go into the artistic works, but the lack of any artistic merit will not deprive the finished work of copyright protection.

Spoken words

The 1988 Act makes it clear that spoken words which are recorded by any means become literary works and therefore qualify for copyright protection. The author of the work, i.e., the speaker owns copyright. As discussed later in this chapter, the Act also recognizes that this form of copyright ownership should not stand in the way of proper news reporting.

Originality

Literary, dramatic, musical and artistic works must be original before they can be protected by copyright. The essence of originality is that the author of the work must have devoted skill and labour to its creation. A slavish copy of an existing work will not be protected, nor would the writing out of the letters of the alphabet or the numbers one to 100. (The creation of a new typeface, or font, of letters and numbers, however, is a copyright work.) A musician who copies a folk tune may have difficulty in showing it to be sufficiently original to prevent others from copying his work.

If you produce logarithmic tables by carrying out all the necessary calculations and work independently, your tables may look exactly like an existing set. But both works would be entitled to copyright protection. The second set would infringe the first only if copied from it. Similarly, if two people independently paint a picture of the same country scene or still life, the finished works may be very similar, but both would be original, being created by independent skill and effort.

Two photographers may take photographs of the same event from more or less the same angle, and very similar photographs may appear in rival newspapers. Each newspaper could prevent the copying of its photograph, but could not prevent other photographers from going out to take similar photographs for themselves.

If two literary or artistic works are objectively similar, it may be difficult for the maker of the later work to prove that it is not copied from the first. For some works, an almost identical result is expected if the same research is carried out (for example, producing a railway timetable). However, articles, books or pictures which have a striking similarity to other works suggest copying. It may be difficult for the author of the work to prove that it was independently created, not copied. It is wise, in such cases, to keep drafting notes, and copies of the various stages of development of an idea.

The difficulties which may arise when two works look or sound similar are illustrated by *EMI* v *Vangelis (1987)* which concerned the popular and profitable theme music from the film *Chariots of Fire*. The composer of an earlier piece, *City of Violets* claimed that Vangelis had heard his tune and subconsciously copied it. The court listened to both tunes, compared them with the assistance of expert evidence, and concluded that Vangelis had *not* infringed the earlier copyright. The dispute ended happily for Vangelis, but the case took several years to come to court and involved high legal costs.

Other copyright works

Copyright exists in any sound recording, film, broadcast (television or sound), or cable programme. These are referred to as secondary copyrights. For example, if a television programme is pre-recorded, copyright will exist in the broadcast itself, in the film that is broadcast, and in the script and any music devised for it. Making a video recording of a television programme may infringe all of these copyrights. Where a broadcast is of a live event, for example the FA Cup Final, then the only copyright created is in the broadcast itself. There is no copyright in a live event.

Sound recording, film, broadcast and cable programme are all defined by statute. For present purposes it is enough to note that video recordings are included as films, so that video piracy is a copyright infringement, and that copyright does not exist in a broadcast or film which itself infringes copyright in another film, broadcast or cable programme. Under the new Act, satellite broadcasts, which can be received by members of the public (but not intersatellite transmissions) are copyright works – again, a change in the law brought about by technological advances.

WHO OWNS COPYRIGHT?

Copyright in literary, dramatic, musical and artistic works belongs to the author of the work. This means the person whose skill and effort produced the work – the writer of the book, not the secretary who types it out, the composer rather than the amanuensis. However, in some cases, the person who takes the material down can be the copyright owner. In *Walter* v *Lane (1900)* shorthand writers from *The Times* had taken down political speeches of Lord Rosebery. Reports were published in the newspaper. *The Times*, it was held, could prevent other newspapers from copying its reports. It owned copyright in *the reports*, which had been produced by the skill and labour of the shorthand writers, although Lord Rosebery (who did not make any claim) was the author of the speech. Other newspapers could have taken down the speeches themselves and published identical reports to *The Times*, but they could not take the short cut of copying from *The Times*. Copyright in such cases protects the material form in which the information is recorded, not the information itself. This principle clearly concerns journalists, who are permitted to 'follow-up' the stories in other publications, but may not 'lift' those stories without permission. Put another way, you are perfectly entitled to use the subject matter of other people's stories but you are not allowed to use their words.

If two or more people jointly create a work and their contributions are indivisible (unlike tune and lyric in a song) then copyright is owned jointly. If a ghost writer produces an autobiography, or a newspaper series, the ghost owns the copyright (subject to any agreement made).

The author has to be a person, that is a living human being, and not a corporation. A team of monkeys tapping away on word processors until they produce a literary work of genius would not be able to prevent it from being copied. Under the 1988 Act, where a work is produced with the aid of, or is generated by, computers, the person who undertakes the arrangements necessary for the creation of the work is its author. (Before 1988, the copyright owner was the person providing the human input.) Difficulties may occur where computer software is created by the input of several people at different stages. Where such collaboration has occurred there may be joint ownership of copyright.

In *Express Newspapers* v *Liverpool Daily Echo (1985)* a provincial newspaper reproduced the *Daily Express*' bingo game winning numbers. Cards had been distributed to readers, and each day a series of number on a grid were printed in the *Express*. People did not have to buy the *Express* in order to take part in the game (this would have been an unlawful lottery). The series of numbers printed each day were generated by computer. However, it was ruled that the *Express* was able to prevent anyone else from reproducing its numbers, since the numbers and grid were an original literary work. The game had been devised by human skill and labour, not simply generated at random by machines.

Photographs

Before 1988 ownership of copyright in photographs had special and different rules. The basic rule was that the person who owned the film in the camera owned copyright in the photograph. Only photographers who used their own films became copyright owners. A modification applied if the photograph was commissioned. If someone commissioned a photograph and agreed to pay for it, then the photograph produced belonged to the person who commissioned it, not the photographer (no matter who owned the film). A freelance photographer using their own film owned copyright in photographs taken on spec, but not on photographs commissioned by some publication.

Copyright, Designs and Patents Act of 1988 brings ownership of copyright into line with literary works. The person who creates the photograph will have copyright in it. Any photographer, whether commissioned or using someone else's film, will be the first owner of copyright. One result of this change is that if you ask someone to take a photograph of you on holiday, whoever you ask will become owner of the copyright in your snap.

The question of copyright ownership in photographs is of fundamental importance to journalists, particularly those in the world of newspapers and magazines. Only the owner, or owners (of the copyright, as opposed to, say, of the film or camera), can give permission to use a photograph. Permission must be obtained from the right person, which may not be easy. In *Daily Mail* v *Daily Express (1987)* the *Daily Mail* had bought exclusive rights to some wedding photographs from a husband whose wife was being kept alive on a life-support system only until her child could be born. The paper obtained an injunction to prevent the *Daily Express* from publishing the same photographs. The *Express* argued that the wedding photographs were owned jointly by the wife and the husband. The *Mail* had obtained consent from only one joint-owner' it could not obtain an injunction in copyright until it had the consent of *both*. The court held that the husband and wife did own the photographs jointly, but upheld the injunction. It was not clear whether wife was clinically dead (and therefore incapable of giving or refusing consent). In those circumstances the *Mail* could successfully argue that it had acquired a good title to the pictures.

Sound recordings and films

The rules about ownership of copyright in film, broadcasts and sound recordings were changed by the new Act. Copyright in films and sound recordings are now owned by the person who makes the arrangements necessary for the making of the film or recording. This would be the producer of a film, or the record company, rather than the director or artistes. (Under the 1956 Act the rules about ownership of copyright in sound recordings were the same as those for photographs – the owner of the material on which the recording was made, or the person who commissioned it.) Broadcasts will be owned by the person making the broadcast. (Under the 1956 Act only the BBC or IBA could own this copyright.) Copyright in individual pre-recorded programmes which are broadcast may belong to the programme-maker. The copyright in cable programmes belongs to the person providing the cable service.

Employees

Where a work is produced by someone *in the course of their employment*, then the normal rule is that copyright is owned by the employer. There must, however, be a contract of employment, or contract of service. In law, this is different from a contract *for* services, or a freelance contract. Copyright will belong to the employer only if it is part of the employee's duties to produce the work. The employer of a computer programmer will own copyright in computer programs produced at work, but not in a bestselling novel written by the programmer.

The contract of employment can agree that the copyright position should not follow this normal rule. Anyone working for themselves owns copyright in any work they produce, unless they assign it to someone else. It is important for anyone working freelance to look carefully at any freelance contract, which may assign copyright.

Newspaper employees

Under the 1956 Act, when a literary, dramatic or artistic work was made by a person employed by the proprietor of a newspaper, magazine or similar periodical, for the purpose of publication in it, the normal employee rule was varied. The proprietor of the publication was entitled to copyright in so far as it related to publication in a newspaper, magazine or periodical.

In all other respects, the author of the work retained all rights to it, for example to permit dramatic adaptation. This special rule could be varied by agreement, giving either the author, or (more realistically) the proprietor, greater rights.

However, the 'journalists exception', as it was known, was abolished by the 1988 Act. This leaves newspaper reports in the same position as all other employees – the proprietor of the newspaper owns the whole copyright. It is a significant loss for journalists. It is an important issue. The right to authorize later use of a work (which may be profitable) as well as the right to sue for infringement, depend on ownership. In *Beloff* v *Pressdram (1973)* political journalist Nora Beloff sued *Private Eye* for breach of copyright when it published a memorandum written by her in the course of her employment with *The Observer*. The original owner of copyright in the memorandum was the newspaper. An attempt by the Editor to assign copyright to Ms Beloff failed, because he had no authority to assign copyrights belonging to The Observer Limited. Ms Beloff had no right to sue, and her claim failed.

Creators of cartoon characters, whether employed by newspapers or magazines should take care that their contract does not give all rights to their characters to the proprietor. When the creator of the cartoon character Desperate Dan left the comic, the *Dandy*, he was forced into a long legal battle to try to keep his character. Merchandising rights to cartoon characters can be valuable commodities, as Walt Disney has shown.

Transfer of ownership

Copyright can be transferred from one person to another, like any other item of property. Copyright can pass as part of an estate on death, or be assigned during the lifetime of the owner. The effect of the rules about ownership above can be altered by agreement. Any assignment of copyright must be in writing.

Formalities

The owner of copyright does not need to go through any formalities (such as registration) to protect a copyright work. No copyright notice need appear on any work. The formula © and name (of copyright owner) and date (of first publication) provides protection under foreign and international laws. The rules on international protection of copyright are complex.

WHAT IS INFRINGEMENT?

Copyright gives its owner the exclusive right to deal with a work in various ways. The copyright owner can permit others to deal with the work. A licence can be given to use the work for one purpose, or generally. For all of the infringing acts below, the consent of the owner is a good defence. As we have seen, it can be difficult to know who owns copyright. An employer may own copyright in a work produced by an employee. If a newspaper is given permission to publish the work by the employee in such a case, it would not have a defence to a copyright claim by the employer. If any of the following acts are done without the permission of the copyright owner, that is a breach of copyright.

Copying

Copying is an infringement of all types of copyright. If an article in one newspaper is taken and reproduced verbatim in another, that is a clear infringement. But the whole article need not be taken. If a 'substantial part' of the original is copied, that will still be an infringement of copyright. To be a substantial part it is not necessary to take most of the original in quantitative terms. It is enough if the most significant or distinctive part is copied.

Whether what is taken is a substantial part is always a difficult question of fact. If the first notes of Beethoven's *Fifth Symphony* were taken by a rival composer, but not the rest, that could be an infringement of copyright (had copyright not expired). Those notes were so distinctive as to be a substantial part. In the more modern technique of sampling, very short extracts are taken from a record. If an extract is a distinctive 'riff' or 'hook', it can amount to an infringement of copyright. The musical example is the easiest to give, but the same principle applies to written works or film clips.

The copying need not be exact. Minor changes will not prevent the infringement from taking place, especially if the changes are intended deliberately to avoid a copyright action. The making of a parody or pastiche may breach copyright. The question depends on the degree of similarity between the parody and the original. In *Williamson* v *Pearson (1987)* an advertising agency took a song from *South Pacific* (*There is Nothing Like a Dame*) and produced a commercial for a bus company praising its waitresses (*There is Nothing Like Elaine*). The owners of the copyright in *South Pacific* obtained an interlocutory injunction. Although the words were totally different, the tune was the same. The question was whether the parody made use of a substantial part of the expression of literary copyright.

The use for which the parody is put appears to be relevant. The courts are more willing to allow parodies which make political or humorous comment, than those which are made solely for commercial reasons.

There is no precise guidance on what will be an infringement and what will not. Every case depends on its own facts, and a comparison of the original article and the copy. In *MacDonalds* v *News Group (1985)* a publisher had obtained an injunction preventing a newspaper from printing extracts from one of its books, *The Killing of The Unicorn*. The newspaper reported on the contents of the book, without using any verbatim quotation from it, except for one picture caption of nineteen words. The court held that the newspaper was not in breach of the injunction. The injunction could only prevent a breach of copyright. The extract of nineteen words could not amount to a substantial part of the book.

Some copying is not a breach of copyright. If you copy a television or sound broadcast for private purposes only, that is not an infringement of copyright in the broadcast itself (although it may infringe copyright in a pre-recorded programme or film). Home taping of live programmes to keep in a private collection, or to watch at a more convenient time, is permitted. It would be an infringement of copyright if you were to sell the video tape or to hire it out. Since the 1956 Act there has been a rule permitting artistes to record cover versions of records. Once a record has been made, later recordings of the same work can be made without the consent of the copyright owner, as long as various conditions are complied with. These include the payment of a compulsory licence fee of 6¼ per cent of the retail price of any records made.

Other infringements

Under the 1988 Act, it is an infringement to issue copies of copyright works to the public (to 'publish' them, under the 1956 Act). Performing a literary, dramatic or musical work in public is an infringing act, as is playing or showing in public any sound recording, film, broadcast or cable programme. This obviously includes using copyright works in lectures or speeches, or in presentations using films, recordings or broadcasts.

Broadcasting a literary, musical, or dramatic work infringes copyright. However, when an artistic work is publicly displayed it can be included in broadcasts or films, and can be photographed, drawn or painted.

Making adaptations of literary, dramatic or musical works is an infringement of copyright. Turning a play into a book, or a book into a play, translating a work, or putting it into pictorial form are all adaptations. Producing a cartoon of a Jeffrey Archer novel would be a breach of copyright. Giving a tune a new arrangement is also an infringement. Copying or publishing the adaptation is an infringement of copyright in the original work. For computer programs, translating a program from one computer language to another is an infringement of copyright.

Commercial misuse of copyright work is further prevented by making the sale, hire, or importation of copyright works an infringement of copyright.

DEFENCES

The law provides various defences to infringement of copyright, the most important of which is 'fair dealing'.

Fair dealing

The defence of fair dealing acknowledges the wider interest of freedom of speech by allowing considerable latitude in the use of copyright material for certain worthy purposes. The Copyright, Designs and Patents Act 1988, limits those purposes to news reporting, to criticism and review, and to research and private study.

(a) News reporting

With the exception of photographs, use may be made of any sort of copyright work providing it is for the purpose of reporting current events. In the cases of newspapers, magazines and any other sort of print media the reproduction must be accompanied by a 'sufficient acknowledgement', i.e., proper identification of the original work by name and author. This requirement does not apply, however, where the reporting of current affairs is by means of television, radio, satellite or cable broadcasting.

(b) Criticism and review

Any sort of copyright work, including photographs, may be copied without liability providing the reproduction is made for purposes of criticism and review. In this area of the fair dealing defence a sufficient acknowledgement of the original work and its authorship must be given in every case, i.e., whether the copying is through the medium of print, radio or television.

(c) Research and private study

Use of copyright works for the purposes of research and private study is permissible. Under this branch of fair dealing there is no requirement for sufficient acknowledgement.

There is no definition of what is meant by fair dealing. Every case will depend on what is taken, and the reasons for which it was taken. In *Associated Newspapers* v *News Group (1986)* the plaintiff obtained, for a limited period, exclusive rights to the letters of the Duke and Duchess of Windsor. These were printed in the *Daily Mail*. *The Sun* published the whole of one letter and part of another. The plaintiff obtained an injunction preventing further publication. There was no interference with free speech, said the court. *The Sun*'s aim was solely to increase readership. Arguments that the publication was for the purpose of criticism or review, or to report current events, failed to impress the court.

The motive of the publisher is relevant. The courts are willing to look behind spurious arguments of the public interest in free speech, when all that a newspaper is interested in is 'spoiling' a competitor's exclusive.

A genuine review of work, and genuine reports of current events are permitted. The reporting in newspapers of matters obtained from advance copies of magazines is routine practice, and acceptable as long as there is an acknowledgement of the source. The magazine gets free publicity. But the amount of material taken must be reasonable too. The lifting of a whole article, including verbatim quotations, could result in an action for breach of copyright.

'Current events' will be generously interpreted to include all varieties of news. In 1991 a High Court judge ruled that the use of BBC film footage of World Cup football matches by its satellite station rival, British Satellite Broadcasting, was fair dealing. BSB illustrated its spoken match reports with BBC clips of goals and other highlights of play. It acknowledged the source and confined itself to short, informative exerpts. The judge acknowledged that contemporary football matches in the World Cup were clearly 'current events' and dismissed the BBC's copyright claim.

Where a book is published and one newspaper has obtained exclusive serialization rights, it is likely to pursue actions against other newspapers publishing details of the book. Particular care should be taken before any extracts are published. Similarly, if an advance copy of a book is provided for a newspaper to enable it to decide how much to offer for the serialization rights, a newspaper should not reproduce extracts if it does not buy the rights.

The fair dealing defence does permit matters of public interest to be reported. In *Hubbard* v *Vosper (1973)* the founder of the cult of Scientology applied for an injunction to stop publication of a book 'exposing' Scientology written by a former Scientologist. The book quoted from books written by Hubbard, and from other writings (including internal memoranda). The court refused an injunction. The defendant showed that he might have a good defence of fair dealing. Although substantial amounts of material were quoted, this did not deprive the defendant of his defence. He was entitled to criticize the philosophy set out in the works, and was not limited to criticizing their literary style.

The fair dealing defence is relevant to investigative reporting where documents are obtained. Government documents, local authority reports, and private papers are the subject of copyright. Quotations from them may be justified by this defence.

The media may also raise a more general public interest defence, like the public interest/iniquity defence to an action for breach of confidence (see Chapter 7).

Although there are no firm guidelines, it has been recognized as a defence to a copyright claim by the Court of Appeal on at least two occasions. In 1984, the *Daily Express* was permitted by the court to publish copyright material concerning the accuracy of a machine used to test drivers' breath for alcohol (*Lion Laboratories* v *Evans*). More recently, the Appeal Court refused to injunct the *Daily Mirror* against publishing extracts from Margaret Thatcher's memoirs on the grounds that the views of the last Prime Minister on certain topics, e.g. contemporary politicians, were clearly a matter of public interest.

The 1988 Act added a new defence. 'Where a copyright work is included 'incidentally' in an artistic work, sound recording, film, broadcast or cable programme, this is not an infringement of copyright. What is incidental is not defined, except that any inclusion of a musical work which is made deliberately is *not* incidental.

Spoken words

Although the 1988 Act recognizes that spoken words which are in any way recorded become the copyright of the speaker, it also allows the media considerable latitude to use or report the words of others without infringing that copyright.

Section 58 provides that where a record of spoken words is made, in writing or otherwise, for the purpose:

(a) Of reporting current events, or
(b) Of broadcasting or including in a cable programme service,

use of the record or of material taken from it is not an infringement of any copyright in the words provided certain conditions are met. Those conditions are that:

(a) The record is a direct record of the spoken words and is not one taken from a previous record or from a broadcast or cable programme.
(b) The making of the record was not prohibited by the speaker and, where copyright already subsisted in the work did not infringe copyright.
(c) The use made of the record or the material taken from it is not of a kind prohibited by the speaker or copyright owner before the record was made.
(d) The use is by or with the authority of the person lawfully in possession of the record.

In essence this means that newspapers and magazines may quote spoken words as often and as fully as they wish providing their purpose is the reporting of current events. Broadcasters and cable TV producers are free to reproduce spoken words for any purpose. If speakers do not wish their words to be used the onus is on them to specifically prohibit such use. These provisions apply whether the words are spoken in private or in public.

Other defences

Copyright is not infringed if works are copied for the purpose of judicial proceedings, or a report of judicial proceedings. The 1988 Act extended this defence to cover proceedings of Parliament, or Royal Commissions. Taking copies of material which is required by statute to be open to public inspection (including public records and company records) is not an infringement.

There are detailed rules about copyright where material is reproduced for educational purposes, or by libraries. These are too complex for inclusion here.

NO COPYRIGHT

Public policy may prevent copyright existing in a work. In 1916, the courts held that a novel entitled *Three Weeks* could not be the subject of copyright, since it had an immoral theme. The same book would be protected today, when even video nasties are the subject of copyright. The rule is very limited.

DURATION OF COPYRIGHT

Copyright is a monopoly right. The law attempts to balance the protection of the author with the need for free flow of ideas and information. Copyright is limited in duration to achieve this balance.

The copyright in all literary, dramatic, musical or artistic works lasts until fifty years from the death of the author. (Under the 1956 Act, copyright in any unpublished work lasted indefinitely, and copyright in photographs was limited to fifty years from first publication.) Copyright in films, sound recordings, broadcasts, and cable programmes under the 1988 Act will last for fifty years from the time they are made or released.

Once copyright has expired, anyone is free to deal with the work as they choose. There is no need to pay licence fees or obtain permission from the owner. This can result in a sudden rush of different editions of the work of a particular author. It can also have financial consequences. For example, the Great Ormond Street Children's Hospital received a great deal of money from the copyright of J. M. Barrie's *Peter Pan*. This stopped when copyright expired at the end of 1987, having serious financial consequences for the hospital. Former Prime Minister Sir James Callaghan introduced a proposal into the new Act to extend copyright exceptionally for this case.

REMEDIES

Injunctions

Permanent injunctions and interlocutory injunctions are available in actions for breach of copyright. The principles and practice are similar to those applicable in other civil actions. (See Chapters 3 and 7.)

Damages

The calculation of damages for breach of copyright is complicated. Under the 1988 Act, three different types of damages are available:

1 Infringement damages
2 Flagrant damages
3 An account of profits

Damages are not available from any defendant who did not know, or had no reason to believe, that copyright existed in the work infringed.

Ordinary infringement damages are intended to compensate the plaintiff for the damage done to his interest. It is reparation for the owner, to put him into the position he would have been in, had the copyright not been infringed. This is normally calculated as the reasonable licence fee the defendant would have had to pay the plaintiff for the right to do what he did.

Flagrant damages are additional to the above. Under the 1956 Act, if the court, looking at the flagrancy of the infringement, and any benefit the defendant obtained from it, was satisfied that 'effective relief' was not otherwise available to the plaintiff, it could award additional damages, as it thought appropriate. The new Act changed the test slightly – the court can award such damages as the justice of the case may require (it need not consider whether the plaintiff can obtain effective relief).

Flagrant damages are to deter the defendant. If, for example, the plaintiff refused the defendant permission to publish something, but the defendant did so regardless, in order to benefit himself financially, the court might award additional damages to the plaintiff. If the owner would not have given permission at any price (to the publication of private papers for example), the damages will be higher. It is similarly the case if publication causes distress to the plaintiff. In *Williams* v *Settle (1960)* a photographer supplied wedding photographs to the press. The photographs had been commissioned by the bride, and so were her copyright (under the law as it then was). The photographer sold them to the press for financial gain, after the bride's father-in-law was murdered. The court awarded flagrant damages of £1,000.

The plaintiff may choose to recover an account of profits, instead of damages. The amount is calculated by reference to the profit made by a defendant, not the loss suffered by the plaintiff. Only profit is recoverable – the defendant is allowed to take into account expenses incurred in connection with producing the infringing articles. The calculation of profits can be a long and very expensive task.

Delivery up

Infringing copies of copyright works belong to the copyright owner. Under the 1988 Act, the owner of copyright can recover infringing copies from anyone possessing them in the course of a business. This enables a copyright owner to demand delivery up (the handing-over) of copies of leaked documents. For example in *Secretary of State for Defence* v *Guardian (1983)* the Government recovered a copy of internal documents leaked to the *Guardian* by Sarah Tisdall (see page 144). The infringing copies belonged to the Minister. The privilege in Section 10 of the Contempt of Court Act 1981 did not protect the *Guardian* from handing over the documents, which identified their source.

CRIMINAL OFFENCES

Certain types of copyright infringement give rise to criminal penalties, as well as a civil claim in damages. The offences are directed at commercial exploitation of copyright. It is an offence to make for sale or hire, to sell or let on hire, to exhibit in public by way of trade, or to import into the UK (other than for private use) any article which you know is an infringing copy. It is also an offence to distribute articles which you know to be infringing copies for the purpose of trade, or to such extent as to affect prejudicially the owner of the copyright. (These offences were created by the 1956 Act and are largely continued under the new Act.)

The criminal offences are used mainly in relation to video pirates (infringing copyright in films) and record pirates (sound recordings). Penalties were increased in 1983 to take account of the gravity of piracy. Penalties include two years' imprisonment and/or an unlimited fine after trial on indictment, or two months' imprisonment and/or a fine of £2,000 after summary trial. The police have powers to search premises when criminal offences are suspected.

OTHER RIGHTS

False attribution of authorship

Damages are available if a person's name is put to a work of which they are not the author in such a way as to imply that they are. Publishing or selling such a work also gives rise to damages. In *Moore* v *News of the World (1972)* Dorothy Squires recovered £100 for false attribution of authorship. The newspaper had interviewed her, and published an article stated to be *by* her. She claimed that she had not used the words published.

Newspapers who make up quotations are at risk of a claim under this section. In the Moore case, the newspaper claimed that it was its usual practice for reporters to put words into the mouths of individuals.

Under the old law, this right applied only to attribution of the authorship of literary, dramatic, musical or artistic works. The 1988 Act extended the right to film directors (who are deemed to be the authors of their films) in line with the new 'moral rights'.

Moral rights

The 1988 Act introduced, for the first time into English law, the European idea of an author's moral right over a work. The author of a literary, dramatic, musical or artistic work has a right to be identified as the author. This also applies to the director of a film. The identification must be clear, reasonably prominent, and in a form (which may include use of a pseudonym) approved by the author or director. The identification must appear in, or on, each copy of the work, or in some other way likely to be brought to the notice of people who obtain copies of the work, or see the film.

This right does not apply automatically. The author must assert *in writing* the right to be identified in this way, whenever the work is made available commercially to the public. Even then, there are some circumstances in which identification is not required, for example where a copyright work is being fairly dealt with by film, radio or television for the purpose of reporting current events. Another limitation on the right covers works produced for the purpose of publication in a newspaper, magazine, or similar periodical. Photographers and journalists do not have a right to a credit.

Damages are available if the author's right to be identified is ignored. There are no guidelines about the appropriate measure of damages. They are meant to cover any financial loss suffered. No damages are to be awarded for hurt feelings. An author or director might be able to show some financial loss in that their name was not brought to public attention in connection with a successful work.

The same authors and directors will have a right not to have their work subjected to 'unjustified modification'; that is, to any addition, deletion, alteration or adaptation. Modifications are justified only if 'reasonable in the circumstances, and not prejudicial to the honour or reputation' of the author or director. There are no guidelines about what will be considered reasonable by this definition. Publication of unjustifiedly modified versions of copyright works to the public infringes this right.

Authors who produce work in the course of their employment cannot complain if their employer consents to a modification (film directors' rights are similarly limited). There is another exclusion for works produced for newspapers or magazines. Editors and sub-editors need not worry about the author's rights as they cut stories or crop photographs. In such circumstances, there is no right in the author to maintain the integrity of such work.

Damages are available – again there are no guidelines as to amount. There is no specific exclusion of damages for hurt feelings. The court may order an injunction to prevent the use of an unjustifiedly modified work, unless a disclaimer is made at the same time dissociating the author or director from the modified work.

9 COURT REPORTING: THE RESTRICTIONS

THE OPEN COURT RULE

Justice should not only be done but should manifestly and undoubtedly be seen to be done.

Lord Hewart in *R.* v *Sussex Justices, ex parte McCarthy (1924)*

The proper administration of law in accordance with the natural rules of justice requires that proceedings of the court should be held openly and in public.

Although the principle may not be universally observed it is undoubtedly recognized throughout the world as being a basic standard by which the quality of legal systems may be judged. Lord Hewart's historic maxim has been redrafted, albeit in less colourful form, into numerous national constitutions and parliamentary statutes. Article 6 of the European Convention of Human Rights which protects the right of every defendant to a 'public hearing' echoes it precisely.

There have been occasions over the years when judges or magistrates have taken it upon themselves to clear their courts of press and public in order to conduct cases *in camera* (behind closed doors). Unless there is good cause recognized by law for taking such a step it is improper and, in itself, would be grounds for appealing whatever verdict is reached.

The principles applicable were given detailed consideration by the House of Lords in the case of *Scott* v *Scott (1913)*. Lord Halsbury put it very simply:

Every court of justice is open to every subject of the King.

Viscount Haldane stipulated that exceptions to the rule were to be strictly limited:

The power of an ordinary court of justice to hear in private cannot rest merely on the discretion of the judge or on his individual view that it is desirable for the sake of public decency or morality that the hearing shall take place in private. If there is any exception to the fixed principle which requires the administration of justice to take place in open court, that exception must be based upon the operation of some other and overriding principle which defines the field of exception and does not leave its limits to the individual discretion of the judge.

Other cases have made it reassuringly clear that the Press plays a crucial part in guaranteeing that 'justice is seen to be done'.

. . . the presence or absence of the Press is a vital factor in deciding whether a particular hearing was or was not in open court. I find it difficult to imagine a case which can be said to be held publicly if the Press have been actively excluded.

Lord Chief Justice Widgery in *R.* v *Denbigh Justices (1974)*.

The open court rule is therefore the norm for legal proceedings. There are, however, numerous exceptions to this rule. In various circumstances, where the interests of justice or national security demand it, courts may sit in camera. There are other occasions where the public is not admitted to a hearing but the Press is allowed in to report it. Another common situation, the rules of which (see below) should be carefully studied by every trainee journalist, is where the court proceedings are open to both Press and the public but there are restrictions upon what may be reported.

For proceedings to take place other than in open court there should be legal authority either through some statutory provision or at common law. The normal reasons are to protect state secrets or national security, trade secrets, patent designs or confidential information (usually only when the action is specifically brought to protect that very information) and where the hearing involves wardship or the custody and guardianship of children. At common law the court has discretion to go in camera if such a course is necessary for justice to be done or, possibly, in order to prevent the proceedings being disrupted by disorderly conduct.

In view of the clearly stated principles it is perhaps surprising, as trainee reporters quickly discover to their annoyance, that a huge amount of the work of the civil courts and a small portion of criminal court work is conducted in chambers. Although such hearings are not in camera they are held in rooms to which neither the Press nor the public are normally admitted.

Most chambers hearings are concerned with pre-trial procedural matters which are dealt with in this way rather than in open court purely for reasons of speed and administrative efficiency. Except on those occasions listed in Section 12 of the Administration of Justice Act 1960, which is given detailed consideration below, there is nothing to prevent any reporter who is given information about what is said in chambers from filing it for publication.

REPORTING RESTRICTIONS

Committal proceedings

In the absence of some good and proper reason for being in camera committal proceedings at the Magistrates Court will always be conducted in open court. Until relatively recently there was also no reason why a full report of what occurred in the proceedings should not be published or broadcast to the general public.

Official attitudes towards the 'free for all' enjoyed by the Press in their coverage of committals began to change at the time of the Bodkin Adams murder trial in 1957. The prosecution evidence adduced at his committal and widely reported by the media suggested that the 'good Dr Bodkin Adams', as he came to be known, had helped a considerable number of his elderly patients on their way to premature meetings with their maker. The extent of that evidence, i.e. the number of alleged murders, was far greater than that which the prosecution felt it prudent to present at his full trial. The prejudicial effect of the Press reports of the committal proceedings was obvious.

A Government committee set up to look at the problem concluded that such reporting was unduly prejudicial and should be banned. The potential for prejudice was no doubt heightened by the common practice of defendants at committal hearing reserving their defence until full trial.

After the committal of the Moors murderers in December 1966, during which reporters were treated to the full lurid detail of eighty prosecution witnesses paraded before the magistrates of Hyde, in Greater Manchester, the committee's report was finally implemented.

Section 3 of the Criminal Justice Act 1967, placed strict limits on the reporting of committals. With some amendments, those restrictions are now set out in Section 8 of the Magistrates Court Act 1980.

In any report of committal proceedings, whether written or broadcast, it is unlawful to publish any details except the following:

1 The identity of the court and the names of the examining justices.
2 The names, addresses and occupations of the parties and witnesses and the ages of the accused and witnesses.
3 The offence or offences, or a summary of them.
4 The names of counsel or solicitors engaged in the proceedings.
5 Any decision of the court to commit the accused, or any of the accused for trial, and any decision of the court on the disposal of the case of any accused not committed.
6 The charges on which the accused is committed or a summary of them and the court to which he was committed.
7 The date and place of the next hearing if there is an adjournment.

8   Any arrangements regarding bail.
9   Whether legal aid was granted.

The form of committal proceedings varies from case to case. Where the defendant accepts that there is a case to answer it is usual for the written statements of prosecution witnesses to be simply handed in. In such cases none of the evidence is given publicly and the only area of danger for the court reporter concerns police objections to bail and the reasons given by magistrates in the event of it being refused. Neither are reportable.

If the committal does not follow the short form set out above, it will consist either of witnesses being called to give their evidence or of their statements being read to the court. Indeed it may be a mixture of both. In these circumstances it should be remembered that it is an offence to publish the evidence given.

There are, however, exceptions to the above rule.

- If the magistrates decide not to commit the accused for trial at the Crown Court and instead dismiss the charges, the restrictions do not apply.
- If they decide that rather than commit to the Crown Court they will try the accused themselves, again the restrictions do not apply.
- Under Section 8(2) of the Act the reporting restrictions will not apply if the accused asks the court to lift them. Where there are two or more defendants and not all of them wish to have the restrictions removed, they will only be lifted if, after hearing representations from all of the accused, the court is satisfied that it is in the interests of justice that they should be.

Where any one of these three exceptions apply, the media are free to report full details of the committal proceedings. They are, of course, also free to publish these details at the conclusion of the Crown Court trial, though it is improbable that they would wish to do so given the passage of time.

Section 8 also makes it clear that the restrictions apply to all remand hearings prior to committal.

Since the situation arises in relation to every criminal case which is destined for trial at the court it is important that reporters understand this area of the law. Reduced to its simplest form, the rule is that unless the court has ordered the lifting of reporting restrictions, media reports of remand and committal hearings may only refer to those matters set out in 1 to 9 above.

However, Section 8 places the restrictions *only* on reports of the actual proceedings. It could hardly breach the section, for example, to publish the fact that the accused was driven to court by his wife in the family saloon car or that large crowds assembled outside the courthouse to witness his arrival. A logical extension of this reasoning suggests that it is perfectly lawful to publish an article which reports the hearing and also refers to undisputed and non-prejudicial background to the case – providing that the latter does not rely upon quotes or information that formed a part of the proceedings.

If a report is published in contravention of the statutory restrictions the proprietor, editor, publisher, TV or radio company or person having *executive* responsibility for the publication will be liable to prosecution in the Magistrates Court. *The Act gives no power to proceed against the reporter at court who filed the story*. If found guilty the maximum fine is £5,000. The Attorney General must give his consent for such a prosecution.

Hearings in chambers

Despite the open court rule an enormous amount of the court's work is conducted in chambers to which, as has been said, neither the press nor the public are admitted. Nearly all pre-trial applications in the County Court and the Queen's Bench Division of the High Court are heard in chambers as are most matters dealt with by the Family Courts.

The average hearing in chambers is unlikely to be of particular interest to the press since it is primarily concerned with technical points of procedure and pleading. Nevertheless, the occasions (e.g. injunction and custody applications) when the media will want to report chambers hearings are frequent enough for it to be worth a reporter's while to learn the legal dos and don'ts which apply.

They can be found in Section 12 of the Administration of Justice Act 1960, which begins by laying down the general rule applicable to the reporting of chambers and in camera hearings:

> The publication of information relating to proceedings before any court sitting in private shall not of itself be contempt of court except in the following cases . . .

Section 12 then goes on to list the occasions on which such reports will constitute contempt:

1 Where the proceedings relate to wardship, adoption, custody, guardianship, maintenance or rights of access to a child.
2 In relation to applications made under the Mental Health Act.
3 Where proceedings are held in private for reasons of national security.
4 Where the information relates to a secret process or discovery which is in issue in the proceedings.
5 Where the court (having power to do so) expressly prohibits the publication of all information relating to the proceedings, or of information of the description which is being published.

Before Section 12 came on to the statute book there was a good deal of doubt as to whether any sort of media coverage of chambers or in camera hearings could be lawful. Although the wording of the section could be more precise, it should at least be welcomed for clarifying the basic principle which is that, apart from those excepted cases set out above, the law permits the reporting of proceedings heard in private.

The practical difficulty for the reporter, of course, is that he is not allowed to be present at such hearings. He must in general, therefore, rely upon interviewing those directly involved outside the doors of the courtroom or chambers.

Although such reporting will not *of itself* incur any liability for contempt it should perhaps be borne in mind that it does not come within the protective formula of being a 'fair and accurate report of legal proceedings held in public'. The publication of any seriously prejudicial matter arising from such circumstances, (i.e. reports of *private* hearings) would still be an offence under the Contempt of Court Act.

For much the same reason, there would be no automatic defence to libel proceedings since absolute privilege does not attach to reports of proceedings which are not heard in open court.

Where particular proceedings do fall within one of the exceptions set out in 1 to 5 above, extreme caution should be exercised. Every reporter and editor should realize that, given the obvious danger of contempt, this is a high-risk area. If reports on, or touching upon, such proceedings are seriously contemplated, legal advice should be taken before publication.

In fact the embargo is not total. Section 12 itself provides that it is lawful to publish the whole or any part of the order made at the hearing unless the judge expressly forbids it. Also, the case law on the meaning of the section has recognized that other things may be reportable.

For example, in *re F. (1977)*, a wardship case, (the names of parties in child cases are not given in law reports) the Court of Appeal exhaustively considered what is meant in Section 12(1) by the phrase 'information relating to the proceedings'. It decided that information about the *ward* could be distinguished from information about the *wardship proceedings* and that while publications containing the latter would constitute contempt those containing the former would not necessarily be unlawful. The fact that someone is a ward of court does not therefore mean that that person cannot be the subject of published stories.

In relation to precisely what sort of information relates to the proceedings as opposed to the ward himself (or herself), the same court stipulated that the embargo covers not only the matters aired during the hearing itself but also all pleadings, affidavits, reports, witness statements and other material which is prepared for use in the case.

The precise application of Section 12 was further clarified by Sir Stephen Brown, the President of the Family Division of the High Court, in the 1988 contempt case brought by Cleveland Council against the *Mail on Sunday*, *The Sun* and the *Daily Mirror*. The case arose from published stories concerning two of the families at the centre of the notorious Cleveland child abuse scandal. The children named and pictured in the articles were wards of court and detailed accounts of the events surrounding the wardship proceedings were published. Despite that, the judge ruled that the newspapers were not in breach of Section 12. The articles were not reports of what happened in the wardship court nor did they rely on, or reproduce anything that was said in, or produced for, the hearing.

In dealing with stories about wards of court, the journalist should take care to check that no injunction is in force affecting publication. Judges often reinforce the general provisions of Section 12 with an injunction specifically prohibiting identification of the ward. Since the penalties for breaching such orders can be very heavy, checks with the court or with the lawyers involved in the wardship case are well-advised.

The reporting restrictions imposed by Section 12 may of course be lifted in whole or in part by the judge, as frequently happens in custody or wardship cases where there is a fear that the child will be forcibly removed from the jurisdiction. At such times, especially when the child's whereabouts are unknown, the courts are generally quick to recognize that publicity via the media may be helpful.

Sexual offences

In 1976 Parliament passed the Sexual Offences (Amendment) Act which introduced the unique concept of anonymity in the reporting of rape cases.

The statute originally decreed that from the time a person was accused of a rape offence neither complainant nor defendant could be identified by the media. 'Accused of a rape offence' was defined in terms of the issue of a warrant or the appearance in court of someone on a rape charge.

The protection of anonymity was, therefore, effective only from the time that the matter was first brought before the court – usually either when a warrant was obtained from a magistrate or at the time of the first remand where there had been an arrest without warrant.

Although this meant that the press could generally publicize the name of a fugitive suspect, it provided absolutely no comfort for the victim who could still be exposed to full and distressing publicity while the crime was being investigated. This clearly could not have been what Parliament had intended and led to strong criticism of the Act.

In 1985 Sir Michael Havers, the Attorney General, was obliged to declare that under the existing legislation there was nothing he could do about the massive media coverage which had effectively identified the young victim of the 'Ealing Vicarage Rape'. The girl had been brutally raped during a robbery at the vicarage and for some time, while the press and TV homed in on the victim, her assailants were unknown and unapprehended. The Attorney General promised that fresh legislation would close the loophole in the law.

The reforms were eventually effected through the Criminal Justice Act 1988, and came into force on 28 September of the same year. Under Section 158 of that Act the 1976 law, i.e. the Sexual Offences (Amendment) Act, was altered in two vital respects. First, the anonymity of the accused in rape offences was removed completely – henceforward the media could freely identify anyone on a rape or rape-related charge (though extreme caution should be exercised in relation to pictures where identification is at issue). Second, the protection against identification afforded to the victim was brought forward to the moment the complaint is first made.

Four years later, Parliament decided that the victims of certain sexual assaults other than rape should be protected in the same way. This objective was duly achieved by the Sexual Offences (Amendment) Act 1992.

As with all reporting restrictions there are penalties for infringement – in this case a maximum fine of £5,000. Every reporter should therefore have a clear idea of the basic rules laid down by the statutes.

1 The Sexual Offences (Amendment) Acts of 1976 and 1992 apply only to England and Wales.

2 The 1976 Act only applies to rape offences, i.e.
   - Rape itself
   - Attempted rape
   - Aiding or abetting either of the above
   - Inciting, counselling or procuring rape
   - Conspiracy to rape
   - Burglary with intent to rape

   The 1992 Act applies to:
   - Indecent assault on a man or woman
   - Buggery and assault with the intent to commit buggery
   - Incest by a man or a woman
   - Intercourse with a girl under the age of thirteen or between thirteen and sixteen
   - Intercourse with or procurement of a mentally handicapped person
   - Indecent conduct towards a child
   - Procurement of a woman by threats or false pretences
   - Administering drugs to obtain intercourse with a woman
   - Incitement by a man of his granddaughter, daughter or sister under the age of sixteen to commit incest with him
   - Attempts to commit any of the above offences

3 The Acts provide that anonymity runs from the time the complaint is first made. However, in terms of exactly what it is that the media is prohibited from publishing, they introduce a distinction between the time of the first complaint and the time when a person is accused.

Section 1 (1) of the 1992 Act (which is mirrored in the 1976 Act) states:

'Where an allegation has been made that an offence . . . has been committed against a person, neither the person's name nor address and no still or moving picture of that person . . . .'

may be published if it would be likely to lead members of the public to identify him or her as the victim. However, Section 1 (2) states that:

'Where a person is accused of an offence . . . no matter likely to lead members of the public to identify a person as the person against whom the offence is alleged to have been committed . . .'

shall be published. It is clear that the reporting restriction becomes greater after a person has been accused. It would, for example, be dangerous under Section 1(2) to publish as part of the crime report the victim's precise job and place of work or, say, the name of her married sister. Such details, however, could not be in breach of Section 1(1). The reason for the less stringent restrictions prior to the alleged villain being 'accused' is to allow the publication of information which may bring forward witnesses or otherwise help the police investigation.

The Act does not define what is meant by 'an allegation' being made but it is reasonable to assume that the courts will interpret this to mean a complaint to the police. The complainant, of course, does not have to be the victim herself. In relation to when 'a person is accused' the Acts define it for practical purposes as when either a warrant is sought or, if there has been an arrest without a warrant, when the person first appears before a court on a rape charge.

4 The prohibitions apply to written publications available to the public, to broadcasts and to cable programmes, i.e. to all written and visual media who publish in England and Wales. There is no automatic restriction against identifying such victims in Scotland.

5 The prohibitions apply 'during the lifetime' of the victim.

6 The judge in the case has discretion to lift the anonymity rule if:
   (a) He is satisfied at trial that there would be a 'substantial and unreasonable' burden on reporting the case and the public interest requires the lifting of the restriction.
   (b) An accused applies to the judge so that potential witnesses may come forward and there is a likelihood of substantial prejudice to his defence unless the restriction is lifted.

If the relevant offence is to be tried summarily (i.e. in the Magistrates Court) this discretionary power may be exercised by the Magistrates.

Judges are likely to be sympathetic to the plight of the press where the matter being tried goes seriously beyond the sexual offence, e.g. in *R. v Hutchinson (1984)* the accused was charged with the murder of three members of a wealthy Sheffield family and the rape of another family member who survived. The victim of the rape, whose surname was the same as her deceased relatives, was also the chief prosecution witness on the murder charges. It was suggested to the trial judge, on behalf of certain factions of the press, that proper reporting of the multiple-murder trial could not take place if the names of the murdered family could not be made public because of the rape issue. The judge ruled that it was in the public interest for the restriction to be lifted in respect of the rape victim.

7　On charges of breaching the anonymity rule, it is a defence to prove that the victim had given his or her *written* consent to the relevant publication. Written consent will not, however, be a defence if it is proved '. . . that any person interfered with the peace or comfort of the person giving the consent with intent to obtain it'.

8　Only newspaper editors (or their equivalents in broadcasting), publishers and broadcasting companies may be proceeded against for an offence under the Acts and the Attorney General must give his consent before a prosecution may be brought.

Divorce cases

Husband and wife disputes have always been a source of good copy for reporters who work at the popular end of the media market. The *News of the World*, the most successful mass-selling newspaper ever, used to boldly proclaim next to its masthead each week 'All Human Life is Here'. For many years readers found that 'all human life' in fact consisted largely of detailed reports from the criminal courts and the divorce courts.

While tales of criminals being brought to justice still dominate their fair share of headlines the steady flow of lurid stories from the divorce courts has been reduced to a trickle. The blame for this (and to many old-school court reporters *blame* is most certainly the appropriate word) lies upon the legislators who have radically reformed the divorce laws.

Because of the comparative ease with which marriages can now be dissolved and because the element of fault is no longer particularly relevant in the proceedings, the vast majority of divorces now go undefended. In practical terms this means no publicly-vented acrimony and no reportable court case. The only part of the process of undefended divorce actions which occurs in open court is when the County Court judge rubber-stamps the decree nisi.

However, even the trickle of defended divorce cases which are fought in open court are not free from restriction for the court reporter.

The Judicial Proceedings (Regulation of Reports) Act 1926, states in Section 1:

It shall not be lawful to print or publish, or cause to be printed or published . . . in relation to any judicial proceedings for dissolution of marriage, for nullity of marriage, or for judicial separation . . . any particulars other than the following

(i) The names, addresses and occupations of the parties and witnesses.

(ii) A concise statement of the charges, defences and counter-charges in support of which evidence has been given.

(iii) Submissions on any point of law arising in the course of the proceedings and the decision of the court thereon.

(iv) The judgement of the court and the observations made by the judge in giving judgement.

These restrictions were extended by later legislation (the Domestic and Appellate Proceedings Act 1968, Section 2 as amended by the Matrimonial Causes Act 1973) to cover proceedings for either of the following:

* A declaration of legitimacy
* Financial provision for a spouse

Reporters should note that the charges and counter-charges can only be reported if evidence has already been given in support of them. In other words, where there is an allegation, say, in a divorce petition about which no evidence is given during the divorce hearing itself, that allegation may not be reported – unless, of course, it is referred to by the judge in the course of delivering his judgement.

As with most reporting restrictions, only proprietors, editors, printers or publishers may be prosecuted and the Attorney General must give his consent to such a course. The maximum penalty is four months imprisonment and/or a fine of £5000.

Family proceedings

Under the Children Act 1989 Magistrates Courts are given wide jurisdiction and powers to deal with family matters. Justices who preside over cases in this area are required to have special training and are selected from a 'family panel'. When sitting they are known as 'family proceedings courts' and handle matters such as care orders, maintenance and adoption.

Family proceedings are open to representatives of newspapers or news agencies, i.e. the press, but are closed to the general public. The court, however, has power '. . .if it thinks it necessary in the interest of the administration of justice or of public decency. . .' to direct that all but the parties, their legal representatives, witnesses and court officers be excluded from the hearing (Magistrates Courts Act 1980, Section 69 as amended by the Children Act 1989).

Where the press are allowed to attend, the reporting of family proceedings is restricted by Section 71 of the Magistrates Courts Act to those same four categories reportable in divorce cases, i.e.

1 The names, addresses and occupations of the parties and witnesses.
2 The grounds of the application and a concise statement of the charges, defences and counter-charges in support of which evidence is given.
3 Submissions on any point of law arising in the course of the proceedings and the decision of the court thereon.
4 The decision of the court and any observations made by the court in giving it.

Overriding and extending these restrictions is the further bar imposed by Section 97 of the Children Act which states that:

'No person shall publish any material which is intended or likely to identify:
— any child as being involved in such proceedings, or
— an address or school as being that of a child involved in such proceedings.'

The Act defines 'child' as being a person under the age of eighteen.

In relation to adoption hearings the controls are tighter. The press is never allowed to be present and reports may cover categories 3 and 4 above but *not* categories 1 and 2.

Once again, only proprietors, editors and publishers (or their equivalents in broadcasting) may be prosecuted and the Attorney General must be give his consent to such a course. The maximum penalty is a fine not exceeding 'level 4' on the Magistrates Court Standard Scale (currently £2,500).

If the application before the magistrates is brought under the Adoption Act 1976, the controls are even tighter. In such cases the charges and counter-charges (if there are any) cannot be reported and under no circumstances can the child be identified in any way.

Indecent matter

The statute which inhibits reporting of divorce cases, i.e. the Judicial Proceedings (Regulation of Reports) Act 1926, also imposes a legal ban on publicizing indecent matter which comes out in evidence or otherwise during proceedings before a court. The Act provides in Section 1:

It shall not be lawful to print or publish, or cause to be printed or published, in relation to any judicial proceedings any indecent matter or indecent medical, surgical or physiological details, the publication of which would be calculated to injure public morals.

Exactly what sort of matters arising from legal proceedings would be so indecent as to injure public morals is not easily definable. Public morality is hardly constant from generation to generation and the populace of today are certainly exposed as a matter of course to sights and sounds which would have offended their forebears in 1926. There have been few, if any, prosecutions brought under this section in recent years.

Young offenders

Prior to 1991 young offenders appeared before and were dealt with by the Juvenile Court. It was presided over by specially-trained magistrates and had jurisdiction over persons upto the age of seventeen.

By the Criminal Justice Act of that year Juvenile courts were replaced by Youth Courts and the jurisdiction was extended to cover young persons upto the age of eighteen. The Act amended all existing legislation on young offenders in order to reflect these reforms.

Although Youth Courts are closed to the public they are open to 'bona fide representatives of newspapers and news agencies' (Section 47 of the Children and Young Persons Act 1933). There are, however, strict controls over what matters may be published. Section 49 of the Children and Young Persons Act 1933, states:

> . . . no newspaper report of any proceedings in a youth court shall reveal the name, address, or school or include any particulars calculated to lead to the identification of any child or young person concerned in those proceedings, either as being the person against or in respect of whom the proceedings are taken or as being a witness therein, nor shall any picture be published in any newspaper as being or including a picture of any child or young person so concerned in such proceedings. . . .

The above limitations, which of course cover both the accused person and witnesses if they are under eighteen years of age, also apply to reports which are broadcast by television or radio (Section 57 of the Children and Young Persons Act 1963).

Reporters should note that it is frequently not sufficient simply to leave out the name of the young person and his parents. The section makes it unlawful to name the youth's school or to reveal any matter which is likely to lead to him or her being identified. Thus, to name an adult who was present at court and describe her as the aunt of the accused could amount to an offence. It should also be noted that the protection of the Act is extended to young witnesses as well as defendants.

The restrictions may be lifted in whole or in part by order of the Home Secretary or the court itself '. . . if satisfied that it is appropriate to do so for the purpose of avoiding injustice to a child or young person' (Section 49 as amended by Section 10 of the Children and Young Persons Act 1969). Publicity may be allowed, therefore, only in order to protect a particular young person (e.g. where an innocent boy or girl is being publicly confused with the accused) and not as a form of punishment or for the protection of the public at large.

The Youth Court is one of the very few types of court in respect of which all reporting is automatically restricted. There are, however, occasions where young offenders are dealt with in other courts. If they are co-charged with an adult they initially appear at the Magistrates Court. If the magistrates do not try the matter to a conclusion they can be sent to the Crown Court or back to the Youth Court. Even when they are charged alone (or with other young offenders) they may end up in the Crown Court if the offence is sufficiently serious.

In either case, and indeed in any other situation where persons under nineteen years of age appear either as parties or witnesses in proceedings other than at the Youth Court, the media may publish their identity unless a specific order is made by the relevant court to prohibit this.

Under Section 39 of the Children and Young Persons Act 1933, orders may be made in relation to any proceedings in any court where a child or young person is appearing as a party or a witness. Once an order is made reporters are subject to exactly the same restrictions as those which apply in the Youth Court.

It should be noted that Section 39 orders are the norm at Magistrates Courts and the Crown Court where the accused, or one of them, is under eighteen (though it is by no means common practice where the young person is simply a witness). If the reporter is in any doubt as to whether the order has been made he should always ask the Clerk of the Court.

Section 37 of the same Act allows any court to be cleared of the public while a young person gives evidence. As with youth proceedings members of the press are permitted to remain.

Orders under the Contempt of Court Act

As the previous sections of this chapter illustrate, there are basically two forms of secrecy which may be imposed upon the proceedings of a court. The first is to have the case, or part of it, heard in camera and the second is to restrict media reporting of it. In practice, the two often overlap.

In respect of both forms, the secrecy is either automatic or it is a matter for the discretion of the particular court. In Youth Courts and most family proceedings, for example, it is decreed by statute that hearings shall be both closed to the public and for the most part unreportable. In contrast, Section 8(4) of the Official Secrets Act 1920 gives the judge in an official secrets trial a discretionary power to clear the public from the court whenever he considers it necessary to avoid prejudice to national security.

Apart from powers bestowed by specific statutory authority the common law has always allowed judges a further discretion to impose secrecy upon proceedings. In *Scott* v *Scott (1913)*, the House of Lords recognized that the open court rule may be set aside whenever the interests of justice demand it. The court's residual powers under the common law has always enabled it also to make orders restricting reporting.

The Contempt of Court Act 1981, was aimed, among other things, at tidying up the legal basis for making discretionary orders which impose secrecy upon the media. The relevant sections did not introduce any significant change to the law; they did however go some way towards formalizing and rationalizing it.

The Act sets out two distinct types of restriction which may be ordered in respect of court reporting. The first is that reporting should be postponed. The second goes further and imposes a total prohibition on the publication of names 'or other matter' which arise during the case.

Postponement
Section 4(2) of the Contempt of Court Act states:

> . . . the court may, where it appears necessary for avoiding a substantial risk of prejudice to the administration of justice in those proceedings, or in any other proceedings pending or imminent, order that the publication of any report of the proceedings be postponed for such period as the court thinks necessary for that purpose.

Since its implementation the use by the courts of Section 4(2) has frequently led to criticism and challenge. Certainly there seems to have been a marked tendency, especially among the lower courts, to make orders on inappropriate grounds or as forms of permanent ban rather than simply postponements of reporting. Once such an order is made the court reporter is usually subject to major inhibition. It is, therefore, of some importance that he or she understands exactly what Section 4(2) means.

1 *Court*:   In this and every other provision of the Contempt of Court Act the reference to court '. . . includes any tribunal or body exercising the judicial power of the state' (Section 19). Thus all the regular courts from the Magistrates Court upwards may make Section 4(2) orders, as may the Coroner's Court, the Industrial Tribunal and any other tribunal established by statute to perform a judicial function.

2 *'Necessary for avoiding a substantial risk of prejudice . . . in those proceedings, or in any other proceedings pending or imminent*: First, it should be noted that, unlike under the strict liability rule set out in Section 2 of the Act, the prejudice which the court has to consider likely before making an order does not have to be 'serious'. Second, the risk of prejudice may apply to the proceedings which are actually before the court or to any other case which is 'pending or imminent'. In practice the old common law position regarding orders postponing the reporting of a case has been changed in only one respect by Section 4(2). The cir-

cumstances which give rise to the risk of prejudice are, of course, no different post-1981. Similarly, in the past those circumstances usually meant that reporting was postponed, either because the court so ordered it or because the media were well aware that publication of the relevant material would be contempt. The single practical difference now is that where a court considers that reporting ought to be postponed *it should specifically order it.* Prior to 1981 it was the position that publication of, say, prejudicial matter heard in the absence of the jury (see below) would amount to contempt whether the judge had made an order or not. Section 4(1) of the Act, however, provides that fair, accurate and contemporaneous reports of open court proceedings which are published in good faith cannot be contempt under the strict liability rule. In the absence of an order being made it would, therefore, be considerably more difficult to establish contempt where a court report has given rise to prejudice. Although the court's discretion is bound to be exercised in response to the particular facts and circumstances of each case there are three situations where a postponement order is regarded as normal practice:

(a)   Where prejudicial matter is heard by the court while the jury is absent – a 'trial within a trial', i.e. when the admissibility of particular pieces of evidence (e.g. confessions) is challenged, and submissions on points of law are invariably heard in the absence of the jury. Prior to the Act few courts would have considered it necessary to make a specific order in these circumstances since the media would know that reporting such matters would be contempt. As discussed above, strict liability contempt will not, however, apply unless there is an order.

(b)   Where the accused is awaiting a further trial or trials for other matters – unlike (a), this would be a case of there being a risk of prejudice to 'other proceedings' rather than those in which the order is made. Obviously the publication of damning evidence or, of a conviction, is likely to influence a future jury against the defendant. Only other proceedings which are imminent or pending may be taken into account under Section 4(2). Effectively this means any other case in which the accused has already been charged or where it is known that he is about to be charged.

(c)   Where the separate trial or trials of other people are likely to be prejudiced by material arising during the proceedings. It is not uncommon for evidence to be given in one trial which is highly prejudicial to separate proceedings against other parties. If the judge considers the risk to be substantial he may make an order postponing publication. Again, the other proceedings must be imminent or pending.

In considering the effect of Section 4(2) the Court of Appeal in the case of *ex parte Telegraph plc (1993)* ruled that before a postponement order is made the court must be satisfied that the risk of prejudice is *substantial* and that the precise order made (as opposed to one which is less severe) is *necessary* in order to avoid that risk.

3   '*Order that the publication of any report of the proceedings, or any part of the proceedings, be postponed for such period as the court thinks necessary for that purpose*:   Journalists should be in no doubt that the Section 4(2) order is a powerful weapon for gagging the media. It can be applied to every word spoken during the trial if the court considers it necessary. The postponement may, moreover, run for a considerable time. What the court may not do is prohibit reporting for all time under the guise of postponing it, nor may it make an order for any reason other than to avoid prejudice in the proceedings or in future proceedings.

Also, the court cannot use Section 4(2) to prevent the publication of any matter which is not 'part of the proceedings'. In 1986 the Divisional Court ruled that magistrates were wrong to make a Section 4(2) order which barred the broadcasting of TV film showing an arrest. The film formed no part of the proceedings before the court.

Prohibition

Section 11 of the Contempt of Court Act states:

> In any case where a court (having power to do so) allows a name or other matter to be withheld from the public in proceedings before the court, the court may give such directions prohibiting the publication of that name or matter in connection with the proceedings as appear to the court to be necessary for the purpose for which it was so withheld.

The section does not give the court any particular powers it did not already possess. Significantly, however, it does confirm that where there is power to impose partial secrecy inside the courtroom itself (by withholding a 'name or other matter from the public') it may impose the same secrecy upon media reporting of the case. The court must already have exercised a valid power to withhold the relevant information from the members of the public sitting at the back of the courtroom.

The circumstances which allow names or other matter to remain secret are effectively the same as those which justify hearings going in camera. Either there is specific statutory authority or power under the common law – the latter exists whenever the interests of justice demand it.

The most common instances of names being withheld are blackmail and Official Secrets cases. The justification for the first is apparently to ensure that victims of blackmail will not be frightened of reporting the crime. In *R.* v

Socialist Worker (1974) the judge in the Janie Jones blackmail case directed that the victims should be referred to as Mr X and Mr Y. An article written by the left-wing journalist, Paul Foot, which was headed 'Y, Oh Lord, Oh Why?' named the two men. Both Foot and the journal were successfully prosecuted for contempt.

Two points worth stressing:

First, Section 11 orders cannot be made in respect of a 'name or other matter' which has already been given in open court. The subject matter of the order must also have been withheld from the public in the courtroom.

Second, Section 11 should be invoked only when the interests of justice would be harmed if the 'name or other matter' were made public. It must not be used simply to spare the embarrassment of defendants or witnesses.

In *R.* v *Evesham Justices, ex parte McDonagh (1988)* magistrates trying an ex-MP on a motoring charge allowed his address to be kept secret because he feared harassment from his former wife. The Divisional Court ruled on appeal that Section 11 orders should be made only where to do otherwise would '. . . frustrate or render impracticable the administration of justice . . . .' The power to restrict publication '. . . was not enacted for the comfort and feelings of defendants'.

PRESS CHALLENGES TO SECRECY ORDERS

Regrettably, courts have frequently shown a willingness to make secrecy orders upon inappropriate grounds. They tend to suit the interests of the accused in that embarrassing publicity is avoided. They are frequently made after an application from defence counsel and are occasionally nodded through unopposed. There are other instances where it is appropriate for the court to postpone publication of certain material but the order which is made is far too wide and amounts either to a blanket ban or a permanent restriction.

Faced with an 'imperfect' order the options open to a newspaper or TV company are limited. It can simply publish a report in defiance of the order and hope to escape punishment for contempt. The problem is that orders of the court, right or wrong, are expected to be obeyed until a higher authority rules otherwise. Defiance is not, therefore, recommended.

There are effectively three ways to challenge orders which are thought to be wrongly made:

1 *Judicial review*

Under common law the High Court has always had power to review the workings and orders of inferior courts. This traditional avenue of appeal for aggrieved parties is now statutorily recognized in the Supreme Court Act 1981 which sets out the limits of, and procedure in relation to, applications for Judicial Review.

There are two drawbacks: first Judicial Review is not available to challenge orders of the Crown Court relating to trial on indictment; and second, because the process is slow, by the time such an application is heard, the relevant report may be stale.

2   *Section 159 Appeal*
Prior to 1988 Judicial Review was the only formal means by which the media could challenge secrecy orders. Section 159 of that year's Criminal Justice Act, however, gave 'any person aggrieved' the right to appeal to the Criminal Division of the Court of Appeal against orders made by a Crown Court Judge.
(a)   Under Sections 4 or 11 of the Contempt of Court Act 1981.
(b)   Restricting public access to all or part of the proceedings (i.e. 'in camera' orders).
(c)   Restricting reporting of all or part of the proceedings (e.g. under Section 39 of the Children and Young Persons Act 1933).

While it is fortunate that media representatives are clearly within the definition of 'aggrieved' persons, it is less than satisfactory that the Section 159 appeal process only applies to Crown Court decisions.

3   *Application to the originating court*
The cheapest, quickest and often most effective way to challenge non-publication orders is to raise the matter with the court which made the order itself.

The media does not have an absolute right to be heard, but there is plenty of guidance from the higher courts to the effect that magistrates and judges should allow representations to be made by or on behalf of the press.

In 1993 the High Court overturned a stipendiary magistrates ruling that he had no power to hear media representations against a Section 4(2) order during the committal for trial of Larry Trachtenburg, one of the accused in the Maxwell affair.

Lord Justice Mann recognized that the media's application was not an attempt by a non-party to be heard on the subject matter of the proceedings. On the contrary, it was a request to be heard on whether those proceedings could be reported. The judge considered that any court contemplating a Section 4 order had an inherent power to take representations on whether it was proper and/or appropriate from those at whom the order is aimed, i.e. the media.

'They are in particular the best qualified to represent that public interest in publicity which the court has to take into account when performing any balancing exercise which has to be undertaken. The need properly to operate Section 4(2) requires that a court should be able to receive the best assistance available when considering the curtailment of the freedom to report.'

Lord Justice Mann went on to express the view that although the power to hear press representations was discretionary . . .

'I expect that the power will ordinarily be exercised when the media ask to be heard either on the making of an order or in regard to its continuance.'

Faced with a gagging order which they wish to challenge *before the court itself* newspapers or broadcasters effectively have two options:

1   If the reporter in court believes that the order has been wrongly made, he or she can set out relevant objections and argument in a note and hand it to the court clerk for on-passing to the magistrates or judge. The note might, for example, point out that a Section 11 order is being made to ban reporting of a name which came out in court earlier in the trial, or it might remind the magistrates that the Section 4 order has no time limit on it. This informal route is frequently very effective. Upon receipt of such a note the court is likely to look carefully at what the statute allows it to do.

2   Alternatively (or additionally if the first option fails) the newspaper or broadcaster can instruct its lawyer to make representations to the court on the propriety of the order. It is usually possible to organize such an application within twenty-four hours of the order being made. As outlined above, the media does not have an absolute right to be heard, but the court will usually exercise its discretion to allow the making of representations, for example:

●   In 1982 *The Observer* defied a blanket ban on reporting the trials of certain nurses at Rampton Hospital. The trial judge agreed to hear its counsel's arguments to the effect that the order was too wide. In the event he agreed to withdraw it.

●   At the end of a 1985 murder case at Newcastle Crown Court *The Sun* published the details of a trial within a trial during which the judge, Mr Justice Taylor, had ruled that damning evidence against the defendant was inadmissable and would therefore not be put before the jury. He had made an order under Section 4(2) which was effectively a prohibition of reporting rather than a postponement. On seeing *The Sun*'s report the judge stated in open court that the newspaper was in breach of his order and said he would refer the matter to the Attorney General for contempt proceedings to be brought. Later the same day he agreed to hear argument from counsel for *The Sun*. It was pointed out that the order was defective since it was expressed as applying for an indefinite period. Moreover since the trial had concluded and there were no other proceedings contemplated the question of prejudice did not arise. The judge agreed that the order should be discharged and no further action should be taken against the newspaper.

• When the stipendiary magistrate refused to hear media objections in the Trachtenburg case in 1993 the High Court ruled (on Judicial Review) that he was wrong. The *Daily Telegraph* duly re-applied to the original court. After hearing counsel's arguments the same magistrate lifted the earlier Section 4(2) order.

PRECISENESS OF ORDERS

By December 1982, the Lord Chief Justice was sufficiently concerned about the loose manner in which secrecy orders under Sections 4(2) and 11 of the Contempt of Court Act 1981, were being made that he issued a practice direction to the junior courts in the following terms:

> It is necessary to keep a permanent record of such orders for later reference. For this purpose all orders made under Section 4(2) must be formulated in precise terms . . . and orders under both sections must be committed in writing either by the judge personally or by the clerk of the court under the judge's directions. An order must state, (a) its precise scope, (b) the time at which it shall cease to have effect, if appropriate, and (c) the specific purpose of making the order. Courts will normally give notice to the press in some form that an order has been made under either section of the 1981 Act and court staff should be prepared to answer an inquiry about a specific case, but it is, and will remain, the responsibility of those reporting cases, and their editors, to ensure that no breach of any order occurs and the onus rests with them to make inquiry in any case of doubt.

The direction is both an assistance and a warning to the press. It ensures that secrecy orders must be drafted with clarity and precision and that the court staff should give every assistance to reporters wishing to find out exactly what was ordered. At the same time, however, it warns that the duty upon editors to obey these orders is extremely heavy. A failure to discover the existence or precise terms of a particular order will not avoid liability for contempt.

TAPE RECORDERS, PHOTOGRAPHS AND SKETCHES

As well as the limitations placed by the law on the content of court reports there are also certain restrictions placed on how those reports are gathered.

Tape recorders

Section 9 of the Contempt of Court Act 1981, makes it a contempt to:

1   Use in court, or bring into court for use, any tape recorder except with the leave of the court.

2 Publish a recording of legal proceedings by playing it to any section of the public, or disposing of such a recording with a view to it being so published.

Although tape recorders are rarely seen on the press benches of a court, a practice direction issued by the Lord Chief Justice in November 1981 indicated that in deciding whether to give leave courts should consider: 'Any reasonable need on the part of the applicant . . . whether a litigant or a person connected with the press or broadcasting.' At the same time he warned that leave should not be granted if there is a risk that the recording would be used for briefing future witnesses or where the sight of, or noise from, the machine could be distracting.

It should be noted (see 1 above) that if leave has not been given it is risky even to enter the courtroom with a tape recorder. Offenders can be sentenced to a maximum of one month's imprisonment or a fine of £2,500. Section 9 also allows the court to order forfeiture of the offending items. Sound recordings made for the purposes of official transcripts of the proceedings are exempt from these restrictions.

Photographs and sketches

Photographs may not be taken in court, nor may sketches be made if they are intended for publication. Under the Criminal Justice Act 1925, Section 41(1):

> No person shall (a) take or attempt to take in any court any photograph, or, with a view to publication, make or attempt to make in any court any portrait or sketch of any person, being a judge of the court, or a juror or a witness in, or a party to, any proceedings before the court, whether civil or criminal, or (b) publish any photograph, portrait or sketch taken or made in contravention of this section, or any reproduction thereof.

For the purposes of Section 41, 'court' is deemed to cover the area within the courthouse and its precincts. Although it is almost common practice and seems to go unpunished, it is illegal to photograph or film defendants or witnesses as they arrive at, and leave, the court.

While sketching inside court is not in itself forbidden, it becomes a breach of Section 41 if it is intended for publication. It is, of course, perfectly proper to make a sketch of a trial or its participants from memory after leaving the court and to publish it.

The maximum penalty for breach of the section is currently a fine of £1,000.

Industrial tribunals

As a 'body exercising the judicial power of the State' the Industrial Tribunal qualifies as a 'court' under the Contempt of Court Act and therefore has the power to make Section 4(2) or Section 11 orders. It can also make Section 39 orders banning the identification of young persons under the age of eighteen.

Because of Department of Employment fears that lurid reporting deterring complainants from bringing valid chains, tribunals have recently been given further significant powers to curtail reporting. The Trade Union Reform and Employment Rights Act 1993 enable tribunals to make an order banning publication of the identity of the person involved in the proceedings where allegations are made of sexual misconduct or conduct relating to sex or sexual orientation. Under the legislation:

> 'Conduct is related to sex whether the relationship with sex lies in the character of the conduct or in its having reference to the sex or sexual orientation of the person at whom the conduct is directed.'

The non-publication order may last up to the time when the tribunal hands down its decision on the case. Thereafter, however, the tribunal can order that the relevant name or names be removed permanently from all publicly-available records of the case.

10 CONTEMPT OF COURT

Of all the risks an editor or TV producer faces in the day-to-day presentation of news and features the one about which he or she is likely to exercise most care is contempt of court. Few working journalists will not have been told early in their training that the punishment for publishing a contempt can be swift and extreme. Grave contempts can result in imprisonment of the editor or journalist, as in the 1949 case of Sylvester Bolam the *Daily Mirror* editor who went to prison over his newspaper's coverage of the arrest of Haigh the mass murderer. There are numerous examples of the courts imposing massive fines for lesser contempts.

Unlike most other legal problems encountered by the media, contempt of court arising from publications is, for the most part, dealt with under the criminal law. While defamation actions may drag on for years through the civil courts and end with quiet settlements out of court, contempt proceedings are vigorously prosecuted, usually by the Attorney General, with the offender facing criminal sanctions if found guilty.

The essence of contempt of court has always been an improper interference with the administration of justice. Its origin lies in the adjunct to the rule of law that the court must be free to decide on those matters before it unhindered and unfettered by any outside influence. Both the law and the courts charged with its administration must be respected and obeyed.

The contempt laws are therefore aimed at those who undermine, obstruct or interfere with the workings of the court. Hence it is a contempt to carry out any act calculated to prejudice the outcome of legal proceedings. Disobedience of orders made by the court is also contempt as is misbehaviour in, or 'scandalizing', the court. Similarly, to undermine the court's authority, e.g. by suggesting that the judge is biased or incompetent, is likely to be viewed as a contempt.

Since 1981 the major part of the law of contempt as far as it affects the media is to be found in the Contempt of Court Act. Prior to the passing of this act the offence and the principles by which it was governed were based solely on the old common law. Centuries of not always consistent judicial pronouncements did little to assist the editor who needed to know in a hurry what could and could not be safely published. While there are many journalists and some media lawyers who claim that the Act has done little to either liberalize or clarify the law, most welcomed the introduction of a single formulated rule by which to judge potentially dangerous stories. The yardstick against which nearly all such stories are now measured is set out in Sections 1 and 2 of the Act. It is known as the strict liability rule.

However, contrary to the expectations of those in the media and, one suspects, many of the legislators, what the 1981 Act failed to achieve was a total *replacement* of the old law of contempt in relation to pre-trial publicity. Since the passing of the Act, the courts have ruled that the old common law offence still exists and, in at least one case, was shown to be flourishing.

This chapter sets out, in turn, both the new law and the pre-1981 law. It deals first and at greater length with the new law, i.e. the strict liability rule, because (despite some confusion arising from recent cases) it undoubtedly has greater relevance to the everyday reporting and publishing of news.

THE STRICT LIABILITY RULE

Strict liability, according to the Contempt of Court Act 1981, applies to any publication which:

Creates a substantial risk that the course of justice in particular proceedings will be seriously impeded or prejudiced.

The Act limits the period during which strict liability applies. The only publications which are subject to the rule are those occurring while proceedings are 'active' within the meaning of the act.

There are, therefore, four elements to the strict liability rule:

1 Strict liability
2 A publication
3 Active proceedings
4 Substantial risk of serious prejudice

Strict liability

In most criminal cases the prosecution must prove *mens rea*, i.e. a guilty mind, in order to succeed. The often quoted maxim that a man is innocent until proven guilty is generally understood to refer to the need to prove both the physical and mental elements of a crime. Thus a man cannot be guilty of theft unless he meant to be dishonest nor is he a murderer without 'malice aforethought'.

There are, however, a large number of offences created by Parliament in which the normal requirement of *mens rea* is dispensed with. In these cases liability is said to be strict.

In relation to strict liability contempt this means that where a publication creates a substantial risk of serious prejudice to proceedings which are active it will be no defence that such an affect was not intended. The prosecution will not be required to prove that the contempt was intentional, reckless or even negligent.

Thus, an editor summoned before the court for contempt cannot hope to escape a finding of guilt by pleading that publication occurred only because he received extensive legal advice to the effect that the article was safe. Such a plea might establish that his personal level of culpability was nil, but it would still amount only to mitigation and not to a defence.

It follows that motivation is irrevelant in contempt proceedings. Newspapers or TV programmes may be able to establish convincingly that they are performing a public service in exposing other wrongdoings of a person already facing charges, but that will be to no avail if their publication creates a substantial risk of serious prejudice to that person's trial. Apart from the limited effect of Section 5 (dealt with below) the Contempt of Court Act does not recognize a defence of public interest.

The only concession made by the Act to a publisher's innocent intent is in relation to genuine and blameless ignorance of the existence of proceedings which might be prejudiced.

The innocent intent defence
Section 3 of the Contempt of Court Act provides that a publisher is not guilty of contempt under the strict liability rule:

> If at the time of publication (having taken all reasonable care) he does not know and has no reason to suspect that proceedings are active.

A similar defence is established by the same section for distributors who take all reasonable care and neither know, nor have any reason to suspect, that the publication being distributed contains material which is in contempt.

In both cases the burden of proving innocent intent lies on he who pleads it. The onus, therefore, rests on the publisher or distributor to satisfy the court that all reasonable care was taken. It is unlikely to avail an editor when publication occurs days after an arrest is made and proceedings have become active. If, however, the subject of a story is arrested or a warrant is issued as, or just before, the presses are rolling and the editor can show that he did not know of nor have reason to suspect it, he can expect to be acquitted. The existence of negligence, of course, destroys this defence.

A publication

Section 2 of the Act provides that the strict liability rule only applies in relation to publications and defines a publication as including:

> Any speech, writing, broadcast or other communication in whatever form which is addressed to the public at large or any section of the public.

It is clear, therefore, that strict liability applies to the normal output of the media, i.e. newspapers, magazines, TV and radio broadcasts. Plays, concerts and speeches at public gatherings are also publications for the purposes of the act.

Active proceedings

Before the 1981 Act journalists were in danger of being in contempt of court only from the time that proceedings were 'imminent or pending'. Exactly when this period began was frequently a matter of some uncertainty. Since criminal proceedings actually commence when someone is charged the only certain thing was that the period commenced before this occurred. However, depending on each set of facts, in one instance the proceedings might be imminent before an arrest was made whereas in another they would become imminent a good while after the arrest took place. A journalist's ability to identify when his story became a potential contempt would generally depend on his knowledge of what was happening behind closed doors in a police station.

This lack of clarity was cured in relation to the new law of contempt by the introduction through the 1981 Act of a set period when proceedings are active. During this period publications are subject to the strict liability rule.

Both the commencement and conclusion of the active period are defined with some precision:

Criminal cases
Criminal proceedings become active with:

1   An arrest without warrant.
2   The issue of a warrant.
3   The issue of a summons.
4   The service of an indictment or other document specifying the charge.
5   Oral charge (except in Scotland).

In practical terms this represents a considerable tightening of the old law. Before 1981 the fact that an arrest was made or a warrant was issued would almost invariably provoke the publication of background and speculation in the press rather than inhibit it. Such stories ceased only when the police let it be known that charges were imminent.

Arrest

It is now clear that once an arrest is made any seriously prejudicial report is a contempt. Journalists therefore need to exercise caution and restraint in their coverage of arrests. While it will normally be unobjectionable to report the fact of the arrest, the name of the person held and general background about the suspect and the crime, other matters, e.g. his criminal record or facts linking him with the crime, should not be published.

Some problems arise when a person is arrested but charges do not follow within a reasonable time. Suspects are frequently arrested and then later released from police custody without being charged. The Contempt of Court Act states that proceedings which became active upon an arrest cease to be active if the suspect is released other than on bail. When the arrested person is freed unconditionally the media are therefore not inhibited by the strict liability rule. However, journalists face real difficulties when the suspect is released without being charged but on police bail. The terms of such bail may be that the suspect simply has to report back to the police station on a date weeks or months in the future. Such persons are frequently never charged. In the meantime, however, proceedings remain active and media coverage in relation to the suspect is subject to the strict liability rule.

Warrants

Similar difficulties may be experienced when warrants are issued. The person named on the warrant might not be apprehended for many months. It may be known to both the police and the media that he has fled the country and is unlikely to return. Press coverage is nevertheless severely restricted from the moment the warrant is issued.

Two factors exist to mitigate the problem for journalists. The first is the provision in the Act that proceedings which became active with the issue of a warrant cease to be active twelve months from the date of that warrant if the suspect has not been arrested during that period. The second is that the Attorney General made it clear before the Act became law that he would not use it to institute contempt proceedings where the media are simply assisting the police with publicity in a 'hue and cry' situation. Newspapers and TV news programmes in practice have nothing to fear from publishing pictures of wanted men or prejudicial descriptions of them, e.g. 'armed and dangerous', if they are clearly acting for the protection and in the interest of the public.

Criminal proceedings are concluded:

1   Upon acquittal or sentence.
2   Upon any other verdict, finding or decision which puts an end to the proceedings.
3   By discontinuance or by operation of law.

In general terms this means that the active period ceases when the proceedings, for whatever reason, are brought to an end. This includes instances where charges are dropped or an order is made by the court that they should 'lie on the file' (i.e. no further action will be taken on them).

Journalists would do well to remember that proceedings remain active until sentence is passed. The strict liability rule continues to apply where a verdict of guilty is returned and the court adjourns for sentencing at a later date. In cases where sentence is to be passed by a judge the media will, in practice, be free to publish extensive background material on the assumption that judges are experienced enough not to be influenced by such publicity. A great deal more care needs to be exercised in cases where the sentence will be passed by magistrates.

Civil cases
Civil proceedings become active when arrangements are made for a hearing. If, as can happen with emergency applications to the court, no such arrangements are made they become active when the hearing commences.

In High Court cases arrangements for a hearing are deemed to be made when the matter is set down in the official court list of forthcoming actions. In other cases the proceedings become active when a date is fixed for the hearing.

Civil proceedings cease to be active when the case is concluded, by settlement or judgement of the court, or, in the case of pre-trial applications, when the specific matter before the court is disposed of.

Appeals
Appellate proceedings become active when leave for appeal is applied for or notice of appeal is lodged. This means that during the period between the end of a trial and the lodging of a notice of appeal the media are not inhibited by the fear of contempt under the strict liability rule.

Substantial risk of serious prejudice

Section 2 (2) of the Contempt of Court Act states that the strict liability rule will only apply to those publications which create a substantial risk of serious prejudice to the course of justice in the revelant proceedings. Every editor and journalist would be well advised to learn by heart the relevant test for contempt. Is there a substantial risk of serious prejudice?

The courts have made it clear that it is a double test – the risk must be substantial and the likely prejudice has to be serious. In the words of Lord Chief Justice Lane (*Attorney General* v *Times Newspapers (1983)*):

> A slight or trivial risk of serious prejudice was not enough nor was a substantial risk of slight prejudice.

The two limbs of the test are separate but similar considerations apply to both. Lord Justice Parker has illustrated how they might be judged: '

> These limitations interact with one another. An article in a newspaper circulating in a part of Devon would, for example, be far less likely, if likely at all, to create a substantial risk of prejudice to proceedings which were due to be tried in Newcastle than would the same article contained in a national newspaper or a local Newcastle newspaper. The converse is equally true. An article in a Devon newspaper would be more likely to have an effect upon a trial in Devon than the same article in a Newcastle newspaper. The nature of the publication and place of trial thus vitally affect the question whether the publication creates risk within Section 2 (2). Whether the risk, if established, is a risk that the proceedings will be seriously prejudiced or impeded will clearly be affected by the content of the publication and the remoteness or proximity (in time) of the trial.
> *Attorney General* v *News Group Newspapers (1986)*

It has been established through the cases since the Act came into force that 'substantial' does not mean 'weighty' but merely signifies a real risk and one that is 'not insubstantial' or 'not minimal'.

The following factors should be among those considered when assessing whether an article is likely to be a contempt:

Mode of trial

Whether or not there is a real risk that a publication will affect the course of justice in proceedings will frequently depend upon the mode of trial. While there may be an enormous risk that a particular story will prejudice a jury trial, the same story would be assumed to have no effect at all on a case tried solely by a judge.

Trials almost invariably fall into one of three categories – by jury, by magistrates or by judge alone.

Greatest care needs to be exercised in relation to proceedings which are conducted before a jury. Jurors are selected from the public at large and, although they are deemed to be men and women of commonsense who are capable of disregarding what is said in newspapers or on television, the courts are diligent in protecting them from the influence of prejudicial publicity.

Lay magistrates have very limited legal training and although the risk of unduly influencing may be less than in the case of jurors, there is still a need for extreme caution to be exercised before publishing material about cases coming before them.

Judges and stipendiary magistrates (fully qualified lawyers) can be expected to use their legal training and experience to disregard almost any sort of material which is not adduced in evidence or argument before the court. That is not to say it is impossible for judges to be prejudiced, and editors will still need to be careful about stories which may be grossly prejudicial.

With the exception of libel and a few other sorts of action all civil actions are now heard by judges sitting alone. In practical terms this means that the risk of contempt in civil proceedings will usually be less than in criminal proceedings.

Date of trial

The proximity in time between the publication and the relevant trial is a factor which could affect both the degree of risk and the seriousness of the prejudice. Jurors exposed to prejudicial matter are far more likely to have it at the front of their minds after one month than after twelve. The Court of Appeal dealt with precisely this point in *Attorney General* v *News Group Newspapers (1986)*. Ian Botham, the famous cricketer, was suing the *Mail on Sunday* for libel over allegations of drug-taking. Some eleven months before the trial was due to take place the *News of the World* announced an intention to publish similar allegations about Mr Botham. The Attorney General applied for an injunction on the grounds that the *News of the World* article would be in contempt of the existing libel action. That action had been set down in the court list and the proceedings were therefore active. The court declared it was not satisfied that publication of the article so far in advance of the trial date would create a substantial risk of serious prejudice. The injunction was refused.

Place of trial

The width of publication and the location of trial are obvious considerations when assessing the element of substantial risk.

As Lord Parker illustrated (see page 146) a story in a local paper in the South-West is unlikely to cause a real risk of prejudice to a trial taking place in the North-East. It is, of course, unlikely that the place of trial will be of much relevance to national newspapers or nationwide broadcasts.

Content of the publication

The content of the article or story is always the major factor on the question of serious prejudice. Whether a story is seriously prejudicial will depend on the particular facts of each case and the specific issues which the court will have to decide. However, there are certain matters (referred to below) which will almost invariably tend towards contempt.

Photographs

In a 1927 case the *Daily Mirror* published a picture of an accused man on the very day he was to appear in front of a witness at an identity parade. The court held that its publication could have prejudiced the mind of the witness. Lord Hewart declared:

There is a duty to refrain from publication of a photograph where it is apparent to a reasonable man that a question of identity arises.

In 1976 an almost identical situation resulted in the *Evening Standard* being fined £1,000 over a photograph of Peter Hain who was charged with stealing from a bank.

Before publishing pictures of a person who has been arrested or is the subject of a warrant care should be taken to ascertain whether identity is in issue. Journalists should always attempt to check this point with the police and defence solicitors.

As discussed above, where the publication of photographs is likely to assist in the apprehension of a dangerous suspect or where a photograph has been issued for use by the police, contempt proceedings will not be brought even though a warrant has been issued and the proceedings are therefore active.

The defendant's character and record

It is a basic rule in criminal proceedings that a defendant's bad character or previous convictions cannot be used against him. Evidence of his criminal record or matters prejudicial to his character are therefore admissable only in exceptionable circumstances. Since such a rule would be meaningless if the jurors (or magistrates) were to learn of such matters through the newspapers or television their publication usually amounts to a grave contempt. In 1949, the *Daily Mirror* covered the arrest of John Haigh, the 'Acid-bath murderer', by publishing a report which suggested that he had committed other gruesome murders. The editor, Sylvester Bolam, was sentenced to three months imprisonment. Even though Haigh was not actually named the Court found that a serious contempt had been committed.

In cases since the 1981 Act the courts have demonstrated that not every derogatory newspaper story about an accused person will be held to have created a substantial risk of serious prejudice. The publicity which followed the arrest of an intruder called Michael Fagan inside Buckingham Palace in 1982 led to five national newspapers being charged with contempt. In stories published by *The Sun* and the *Sunday People* it was alleged that Fagan had been a 'junkie' and that he was a liar. The court found that in the circumstances of the case the risk of serious prejudice was not substantial.

While the decision on the Fagan case does indicate that the courts are prepared to interpret the strict liability rule liberally, editors should think hard before publishing details of an accused's bad character. Anything which tends to show he is the type of person who would commit the crime with which he is charged or which suggests that he should not be believed is likely to attract a charge of contempt.

Undermining or intimidating witnesses
Similarly, articles or stories which suggest that a witness is untruthful might easily be held to have prejudiced the course of justice in a trial at which he is to give evidence.

A publication which seeks to persuade witnesses to refrain from giving evidence or to change their testimony would probably constitute a serious interference within the meaning of the strict liability rule.

Anticipating the verdict
Especially in the case of jury trials, there are obvious contempt dangers in media stories which predict the outcome of the case or comment on the worth of particular pieces of evidence.

'Without prejudice' negotiations and payments into court
In civil proceedings communications between the parties which are conducted on a 'without prejudice' basis are protected against disclosure to the court. To publicize such communications would almost certainly amount to contempt.

The same applies to payments into court in civil cases. They too are protected against disclosure and should not be publicly revealed.

DEFENCES

Other than the limited defence of innocent publication or distribution (see page 142) the 1981 Act recognizes only two instances where the publication of material which creates a substantial risk of serious prejudice will not be a contempt of court – contemporary reports of proceedings and discussion of public affairs.

Contemporary reports of proceedings

Section 4 of the Act states that:

> A person is not guilty of contempt of court under the strict liability rule in respect of a fair and accurate report of legal proceedings held in public, published contemporaneously and in good faith.

To qualify for Section 4 protection a report must therefore:

1 Be fair and accurate.
2 Relate to proceedings heard in public, i.e., in open court (as opposed to in chambers or 'in camera').

3 Be published contemporaneously, i.e., during or as soon as practicable after the hearing.
4 Be published in good faith, i.e., without a malicious motive.

Such reports are also safe from libel proceedings (see Chapter 2).

The same section of the Act gives the court powers to postpone reports of the proceedings or any part of them if otherwise the administration of justice in those proceedings is likely to be prejudiced. These powers are discussed fully in Chapter 9.

Discussion of public affairs

Section 5 of the Act provides that:

> A publication made as, or as part of, a discussion in good faith of public affairs or other matters of general public interest is not to be treated as a contempt of court under the strict liability rule if the risk of impediment or prejudice to particular legal proceedings is merely incidental to the discussion.

This defence did not exist before 1981. Its introduction was recommended in the 1974 report of the Phillimore Committee on contempt which concluded that it was wrong that publicized debates about matters of general public interest should be brought to a halt simply because legal proceedings arise which reflect the issues being debated.

In *Attorney General* v *English (1982)* the House of Lords held that a *Daily Mail* article by Malcolm Muggeridge which argued for a 'Pro-Life' candidate in a by-election and in so doing referred to an alleged practice among doctors of allowing deformed babies to die was not in contempt of the contemporaneous trial of Dr Leonard Arthur on a charge of murdering a Down's syndrome baby. The Law Lords, who heard the case on appeal, echoed the Phillimore report by stating that what Section 5 was intended to prevent was the 'gagging of bona fide discussion of controversial matters of general public interest merely because there are in existence contemporaneous legal proceedings in which some particular instance of those controversial matters may be in issue.' They found that although Mr Muggeridge's article was likely to create serious prejudice in Dr Arthur's trial it met the requirements of the Section 5 defence and was not, therefore, a contempt. In other words, they decided that the report was part of a bona fide discussion of a matter of public interest and the prejudice was merely incidental to that discussion.

SCOPE OF THE 1981 ACT

The strict liability rule under the 1981 Act will, according to Section 19, apply to the proceedings of 'any tribunal or body exercising the judicial power of the state'.

Apart from cases heard in criminal and civil courts, the 'proceedings' which must not be prejudiced include the hearings of all statutory tribunals. The rule covers Coroner's Courts, courts-martial, employment tribunals and sex discrimination tribunals. The Act does not, however, apply to professional disciplinary hearings, e.g. those administered by the Law Society or the General Medical Council.

THE OLD LAW OF CONTEMPT

The position at common law in relation to pre-trial publicity is that a person is guilty of contempt if he publishes material calculated to prejudice or interfere with proceedings which, at the time of publication, were 'pending or imminent'.

For a prosecution to succeed it is necessary to establish either that the publisher intended to cause the prejudice or was at least reckless in that he was aware of the future proceedings and knew the nature of what he published.

While there is plenty of uncertainty about the precise meaning of 'imminent', it is reasonably clear that proceedings become 'pending', on criminal matters, when a person has been arrested and is about to be charged. This period, i.e. between arrest and charge, is now also covered by the strict liability rule introduced by the 1981 Contempt of Court Act.

Although there is a good deal of judicial comment on record to suggest that contempt could be committed by publishing prejudicial matter in advance of an arrest, there was, in fact, only one British case prior to 1988 which supported this contention. In *R. v Beaverbrook Ltd (1962)*, fines of £5,000 against the newspaper company and £750 and £500 against the *Daily Express*'s Northern and London editors respectively were imposed for prejudicial reports about a man who, at the time of publication, was obviously about to be arrested.

However, in the 1988 case of *Attorney General v News Group Newspapers*, the High Court not only cleared up any doubt which may have existed as to whether the old 'pending or imminent rule' had survived the introduction of the 1981 Act – it also greatly extended the concept of 'imminence'. The case arose after *The Sun* newspaper had announced on its front page in March 1986, that it was funding a private prosecution against an Essex doctor who was alleged to have raped a nine-year-old girl. The accusations had been made to the police by the girl's mother some months before. Although there was medical evidence that the girl had indeed been raped, the only apparent evidence against the doctor was the word of the girl herself. Because of her age, the Director of Public Prosecutions took the view that a conviction was unlikely and therefore decided not to prosecute.

Unfortunately, in announcing that it was going to finance the mother's case against the doctor, *The Sun* also gave the clear impression, through interviews with other members of the girl's family, that he was guilty of the crime. In fact, he was not arrested and charged until fifty-three days after the relevant report. Despite the significant passage of time between the publication and the commencement of proceedings, the court held that in the particular circumstances (especially the fact that *The Sun* itself was paying for the prosecution) the proceedings were imminent and fined the newspaper £75,000 for contempt.

The decision of the court in that case seemed to have the unfortunate effect of greatly extending the restraints imposed upon the media by the contempt laws. Certainly, prior to it few people would have supposed that a report published more than seven weeks before a person was arrested could possibly have been punishable as a contempt.

Indeed, doubts about the validity of the court's decision were openly expressed by the judges presiding over a similar contempt case heard in the High Court three years later. In *Attorney General* v *Sport Newspapers (1991)*, the editor and publishers of the *Daily Sport* faced charges of contempt after publishing the previous convictions (including rape) of a man being sought by police in connection with a missing schoolgirl.

The prosecution failed because the court was not satisfied that the defendants had the necessary intent to cause prejudice. However, even though their decision did not turn on whether proceedings were 'pending or imminent' at the time of publication, one of the judges emphatically declared his belief that *The Sun*'s 1988 case was wrongly decided and the other expressed reservations about it.

At the time of writing, the exact meaning of 'imminence' in relation to common law contempt is, therefore, not entirely clear.

INJUNCTIONS

As well as controlling pre-trial publicity, the judiciary's inherent power to punish for contempt is the key to enforcement of court orders. In a sense, it is the stick which guarantees the Rule of Law. Every citizen should know that disobedience of an order of the court will lead to punishment. Since there is no limit to the fines or terms of imprisonment which can be imposed, the contempt law is the court's ultimate weapon.

An injunction applying prior restraint to publication is the court order most commonly encountered by the media. It can take many forms. For example, an author or a photographer whose copyright has been infringed by a particular newspaper might obtain an injunction to prevent further infringement. Similarly, if a breach of confidence is apprehended the person with rights in the confidential information can ask the court to prevent its improper disclosure. In the family courts, it is extremely common for injunctions to be granted against the media at large in order to protect minors against publicity which might be harmful. Less common, but by no means infrequent, are injunctions banning the publication of libellous material. As discussed in Chapter 3, if the defendant in libel proceedings asserts that a defence of justification can and will be pleaded, the court will not usually restrain publication.

Most editors and producers will understand the import of an injunction which has been granted specifically against his or her newspaper or programme. Once the order has been served or proper notice of its existence has been given (which can be by telephone, letter or fax), any breach of its terms will almost certainly result in punishment for contempt of court.

Similarly, where in a custody case an injunction forbidding identification of the relevant child is granted against '. . . all local and national newspapers, TV and radio stations . . .' the ambit and significance of the order is clear to all who receive notice of it.

What is less known is that one can also be in contempt for publishing material which is the subject of a restraining injunction granted against another separate newspaper, TV or radio station.

Example: newspaper A is injuncted against publishing the confidential medical records of Mr X. Newspaper B subsequently publishes the material which is the subject of that injunction. If it is established that Newspaper B had notice of the injunction's existence, the court can punish its publishers and editor for contempt.

This principle of third-party contempt arose from the long-running *Spycatcher* litigation of the mid-1980s.

In 1986, injunctions pending trial were granted against *The Guardian* and *The Observer* to restrain them from publishing extracts from Peter Wright's book *Spycatcher* on the grounds that the material was subject to a duty of confidentiality owed by Wright to his former employer, the British Government.

Knowing of the injunction's existence, *The Independent* and the *Sunday Times* each carried stories which included parts of the banned material. Both were fined £50,000 by the High Court for contempt. The rationale was that by publishing the material which was at the heart of the restraining order they had destroyed its confidentiality and thereby completely negated the central issue in the forthcoming trial between the British Government and *The Guardian* and *The Observer*.

The issue was appealed all the way up to the House of Lords. In the process the fines against the newspapers were lifted but the principle of third party publishers being liable in contempt for breaching injunctions which were made against other branches of the media, but about which they had knowledge, was upheld.

11 JOURNALISTS' SOURCES

Of all the valuable commodities cherished and jealously guarded by journalists a long contact list of reliable sources is the foremost. Every reporter has his own contact list which has usually been in existence, growing year by year, since its owner had his or her first job as a trainee.

The system by which contacts and sources of information are built up rests essentially on mutual trust and cooperation. On the one hand the journalist relies on being given accurate information upon which to base his or her story and on the other the source relies, where necessary, on not being identified or otherwise compromised. In such circumstances it is a cardinal rule of journalism that the identity of the source remains confidential.

Given the fact that people who speak to reporters on this basis are frequently breaking some duty of confidence they themselves owe to a third party, e.g. an employer, it is not surprising that the journalistic principle of protecting sources clashes from time to time with the rather different priorities of tribunals and courts of law.

The outcome of such clashes has varied according to the circumstances of each case, but courts have been known to take a hard line. In 1963 three journalists were ordered by the Tribunal of Inquiry looking into the case of Vassal the admiralty spy, to reveal the sources for stories they had written at a very early stage in the scandal which accurately identified the traitor. The Tribunal considered that knowing how the journalists got their information would assist it in discovering how security could be tightened. All three refused and two of them went to prison for contempt; the third reporter escaped such drastic punishment only because his source came forward voluntarily –*Attorney General* v *Mullholland and Foster (1963)* and *Attorney General* v *Clough (1963)*.

In the case against Mullholland, Lord Denning identified the interests of justice as being the primary consideration in deciding whether to order disclosure:

The judge . . . will not direct him to answer unless it is not only relevant but also a proper and indeed necessary question in the course of justice to be put and answered.

In Clough's case Lord Parker cited 'the interests of the state' as being the dominant consideration.

Whether or not a court or tribunal orders a journalist to reveal the identity of his or her source is, of course, always a matter of discretion for the judge. It is clear from the old cases that, although journalists do not have the absolute privilege against disclosure which cloaks the lawyer/client relationship, the courts were reluctant to force them to betray their sources unless the interests of justice or of the state demanded it. Indeed after the Mullholland case the Attorney General told the House of Commons, somewhat defensively, that in the previous eighty years there had only been about six instances where such disclosure had been required.

SECTION 10 OF THE CONTEMPT OF COURT ACT 1981

Both the principle itself and the considerations which may override it are set out in statutory form by Section 10 of the Contempt Act 1981.

No court may require a person to disclose, nor is any person guilty of contempt of court for refusing to disclose the source of information contained in a publication for which he is responsible, unless it is established to the satisfaction of the court that it is necessary in the interests of justice or national security, or for the prevention of disorder or crime.

The strength of the protection afforded by Section 10 was tested in *Secretary of State for Defence* v *Guardian Newspapers Ltd (1983)*.

On 31 October 1983, under the headline 'Heseltine's Briefing to Thatcher on Cruise', *The Guardian* published a confidential memorandum prepared by the Secretary of State for Defence on the question of Cruise missiles and their arrival in Britain. The Government demanded the return of its document and the newspaper, realizing that the marks on their copy of the memorandum would identify their source, cited Section 10 of the Contempt Act and refused. The conflict was between protection of a journalistic source and national security. In each of the courts, right up to the House of Lords (there, by a bare three to two majority), national interest prevailed. According to the Master of the Rolls, Lord John Donaldson, there was hardly a contest:

The maintenance of national security requires that trustworthy servants in a position to mishandle highly classified documents passing from the Secretary of State for Defence to other Ministers shall be identified at the earliest possible moment and removed from their positions. This is blindingly obvious. Whether or not the Editor acted in the public interest in publishing the document was not the issue. The Secretary of State's concern was quite different. It was that a servant of the Crown who handled classified documents had decided for himself whether classified information should be disseminated to the public. If he could do it on one occasion he might do it on others, when the safety of the state would be truly imperilled.

In fact the Master of the Rolls made one mistake. The source, as it turned out when the newspaper handed back the document was not a 'he' but a 'she'. Sarah Tisdall, a junior civil servant in the Foreign Office, was sentenced to six months imprisonment.

The Guardian, as it admitted in its public soul-searching after the sentencing of Miss Tisdall, should have destroyed the document before the Government commenced its proceedings. While the courts may have sympathy for a journalist who does not wish to divulge information carried in his head they do not look kindly when the journalist refuses to hand over physical property (i.e. documents) which belong to someone else.

The other highly relevant factor is that memorized names cannot be seized under a search warrant whereas pieces of paper can. The Tisdall affair contained valuable lessons for all editors and reporters.

In *X* v *Y* *(1987)*, a *News of the World* reporter, David Leslie, was given information from medical records owned by a local health authority to the effect that two doctors were suffering from AIDS. The health authority sued to prevent publication of their confidential information and to force Leslie to reveal the name of his source. It was argued that the interests of justice demanded that the person who wrongly divulged medical records should be identified because he or she had committed a criminal act and in order to prevent any further disclosures. The judge granted an injunction to restrain the publication but refused to order that the reporter name his source. The health authority, he said, had not established that such disclosure was necessary in the interests of justice.

Just what the vital phrase 'in the interests of justice' means in the context of Section 10 of the Contempt of Court Act was, to some extent, explained by a 1990 case which, like the Sarah Tisdall matter, went all the way to the House of Lords.

The issue was whether or not William Goodwin, a trainee journalist employed on a trade magazine called *The Engineer* should be ordered by the court to surrender his notes so that his source could be indentified. The source had provided Goodwin with highly confidential information obtained from a missing copy of the plaintiff company's corporate business plan. The reporter's pre-publication telephone calls to the company's offices and to its bankers alerted the company to the fact that he was in possession of information which must have come from the missing document.

An injunction restraining publication of the confidential material was obtained and Goodwin was ordered by the judge to hand over his notes so that the person who stole the business plan could be indentified. Backed by the National Union of Journalists he appealed.

In finding against him the House of Lords ruled that 'in the interests of justice' should be given a wide meaning and need not necessarily be confined to situations where court proceedings were already in existence or were about to be commenced. The phrase should be construed so that:

> . . . persons should be enabled to exercise important legal rights and to protect themselves from serious legal wrongs whether or not resort to legal proceedings in a court of law will be necessary to protect these objectives. Thus, to take an example, if an employer of a large staff is suffering grave damage from the activities of an unidentified disloyal servant, it is undoubtedly in the interests of justice that he should be able to identify him in order to terminate his contract of employment, notwithstanding that no legal proceedings may be necessary to achieve this end.

The Court emphasized that:

> The judges's task will always be to weigh in the scales the importance of enabling the ends of justice to be attained, in the circumstances of the particular case on the one hand, against the importance of protecting the source on the other hand. In this balancing exercise it is only if the judge is satisfied that the disclosure in the interests of justice is of such preponderating importance as to override the statutory privilege against disclosure that the threshold of necessity will be reached. (*Lord Bridge*)

Among the factors affecting the balancing exercise, said the Lords, would be the nature of the information obtained from the source:

> . . . the greater the legitimate public interest in the information the source has given to the publisher or intended publisher, the greater will be the importance of protecting the source.

> . . . and the manner in which the source obtained it . . .

> . . . If it appears to the court that the information was obtained legitimately this will enhance the importance of protecting the source. Conversely, if it appears that the information was obtained illegally, this will diminish the importance of protecting the source unless, of course, this factor is counterbalanced by a clear public interest in publication of the information, as in the classic case where the source has acted for the purpose of exposing iniquity.'

Despite the ruling against him, Goodwin continued his refusal to surrender the relevant notes and was fined £5,000.

As a general rule, a person is not compelled to divulge names or any other information unless ordered to do so by a court of law, a Tribunal of Inquiry (set up under the Tribunals of Inquiry (Evidence) Act 1921) or a

Parliamentary Committee. Thus in the normal course of civil litigation, say for libel or breach of confidence, a newspaper or broadcasting station is not bound to reply to a plaintiff's request for the identity of sources.

Similarly, one is not obliged to supply information requested by the police – the duty of the citizen does not require active cooperation (though a charge of obstruction may follow if the police are deliberately misled).

SECTION 6 OF THE OFFICIAL SECRETS ACT 1920

There is, however, an exception to the general rule. Section 6 of the Official Secrets Act 1920 states that:

> Where a chief officer of police is satisfied that there is reasonable ground for believing that an offence under Section 1 . . . (of the Official Secrets Act 1911) . . . has been committed and for believing that any person is able to furnish information as to the offence or suspected offence, he may . . .

(a) with the permission of the Secretary of State, authorise a senior police officer to require the person to reveal the relevant information, or,

(b) in a case 'of great emergency' he may require that the information be revealed without first obtaining the Secretary of State's permission.

Any person who fails to comply with such a requirement or knowingly gives false information commits an offence.

POLICE POWERS UNDER THE POLICE AND CRIMINAL EVIDENCE ACT 1984

The 1981 Royal Commission on Criminal Procedure recommended that existing police powers of search and seizure, which were based either on the common law or a haphazard selection of statutory provisions, needed to be supplemented and rationalized.

The Government took up the general proposals of the Commission in the Police and Criminal Evidence Act 1984. At the Bill stage fierce criticism for the proposed measures in relation to police powers to search for evidence came from doctors, lawyers, journalists, the clergy and advice organizations. They argued that the Bill as it stood contained wholly inadequate safeguards in respect of information which was held under a duty of confidence. It was foreseen that, like journalists and their sources, there would be many occasions where people would defy a law that required a breach of professional trust.

In order to accommodate mounting public pressure generated by these powerful groups, the Government conceded a number of significant amendments to the proposed powers of search. In particular it created special categories of material, i.e. 'excluded material' and 'special procedure material', which would be exempt from the normal search procedures. Those categories, which consist of various types of confidential information, e.g. the records of doctors, clergymen and advisory agencies, may still be ordered to be disclosed to the police, but only if stricter tests of necessity are satisfied.

The provisions which were finally enacted are far from simple.

NORMAL POWERS OF SEARCH

Section 8 of the Act allows a police constable to apply to a Justice of the Peace for a search warrant. The JP will grant it if he

. . . is satisfied that there are reasonable grounds for believing:

(a)   that a serious arrestable offence has been committed; and
(b) that there is material on premises specified in the application which is likely to be of substantial value . . . to the investigation of the offence; and
(c) that the material is likely to be relevant (i.e. admissible) evidence; and
(d) that it does not consist of or include items subject to legal privilege, excluded material or special procedure material. . . .

In addition the police must satisfy the JP of any of the following:

- It is impractical to communicate with any person entitled to grant entry or access to the premises.
- Entry to the premises will not be granted unless a warrant is produced.
- That the purpose of the search may be 'frustrated or seriously prejudiced', unless the police can secure immediate entry.

Section 15 of the Act stipulates that every warrant must specify the name of the officer who applied for it, the date of its issue, the statutory authority for its issue, the premises to be searched and, so far as practicable, the articles or persons sought. Each warrant authorizes one search only (a return visit will therefore require a fresh application to a JP) and the person whose premises are searched should be supplied with a copy of the warrant.

EXCLUDED AND SPECIAL PROCEDURE MATERIAL

As indicated above, the normal search warrant procedure under Section 8 will not apply if the items which the police require to see consist of material which is subject to legal privilege, excluded material or special procedure material.

The first of these three categories (legal privilege) is effectively off limits to the police. In relation to the second and third, i.e. excluded material and special procedure material, the police may be given *access* if they satisfy the requirements set out in Schedule 1 of the Act.

Items subject to legal privilege

Legal privilege (or legal professional privilege as it is better known) attaches to: (a) communications between a lawyer and his client or his client's representative for the purpose of giving legal advice *or* in connection with, and for the purpose of, legal proceedings (b) communications between either a lawyer, his client or his client's representative on the one side and 'other persons' on the other side in connection with, or in contemplation of, legal proceedings and for the purposes of such proceedings.

With one exception, items which are subject to legal professional privilege are totally exempt from police powers of search and seizure. The exception is if the relevant material is held 'with the intention of furthering a criminal purpose'.

Excluded material

Excluded material means:

1 Personal records which a person has acquired or created in the course of any trade, business, profession or office and which he or she holds in confidence.
2 Human tissue or tissue fluid samples held under a duty of confidence for medical purposes.
3 'Journalistic material' consisting of documents or records which is, and since its acquisition or creation has always been, held under an 'undertaking, restriction or obligation' of confidence.

Section 13 of the Act defines journalistic material as 'material acquired or created for the purposes of journalism' and in the possession of the person who acquired or created it for those purposes.

Special procedure material

Special procedure material is either of the following:

1 Business or professional records (not *personal* records which come within excluded material) held under a duty of confidence.
2 Journalistic material other than excluded material, i.e. items which

come within the Section 13 definition – '. . . acquired or created for the purposes of journalism' and in the possession of the person who acquired or created it for those purposes – but do not qualify as excluded journalistic material as defined in 3 above (in other words, non-confidential material).

Under Schedule 1 applications for access to excluded and special procedure material must be made to a circuit judge rather than to a JP. The person at whom the application is aimed should be given notice of it and has a right to be heard.

If the judge is satisfied that one of the 'sets of access conditions' stipulated in the Schedule exists he may make an order that the person in possession of the relevant items shall either produce them to a constable for him to take away, or give a constable access to them.

The order must be complied with within seven days or such longer period as the judge may specify.

ACCESS CONDITIONS

The first set of access conditions applies to special procedure material and requires the police to establish that there are reasonable grounds for believing:

1   That a serious arrestable offence has been committed.
2   That there is special procedure material on the premises.
3   That it is likely to be of substantial value to the relevant investigation.
4   That it is likely to be admissable evidence.

The police must also show that other methods of obtaining the material have failed or have not been tried because they were bound to fail. Finally, they must show that it is in the public interest for the order to be made.

The second set of access conditions relates just to excluded material. It provides that such items may be made available to the Police under an order if the judge is satisfied that there are reasonable grounds for believing they exist on the premises specified, and if a search warrant would have been granted under any legislation prior to the police and Criminal Evidence Act.

Failure to comply with access orders is punishable as a contempt of court.

It does not help the understanding of these extremely complex statutory provisions that there have been very few cases to illuminate the law and procedures involved. *Commissioner of Metropolitan Police* v *Mackenzie (1987)* is one of them which has assisted slightly. In that case, the Vice Squad wished to obtain various statements and other documents which *The Sun* newspaper had gathered during an investigation into under-age homosexual prostitution ('rent boys'). The application was against *The Sun*'s editor personally. Since the police were unable to establish that Mr Mackenzie had himself ever been in possession of the evidence, that alone doomed their application to failure – it should have been brought against the newspaper company which was the employer of whoever actually had possession of the material. However the editor was also able to show that most of the statements sought had come into existence for the purposes of defending libel proceedings being faced by the newspaper. They were, therefore, covered by legal privilege and were wholly exempt from the access provisions of the Act.

12 OBSCENITY, INDECENT DISPLAYS AND RACIAL HATRED

OBSCENITY

Any law based upon prevailing attitudes towards morality and aimed primarily at literature and pictures is bound to give rise to controversy. This certainly has been the case with the obscenity laws.

The problem is the difficulty in reaching any sort of consensus about which words or images are so harmful to society that their production and distribution should be punishable under the criminal law. Attitudes are bound to differ greatly between people of different age, class and creed.

Despite this there have been prosecutions aimed at the publication of obscene matter for well over 200 years. Until recently the offence was dealt with under the common law charge of obscene libel. The test applied in such cases was formulated by Lord Chief Justice Cockburn in *R. v Hicklin (1868)*:

> . . . whether the tendency of the matter charged as obscene is to deprave and corrupt those whose minds are open to such immoral influences and into whose hands a publication of this sort may fall.

The old common law offence was effectively replaced in 1959 by the Obscene Publications Act which maintained the test of tending to deprave and corrupt but otherwise went some way to liberalizing the law.

The problems of agreeing upon what constitutes obscenity remain and enforcement is not easy. Prosecutors have the daunting challenge of correctly gauging the jury's view of what tends to deprave and corrupt. When they get it wrong, as in the cases of *Lady Chatterley's Lover* (1960) and *Inside Linda Lovelace* (1976), all they achieve is to give the prosecuted work a massive sales boost.

Under Section 2(1) of the Obscene Publications Act 1959, 'any person who, whether for gain or not, publishes an obscene article or who has an obscene article for publication for gain (whether gain to himself or gain to another)' is liable to fines or imprisonment. (Up to £2,000 or six months at the Magistrates Court; three years or an unlimited fine at the Crown Court.)

The Act specifically exempts television and radio transmissions.

The test of obscenity is set out in Section 1:

> . . . an article shall be deemed to be obscene if its effect or (where the article comprises two or more distinct items) the effect of any of its items is, if taken as a whole, such as to tend to deprave and corrupt persons who are likely, having regard to all relevant circumstances, to read, see or hear the matter contained or embodied in it.

- *Article* means 'any description of article containing or embodying matter to be read or looked at or both, any sound record, any film or other record of a picture or pictures.'
- *Publishes* means 'distributes, circulates, sells, lets on hire, gives or lends'. It also includes *offering* an article for sale or for letting on hire.
- Having an obscene article for publication for gain is also an offence. A person 'has' an article if it is in his ownership, possession or control.

Deprave and corrupt

In order to convict for obscene publication the court must be satisfied that the effect of the material would be 'to tend to deprave and corrupt'. The prosecution is not required to prove the specified effect by reference to any resulting sexual or other physical act by a reader or viewer. It is enough to establish a tendency to deprave and corrupt acting upon the mind or emotions of the likely recipient.

The prosecution of *Lady Chatterley's Lover* by D. H. Lawrence (*R. v Penguin Books Ltd (1960)*), which was the first major test case for the Act, produced the authoritative working definition of the key words in Section 1. According to Mr Justice Byrne:

> Deprave means to make morally bad, to pervert, to debase, to corrupt morally.

> Corrupt means to render morally unsound or rotten, to destroy the moral purity or chastity, to pervert or ruin a good quality, to debase, to defile.

The test is stringent: it is not enough that the publication would simply shock or disgust, or even that a reader or viewer would be led morally astray.

The tendency to deprave and corrupt, moreover, is not confined to an effect of a sexual nature. In R. v *Calder and Boyers (1968)*, *Last Exit to Brooklyn* was prosecuted largely for the influence it would have in relation to drug-taking. Other cases have involved tendencies towards brutality and violence.

Intention irrelevant

The requirement of *mens rea*, i.e. guilty intention, which is an essential part of most offences under the criminal law is, for the most part, dispensed with in obscenity cases. The test for obscenity will be satisfied if the prosecution establishes the *fact* of publication and the *effect* of the published article. The intention of the author or publisher is irrelevant. In the *Last Exit to Brooklyn* case it was argued to no avail that the author's only intention was to sufficiently shock the readers so that they would shun the life of degradation he portrayed.

However, the degree of knowledge possessed by those who disseminate obscene material is relevant to establishing the defence allowed by Section 2(5) of the Act.

> A person shall not be convicted . . . if he proves that he had not examined the article in respect of which he is charged and had no reasonable cause to suspect that it was such that his publication of it would make him liable to be convicted. . . .

The onus of proving innocent dissemination in the terms of Section 2(5) rests on the defendant.

Contemporary standards must apply

In deciding whether it tends to deprave and corrupt, juries and magistrates must judge an article by the standards of the day. The law recognizes that society's views about what constitutes obscenity changes with time and that material which would have been judged to be unacceptable twenty years ago would not necessarily be so today.

Although it may be a prosecutor's nightmare to predict their verdict in obscenity cases, there is no doubt that a jury of twelve randomly-selected members of the community provides the best available interpretation of contemporary standards of morality. Juries cannot, of course, create binding precedents but in relation to the facts and circumstances of any given case they establish the acceptable levels of tolerance to indecent material.

'Persons who are likely . . . to read, see or hear. . .'

The Act stipulates that the tendency to deprave and corrupt must exist in relation to 'persons who are likely, having regard to all relevant circumstances, to read, see or hear' the article. In considering the effect of a publication the court therefore, should first identify the likely readers or audience.

Obviously the nature of the article would dictate how difficult this task will be. A magazine sold in an 'adults only' sex shop would, for example, have a limited likely readership which would normally exclude young children. A national newspaper, on the other hand, is available and likely to be read by almost every section of the community.

Once the jury or magistrates have identified the 'persons . . . likely . . . to read, see or hear' they may convict if they are satisfied that the effect of the article was to tend to deprave and corrupt 'a significant proportion' of those persons (laid down in the case against the *Last Exit to Brooklyn*). In other words the effect does not have to be upon all the likely readers, nor upon the average reader, nor even upon the majority of readers.

In *DPP* v *Whyte* (1972) it was argued that since the article in question would be purchased only by persons who were already depraved and corrupt its effect would be negligible. The House of Lords decided that it was wrong to consider the effect only upon the category of *most* likely readers (in this case people who were already corrupted) and that all categories of likely readers should be included.

'Taken as a whole'

In considering whether it is obscene the court must consider the article as a whole. It is wrong to judge it by reference to isolated extracts. Where the prosecution concerns a book, the judge will therefore normally instruct the jury to read it from cover to cover in order to establish its effect.

However, where the relevant publication consists of a number of separate and independent items, as with most newspapers and magazines, the court may convict if any single item satisfies the test of obscenity and despite the fact that the rest of the publication is harmless. In *R.* v *Anderson* (1974), the prosecution of *Oz* magazine, the Court of Appeal affirmed that, though some parts of the issue were unobjectionable the publication as a whole was tainted by those that were.

Search, seizure and forfeiture

Under Section 3 of the Obscene Publications Act 1959, a JP may, if satisfied that there is reasonable ground of suspecting that obscene articles are kept for publication for gain in any premises, stall or vehicle in the area of his or her jurisdiction, issue a warrant which empowers the police to enter and search the premises and seize offending material.

Such warrants (like most warrants) are obtained by a police officer swearing an information before a magistrate to the effect that he or she has reasonable cause to believe that material which contravenes the Act exists at a given location. The warrant is good for fourteen days from the date of issue. If obscene articles are found it also enables the seizure of any documents found at the premises which relate to a trade or business carried on there.

Where offending articles are seized, a summons may be issued to the occupier of the relevant premises to attend court and 'show cause why' they should not be forfeited. The 'owner, author, maker . . . or any other person through whose hands they had passed before being seized . . .' may also turn up at court on the specified day in order to oppose forfeiture.

The 'public good' defence

Although an article is obscene, the publisher will escape conviction if he establishes that it is justified as being for the public good. The defence is set out in Section 4 of the Act.

> . . . a person shall not be convicted of an offence against Section 2 of this Act (i.e. publishing obscene material or having it for gain), and an order for forfeiture shall not be made . . . if it is proved that publication of the article in question is justified as being for the public good on the ground that it is in the interests of science, literature, art or learning, or of other objects of general concern.

Section 4 provides for a separate defence if the obscene article consists of a film or film soundtrack. In such cases there will be no conviction if it is proved that the publication '. . . is justified as being for the public good on the ground that it is in the interests of drama, opera, ballet or any other art or literature or learning.'

Whether or not the publication of an obscene article is justified as being for the public good will, whenever it is raised, always be a matter for the jury or magistrates to decide. However, Section 4 does allow both the defence and prosecution to call expert witnesses to give evidence '. . . as to the literary, artistic, scientific or other merits of an article . . .' in order '. . . either to establish or negative . . .' the particular ground of defence raised.

Where the accused person seeks to establish the public good defence, the court (i.e. jury or magistrates) should, according to the *Last Exit to Brooklyn* case, approach the issues in the following way:

1 They should first decide whether or not the article is obscene. Only if they find that it is need they go on to consider the defence of public good.
2 They must then on the one hand assess the number of readers or viewers which the article would tend to deprave and corrupt, the strength of that tendency and the nature of the depravity and corruption. On the other hand they ought to consider the strength of the literary, sociological or ethical merit in the article.
3 Having weighed up all these factors they should decide whether on balance the publication is proved to be justified as being for the public good.

The onus of proof in establishing the defence rests on the defendant.

INDECENT DISPLAYS

Under the Indecent Displays (Controls) Act 1981, it is an offence for a person to display or cause or permit to display any indecent matter. The Act says that matter is 'displayed if it is visible from a public place' and 'public place' means any place to which the public have or are permitted to have access except:

(a) a place where the public have to pay in order to see the display; or
(b) a shop or any part of a shop to which the public can only gain access by passing beyond the following warning notice:

WARNING
Persons passing beyond this notice will find
material on display which they may consider
indecent. No admittance to persons under 18 years
of age.

The exceptions in both (a) and (b) above only apply if persons under 18 years of age are not permitted access to the display.

The Act does not apply to displays by way of TV broadcast, art gallery, museum, theatre, or cinema. Also exempted are displays which are authorized by and on the premises of the Crown or any local authority.

The police may seize any article upon reasonable suspicion that it is indecent matter which is on display and thereby constitutes an offence under the Act.

Regrettably those who drafted the legislation chose not to define or give guidance on the meaning of 'indecent matter'.

INCITEMENT OF RACIAL HATRED

By the Race Relations Act 1976, Parliament added a provision to Section 5 of the Public Order Act 1936 which was aimed at the incitement of racial hatred.

Under Section 5A of the 1936 Act:

A person commits an offence if:

(a) he publishes or distributes written matter which is threatening, abusive or insulting; or
(b) he uses in any public place or at any public meeting words which are threatening, abusive or insulting,

in a case where, having regard to all the circumstances, hatred is likely to be stirred up against any racial group in Great Britain by the matter or words in question.

The fact that the person responsible for the threatening, abusive or insulting words or written matter did not intend to stir up racial hatred will not be a defence if the court is satisfied that this was their likely effect.

However, as with obscene matter (see above), if the offensive statements are contained in written material the accused has a defence if he can:

> . . . prove that he was not aware of the written matter in question and neither suspected nor had reason to suspect it of being threatening, abusive or insulting.

Section 5A also provides that the offence cannot be committed in relation to either of the following:

1   Fair, accurate and contemporaneous (or as near contemporaneous as reasonably practicable) reports of court proceedings.
2   Fair and accurate reports of proceedings in Parliament.

It should be noted that the prosecution are required to prove two distinct elements:

1   That the words were threatening, abusive or insulting.
2   That they were likely to stir up hatred against a racial group in Great Britain.

Statements which stir up race hatred, even if that was the clear intention of the maker, will not therefore amount to an offence unless they are also threatening, abusive or insulting.

For the purposes of Section 5A 'racial group' means 'a group of persons defined by reference to colour, race, nationality or ethnic or national origins.'

Any proceedings brought under Section 5A in respect of incitements to racial hatred must be authorized by the Attorney General. It is very rare for him to give his consent to such prosecutions.

One recent case where the Attorney General invited the Director of Public Prosecutions to initiate police inquiries with a view to prosecution involved a cartoon in *The Sun* newspaper. In May 1986, the Press Council adjudicated in favour of *The Sun* on a complaint that one of its front-page headlines which contained the phrase 'Arab Pig' was racist. The newspaper celebrated its victory by publishing a cartoon which depicted a number of pigs demonstrating outside its offices with the caption: 'Trouble, now the pigs object to being called Arabs'. The publication led to numerous complaints and demands, particularly from pro-Arab groups, that *The Sun* should be prosecuted for inciting racial hatred. In the event, after careful consideration of the police report, the Attorney General decided against a prosecution.

It should be noted that the reporting or broadcasting of racially extreme speeches or literature in news reports may itself attract a prosecution if the effect is that '. . . hatred is likely to be stirred up against any racial group . . .'.

13 ELECTIONS AND PARLIAMENT

ELECTIONS

Political elections in Britain have not always been the by-and-large civilized and well-ordered affairs that they are now. Readers of Charles Dickens will, for example, have some idea of the widespread corruption and malpractice which used to be a regular feature of Parliamentary elections.

To stamp out such tendencies detailed laws were introduced to regulate and control every aspect of electioneering. Most of them are aimed at the direct participants in elections, i.e. voters, candidates and organizers, but there are two areas of illegal practice which are of direct concern to the media. They relate to false statements and expenses.

False statements about candidates

Section 106 of the Representation of the People Act 1983, states:

Any person who . . . before or during an election, for the purpose of affecting the return of any candidate at the election, makes or publishes any false statement of fact in relation to the personal conduct or character of the candidate shall be guilty of an illegal practice unless he can show that he had reasonable grounds for believing, and did believe the statement to be true.

The offence may be committed both by the maker of a false statement and by anyone, e.g. a newspaper or broadcasting station who publishes it. There are four elements which need to be proved by the prosecution:

1 That the statement was one of fact (rather than opinion)
2 That it referred to the personal character or dealings of an individual candidate.
3 That the statement was made in order to affect the chances of the candidate being elected (in essence, that it was politically motivated.
4 That it was false.

Even if the jury is satisfied that all four elements exist the maker or publisher of the false statement is still entitled to be acquitted if he can establish that at the relevant time he believed it to be true and had reasonable grounds for his belief.

Since the damage done by false statements of a personal nature, especially when published through the media, is likely to be far greater in relation to an election candidate than otherwise, the Representation of the People Act makes specific provision for their restraint. To this effect, Section 106 goes on to empower either the High Court or the County Court to grant injunctions against persons who make such statements in order to prevent the repetition of 'a false statement of a similar character about a candidate'.

The section provides that '. . . *prima facie* proof of the falsity of the statement shall be sufficient . . .'. In this respect, the law places election candidates in a more favoured position than other victims of untruths. In normal circumstances one must establish that the statement was not only false but also defamatory in order to stand any chance of restraining it by injunction.

The Defamation Act 1952 adds a further peril to inaccurate reporting of elections. Section 10 specifically excludes 'defamatory statements published by, or on behalf of, a candidate in any election to a local government authority or to Parliament' from the protection of the defence of qualified privilege.

Election expenses

The provision and payment of expenses incurred by an election candidate is strictly controlled by the law. Under Sections 72–76 of the Representation of the People Act 1983, payment of all such expenses must be made through the candidate's election agent. By Section 75, the Act makes it an offence to incur expenses with a view to procuring the election of a Parliamentary or local government candidate except with his or his agent's authorization.

It is, therefore, illegal for supporters or well-wishers to advertise in order to enhance their chosen representative's chances of being elected. However, the law does not prevent media support through editorial comment or the publication of a particular candidate's views or through the disparagement of his opponents, provided it is not paid for. Similarly, advertising directed at advancing the general interests of a political party rather than an individual candidate is permissable.

- In *R.* v *Tronah Mines Ltd (1952)* it was held that newspaper advertisements condemning Labour's financial policies which appeared during an election were not illegal since they did not relate to any particular constituency. Mr Justice McNair ruled that the law 'does not prohibit expenditure, the real purpose or effect of which is general political propaganda, even although that general political propaganda does incidentally assist a particular candidate among others.'

• The same conclusion was reached by Mr Justice Potts in *The Labour Party* v *News Group Newspapers (1987)*. An organization calling itself Committee for a Free Britain had, in the middle of an election campaign, placed anti-Labour advertisements which focused on the views of 'Betty Sheridan from Haringey' and 'Mark Jenks from Mansfield'. The Labour Party sought an injunction to restrain their republication. The judge found that since the particular wording of the advertisements 'only makes sense in the national context' there was no breach of Section 75.

However, where expense is incurred primarily to oppose (rather than support) a candidate it will still be illegal. In *R.* v *Luft (1977)*, money was spent on publicity and literature which encouraged people in three individual constituencies not to vote for National Front candidates. The case went to the House of Lords where it was confirmed that if the dominant motive was to oppose one candidate it follows inevitably that the expense was intended to secure the election of one or other of his opponents.

Broadcasting controls

Section 93 of the Representation of the People Act 1983, places complicated controls on programmes which concentrate on any particular constituency during election time. The restrictions are broadly as follows:

1 Every candidate in the relevant constituency must consent to the transmission of the programme.
2 All candidates who take an active part in the programme have what journalists commonly refer to as 'copy approval', i.e. they have the right to edit in or edit out in relation to their own contributions to the broadcast.

The law thus gives candidates significant powers to control or, if they wish, disrupt programmes about their constituency. However, either because the candidates are too busy electioneering or because they are grateful for the chance of any TV or radio coverage there seem to be few major disputes over programme contents.

PARLIAMENTARY PRIVILEGE AND CONTEMPT

The Members and the proceedings of Parliament are cloaked with certain traditional rights and privileges aimed at safeguarding the freedom and independence of the individuals and the dignity of the institution.

Foremost among these privileges are the following:

- Complete freedom of speech for members during debates and official proceedings.
- The power of each House to regulate its own procedures. This includes the power to punish both members and outsiders for breach of privilege or, as it is better known, contempt of Parliament.

Freedom of speech

Statements made in the course of proceedings in either House of Parliament or in a committee of either House are absolutely privileged against civil actions. Members may not, therefore, be sued for libel in respect of any defamatory allegation or imputation made during official Parliamentary business.

There are, of course, numerous examples of MPs using their privileged position to 'publish the unpublishable'. The spies, Kim Philby and Anthony Blunt, were exposed by being named in the House of Commons and more recently Geoffrey Dickens MP has on a number of occasions named suspected sex offenders.

Media reports of Parliamentary proceedings have qualified privilege.

Some doubt exists as to whether there is also privilege against criminal prosecution for statements made in Parliament. The Contempt of Court Act expressly allows a defence for reports of judicial proceedings but notably omits a similar provision in respect of Parliamentary proceedings. On the other hand the statutory offence of inciting racial hatred specifically excludes from prosecution anything said in Parliament.

Contempt of Parliament

Contempt of Parliament consists of any acts or words which disrupt or impede the proper working of either House of Parliament or which obstruct, intimidate or wrongly influence members in the discharge of their duty.

There is no clear list of what will constitute contempt. However, the following broad categories of conduct have led to disciplinary action in the past:

Misbehaviour
Conduct which disrupts proceedings, e.g. shouting or throwing things from the strangers' gallery, is punishable as contempt.

Disrupting, obstructing, influencing, etc.
This is the broadest category of contempt of Parliament and encompasses any conduct which has a tendency to impede the proper functioning of either House or its members:

* In 1957, during the aftermath of the Suez crisis the *Sunday Express* and *Romford Recorder* published articles which suggested that MPs were gaining improper advantages in relation to the rationing of petrol. Both editors were summoned to the House of Commons and reprimanded for contempt.
* In 1947, Gerry Allighan MP was expelled from the House of Commons for contempt after writing an article alleging that members were receiving payments for passing confidential information about Parliamentary business to journalists. It subsequently emerged that Allighan himself was one of those who had been 'leaking' material.
* In 1957 the *Sunday Graphic*, incensed at a Parliamentary question tabled by Arthur Lewis MP which suggested that money raised for the Hungarian Relief Fund should go to help Egyptian victims of the Suez bombing campaign, published his home telephone number and invited its readers to ring him. It was held to be a contempt.

However, like judges, Members of Parliament are nowadays more resilient and accustomed to strident criticism than they used to be. It is highly unlikely that robust but honest attacks in the media on Parliament or its members would lead to findings of contempt – although action might easily be taken over reports which seem to be malicious.

Improper disclosure and breach of embargo
In the past various newspapers have been liable for contempt after publishing 'leaked' details of confidential Parliamentary business:

* In 1967, Tam Dalyell MP was reprimanded for disclosing to *The Observer* details of evidence given to a Select Committee of the House of Commons which was investigating chemical warfare research at Porton Down.
* In 1972, the *Daily Mail* revealed advance information about proposed increases in the civil list. Again, it was held to be contempt.
* In 1975, *The Economist* published material from a leaked Select Committee report on a wealth tax. This was held to be contempt.

Procedure

In cases of suspected breach of privilege or contempt, the matter is first referred by an individual MP to the Speaker for a ruling on whether there is a *prima facie* case. If he rules that there is a case to answer the issue is placed before the all-party Committee of Privileges.

After private deliberations during which the accused and/or witnesses may be called (but have no right otherwise to be present), the Committee decides whether a contempt has occurred. If the answer is in the affirmative it reports the offender to a sitting of the whole House with a recommendation as to punishment.

The guilty party may be reprimanded, banished or suspended from Parliament or even imprisoned in the Clock Tower of the House of Commons!

14 OFFICIAL SECRETS ACT AND D-NOTICES

In 1989, the legislation covering official secrets underwent drastic and long-overdue reform. Sections 1 and 2 of the Official Secrets Act 1911 – until then the prevailing law – had been rushed through Parliament, some eighty years earlier amidst the public hysteria over national security which dominated the period leading up to the First World War. Given the speed and circumstances in which they found their way on to the statute books it is perhaps not surprising that both sections attracted a great deal of criticism over the years. However, it was Section 2 which had been the particular focus of regular and damning attacks from judges, politicians and the media.

Recognizing the force of those attacks, in July, 1988, the Government published a White Paper setting out its proposals for the reform of Section 2. Based upon these proposals the Official Secrets Act, 1989, received the Royal Assent ten months later.

After covering Section 1 of the 1911 Act, which remains on the statute book, this chapter will deal with the main provisions of the more recent legislation.

SECTION 1: SPYING

Section 1 of the 1911 Act states:

If any person for any purpose prejudicial to the safety or interests of the State:

(a) approaches, inspects, passes over or is in the neighbourhood of, or enters any prohibited place within the meaning of this Act, or

(b) makes any sketch, plan, model or note which is calculated to be or might be or is intended to be directly or indirectly useful to an enemy; or

(c) obtains, collects, records or publishes or communicates to any other person any secret official code word or pass word, or any sketch, plan, model, article or note, or other document or information which is calculated to be, or might be, or is intended to be directly or indirectly useful to an enemy,

. . . shall be guilty of an offence.

The maximum sentence is fourteen years imprisonment. The meaning of 'prohibited place' is set out at extreme length in Section 3. It effectively includes every Government and military building, however insignificant, as well as all means of communications, e.g. roads and railways, and essential services, e.g. gas and electricity stations.

The most likely area of danger in Section 1 as far as the media are concerned is (c), i.e. obtaining or communicating secrets. However the prosecution in any trial would be required to establish 'a purpose prejudicial to the interests of the state'.

In the 'ABC' case in 1978 charges under precisely this part of Section 1 were brought against two journalists, Duncan Campbell and Crispin Aubrey, and a former soldier, John Berry, in respect of information about signals intelligence and defence installations. The purpose which the prosecution alleged was prejudicial to the interests of the state was the publication of the information in the magazine *Time Out*.

On the fifteenth day of the trial, Mr Justice Mars-Jones strongly made it known that he considered the charges to be 'oppressive'. The following morning they were withdrawn on the instructions of the Attorney General. The judge, however, did not close the door on future prosecutions against journalists: 'I find it impossible to say that Section 1 can only be applied to cases of spying or sabotage.' He suggested that henceforth Section 1 charges should be brought only in the clearest and most serious cases.

THE OFFICIAL SECRETS ACT 1989

Objectives and principles

As stated above, the 1989 legislation was introduced to replace Section 2 of the 1911 Act which, during its 80-odd years of life, had probably been the subject of more criticism than any other law on the statute book. Margaret Thatcher's Home Secretary had described it as 'unworkable', various judges over the years had condemned it, and the Franks Committee, which investigated the reform of the Official Secrets legislation after all three defendants were acquitted in 1970 in a case involving the publication of an army document in the *Sunday Telegraph*, recommended its abolition.

It was the generality of Section 2 which the Franks Committee and other critics found most objectionable. It penalized the disclosure of any information obtained by a person holding office under the Crown or by a Government contractor in the course of his duties, however trivial the information and irrespective of the harm likely to arise from its disclosure.

The central objective of the Government's new legislation was, according to the 1988 White Paper, to attain a better definition of when the disclosure of official information became a criminal offence:

The objective of the Government's proposals is to narrow the scope of the present law so that the limited range of circumstances in which the unauthorised disclosure of official information needs to be criminal is clearly defined. This will ensure that no one need be in doubt in what circumstance he would be liable to prosecution, and enable the courts to enforce the law without any overdue burden of proof being placed either on the defence or the prosecution.

The principal yardstick adopted to justify the imposition of criminal sanctions for wrongful disclosure is the degree of harm to the public interest which may result.

Thus, it will not be enough that the disclosure is undesirable, a betrayal of trust or an embarrassment to the Government. Where the harm arising from improper disclosure is not sufficient to warrant recourse to the criminal law, the Government, through its White Paper, said that it will be content to rely upon the Civil Service disciplinary code or upon the civil law of confidence in order to protect its interests.

Henceforth the criminal law in relation to official secrets applies only to *six* clearly defined categories of information. Other classes of official information, such as Cabinet documents and advice to ministers, will not be specifically protected. The White Paper stated:

Documents of this kind will be protected by the proposals if their subject matter merits it, but their coverage *en bloc* would fuel suspicions that information was being protected by the criminal law merely for fear of political embarrassment.

Under the 1989 Act, liability for disclosure falls on those who improperly disclose information in one of the six categories 'knowing or having good reason to know that to do so is likely to harm the public interest.'

For Crown servants, knowledge of the likely harm will be presumed though they may argue in their defence that they could not reasonably have been expected to foresee the harmful consequences. In relation to other persons (e.g. journalists) the prosecution will have to prove that the discloser knew that harm to the public interest was likely to result. The question will, of course, ultimately be one for the jury.

Finally, the legislators rejected as possible defences the notions of disclosure in the public interest and disclosure only after some prior publication. With regard to the former, the White Paper said that the question of criminality should not depend on motivation but '. . . on the nature and degree of the harm which their (*defendants*) acts may cause.' In relation to prior publication, it is pointed out that newspaper stories may carry little weight in themselves, but if they are then confirmed by, say a senior Government official, disclosure of the information would be more damaging.

Protected categories of information

The six areas of information covered by the 1989 Official Secrets Act are:

1 Security and intelligence matters.
2 Defence.
3 International relations.
4 Information useful to criminals.
5 Interception and phone-tapping.
6 Information entrusted in confidence to other states or international organizations.

The Act broadly applies to three categories of information disclosure; first, those in the security services whose primary function is, of course, to keep secrets; second, those Crown servants and government contractors who from time to time deal with highly sensitive information; and, third, those (e.g. journalists) who have received protected information from someone who belongs to either of the first two categories.

In terms of what must be proved to establish criminality, Sections 1 to 6 of the Act lay down a complicated sliding scale of culpability contingent upon which of the three categories the disclosure falls into. For example, in the case of a member of the security services all the prosecution would need to prove is the disclosure itself. If the person disclosing is a Crown servant or Government contractor, however, guilt will be established only if it is proved that the disclosure was, or was likely to be, damaging. Where the accused person is in the third category, i.e. not connected to Government, the burden of proof is higher still, and the prosecution must establish that he or she was aware of the protected nature of the information disclosed, knew that it had come from a 'classified' source and envisaged that the disclosure was or would be damaging.

Given the complex nature of these statutory provisions, the simplest way to described their effect is to go through sections 1 to 6 in turn. It will be seen that the first four sections cover only Crown or Government employees and contractors. Section 5, however, has direct application to journalists or anybody else who, having received the sort of information or material described in Sections 1 to 4, goes on to make unlawful and damaging disclosure of it.

Section 1: Security and intelligence matters

Section 1 applies to 'any information, document or other article relating to security or intelligence' which is disclosed without lawful authority by any person who is or has been:

(a) A member of the security or intelligence services or a person who has been notified by a Minister of the Crown that he is subject to Section 1 as if he were a member of those services.

(b) A Crown servant or Government contractor.

If you fall within (a) above an unauthorized disclosure is automatically an offence and the only defence available is to establish that you 'did not know and had no reasonable cause to believe' that the material disclosed related to security or intelligence.

The pre-legislation White Paper explained why disclosures by the security and intelligence services should be treated in such an uncompromising way:

> 'They are harmful because they carry a credibility which the disclosure of the same information by any other person does not, and because they reduce public confidence in the service's ability and willingness to carry out their essentially secret duties effectively and loyally. They ought to be criminal because those who become members of the services know that membership carries with it a special and inescapable duty of secrecy about their work'.

If you are in category (b), i.e. Crown servants (who are not members of the secret service) or Government contractors, the offence is committed only if the unauthorized disclosure is 'damaging' within the meaning of the Act, i.e. causes or is likely to cause damage to the work of, or any part of, the security and intelligence services. As with category (a), if you prove that you did not know or have reasonable cause to believe that the information related to security or intelligence you will have a valid defence. It is also a defence to show that you neither knew nor had reasonable cause to know that the disclosure would be damaging.

Section 2: Defence

This section applies only to Crown servants and Government contractors, past and present.

As with security and intelligence, unauthorized disclosure of any information, document or other article 'relating to defence' is a criminal offence if it is damaging.

In this context, a disclosure is 'damaging' if it:

- Damages the capability of the armed forces.
- Leads to loss of life or injury to members of the armed services.
- Leads to serious damage to the equipment or installations of the armed forces.
- Endangers the interests of the United Kingdom abroad.
- Is of information which, if disclosed without authority, is likely to have any of the above effects.

Information 'related to defence' is given a very wide definition and includes the size, development, operations and training of the armed forces, the development and production of weapons and other equipment, military planning and defence policy and strategy.

Again, it is a defence for the accused under this section to prove that they did now know or have reasonable cause to believe either that the information related to defence or that the disclosure would be damaging.

Section 3: International relations

Like its predecessor, this section applies only to present or former Crown servants or Government contractors who make damaging disclosures. In this case, the protected material is any information, document or other article either relating to international relations or which is both confidential and was obtained from a foreign state or an international organization. The disclosure will be 'damaging' if it:

- Endangers the interests of the United Kingdom abroad.
- Seriously obstructs the promotion or protection by the United Kingdom of those interests.
- Endangers the safety of British citizens abroad.
- Is of information which, if disclosed without authority, would be likely to have any of the above effects.

International relations are defined as the relations between states and/or international organizations and include any matter concerning a foreign state or international organization which is capable of affecting the United Kingdom's foreign affairs.

Once again, the Crown servant or Government contractor will escape liability upon proof that he or she neither knew nor had reasonable cause to believe that the information was protected under this section or that the disclosure would be damaging.

Section 4: Crime and special investigation powers

As stated above, the 1989 Act creates six classes of protected material. Two of them, namely information of use to criminals and information about phone-taps and other forms of interception, are covered by Section 4.

The section applies only to persons who are, or have been, Crown servants or Government contractors.

In relation to the general 'of use to criminals' category, criminal liability is incurred if the unauthorized disclosure:

- Results in the commission of an offence.

- Facilitates an escape from legal custody, or prejudices the safekeeping of persons in legal custody.
- Impedes the prevention or detection of offences or the apprehension or prosecution of suspected offenders.
- Is likely to have any of the above consequences.

As usual, those charged with unlawful disclosure of such information will establish a valid defence if they can prove that they neither knew nor had reasonable cause to believe that the disclosure would have any such effect.

The second leg of Section 4 makes it an offence to disclose without lawful authority:

- Any information obtained through a phone-tap or other form of interception authorized by a warrant issued under Section 2 of the interception of Communications Act 1985.
- Any information obtained through actions which are authorized by a warrant issued under Section 3 of the Security Service Act 1989.
- Any information, document or other article relating to the phone-tap or other form of interception under either of the two statutory sections set out above.

In order to protect both the effectiveness of the interception and the security of that which is intercepted, the Act protects the practice (i.e. who is being 'bugged' and how) as well as the content.

Again, the Government's White Paper produced the rationale:

'It is an exceptional but vital instrument which is used for the protection of society when other means are not available. Successive governments have recognized that properly controlled interception for limited purposes, such as national security or the prevention and detection of crime, is not only justified but essential in the public interest'.

Alongside security and intelligence matters, this class of information is accordingly given the highest level of protection by the Act. In order to secure a conviction the prosecution need prove only an unauthorized disclosure. The only defence then available to the accused is that he or she did not know and had no reasonable cause to believe that the information disclosed fell within the protected category.

Section 5: Information resulting from unauthorized disclosure

As has been seen, the first four sections of the Official Secrets Act 1989 are aimed solely at those employed by or contracted to the Crown or the Government. It is considered to be a fundamental principle of state and military security that those public servants entrusted with sensitive information honour the commitment to confidentiality and/or secrecy which is part of their contract of employment. Sections 1 to 4 serve, where appropriate, to add the sanction of the criminal law to that contractual commitment.

Logic, of course, dictates that where protected information has been passed on without authority and then used to the detriment of the State, the criminal sanction must extend beyond the public servant who breached security. As every policeman knows, if there were no receivers there would be no thieves.

The function of Section 5 of the Act is, therefore, to catch the receiver of information disclosed in breach of Sections 1 to 4.

Here, at last, is where the 1989 Act can bite directly upon journalists. The section makes it an offence for any person to disclose without lawful authority any information, document or other article which:

(a)   Falls within the protected classes to which Sections 1 to 4 apply.
(b)   Has come into his or her possession as a result of unauthorized disclosure by those persons to whom Sections 1 to 4 apply.
(c)   Has come into his or her possession as a result of unauthorized disclosure by someone to whom the information was properly entrusted in confidence by a Section 1 to 4 person.

In order to secure a conviction under Section 5 the burden of proof imposed upon the prosecution is of the highest order. It must be proved that the disclosure was damaging within the meanings laid down in the other sections and that the accused person disclosed the information knowing or having reasonable cause to believe:

- That is fell within the protected categories described in Sections 1 to 4.
- That it had come into his or her possession as a result of an unauthorized disclosure as described in (b) or (c) above.
- That the disclosure would be damaging.

Section 6: Information entrusted in confidence to other states or international organizations

As seen above, Section 3 protects confidential information obtained from a foreign state or international organization. Section 6 affords protection to information travelling in the opposite direction, i.e. sensitive material which the United Kingdom entrusts in confidence to the Governments or Government departments of other countries.

Like Section 5, this section also bites upon those outside government service and can therefore be used against journalists. In one respect it is wider than Section 5, since for the offence to be committed it is not necessary that the information came from a Crown servant or Government contractor.

Section 6 makes it an offence for a person to make a damaging disclosure without lawful authority of any information, document or other article which:

(a) '. . . relates to security or intelligence, defence or international relations'.
(b) Has been communicated in confidence by or on behalf of the United Kingdom to another state or to an international organization.

The prosecution must prove:

● That the information came into the accused's possession without the authority of the relevant foreign state or international organization to whom it was entrusted and without that state or international organization having previously made it available to the public.
● That the accused knew or had reasonable cause to know that the information fell within the protected classes set out in (a) and (b) above and that the disclosure would be damaging.

For the purpose of Section 6, the terms 'damaging', 'security or intelligence', 'defence', and 'international relations' have the same meanings as in Sections 1 to 3 of the Act.

Under Section 8 of the Act, the authorities can issue an 'official direction' for the return of any document or other article which is covered by Sections 1 to 6. Failure to comply with such a direction is an offence.

THE D-NOTICE SYSTEM

Apart from the formal system of secrecy enforcement operated through the Official Secrets Act, the Government and the media have an alternative and altogether more civilized form of coexistence in respect of sensitive information relating to national security.

D-notices represent a voluntary system by which the Government advises the Press that the publication of a certain piece of information would be damaging to the national interest. The notices themselves are formal letters circulated by the Defence, Press and Broadcasting Committee to newspaper editors and their equivalents in TV and radio broadcasting. According to a former secretary of the committee, they amount to requests to the effect of: Please do not publish unless you take advice. (Colonel 'Sammy' Lohan in *Attorney General v Clough (1963)*)

They do *not* have the force of law.

The committee consists of representatives from the civil service, the armed forces and the press. It meets about twice a year to review the existing D-notices; since 1962 there have been nine in operation, mostly concerned with defence plans, equipment and installations and with security or intelligence.

15 PROMOTIONS

Ask any editor to identify his newspaper's most valuable commodity and without hesitation he or she is likely to say its readers. Radio and television producers would answer the same question by nominating their listeners or viewers. Success is measured by the size of readership or audience, and competition at all ends of the media industry is fierce.

The circulation wars which have been going on between newspapers for decades have more recently spilled over into broadcasting. It is easy to see why when profits of commercial radio and television companies are usually dictated by share of the market, (i.e. percentage of the available listeners or viewers).

Promotions are the traditional weapons of such wars. Massively publicized offers of free houses, cars and holidays have always been seen by the popular press as the best way to secure a quick increase in readership. When, in 1981, *The Sun* introduced Bingo to its readers, it achieved a circulation gain of something like 500,000, (then about one and a half times the total daily sale of *The Times*). The 'serious' press found it hard to ignore the commercial attractions of such devices and both the *Daily Telegraph* and *The Times* now run promotional games.

Whether they involve pure luck or the exercise of skill, games which offer prizes to the public are closely controlled by statute law. The Lotteries and Amusements Act 1976 lays down rules by which the legality of all forms of promotional game played by the media may be measured.

LOTTERIES

The 1976 Act provides that, apart from a few stipulated exceptions which do not include games run by and through the media, all lotteries are unlawful.

Definition of lottery

Unfortunately the statute does not define the word 'lottery'. Case law, however, has filled the gap by establishing that the essential ingredients of a lottery are threefold:

- There must be a distribution of prizes.
- An element of pure chance must be involved in winning the prizes.
- Each participant must make a contribution towards his chance of winning a prize.
  Readers Digest Association Ltd v *Williams* (1976)

A lottery is therefore defined as the distribution of prizes by lot or chance where those participating have secured their chance of winning by a payment or some other material consideration.

Over the years numerous promotional schemes have received judicial scrutiny to ascertain whether they are illegal as lotteries. Since it is invariably clear from the start that there is a distribution of prizes, the cases have tended to involve one or other of the two following points:

1 Are the prizes distributed by pure chance?

If merit or skill plays a part in the allocation of the prizes it is not a lottery. It is precisely for this reason, i.e. to inject an element of skill, that so many promotional games which might be accused of being simply lucky draws ask participants to write down in x number of words why they think the product being promoted is wonderful.

2 Is the game genuinely free to enter or does the participant have to make some payment?

Where the person must purchase a product in order to participate in a game of chance consideration is deemed to have been given and it is a lottery. Thus, if the entry voucher is contained in a packet of cigarettes or tea, or is inside a newspaper and a purchase is necessary to obtain it, the scheme is illegal.

It is irrelevant that the entry is free with the product, i.e. no extra charge is made. It is also irrelevant that the purchaser of the product is not made aware that there is a voucher inside (and therefore there is no extra inducement to buy). In each case it will still be a lottery unless the chance to win (i.e. the voucher or its equivalent) can be obtained freely and without giving any consideration.

Newspaper Bingo is a good example of a scheme which clearly does induce participants to buy the product, but which has managed to avoid making the purchase a *requirement* of the game. It achieves this by:

1 Delivering the Bingo card (i.e. the entry voucher) free to the homes of would-be participants.

2   Ensuring that the daily Bingo numbers are given out free to whoever requests them, e.g. by phoning the newspaper office. Therefore, although they are published each day in the paper, players do not have to buy it to get their numbers.

The same stratagem is seen in most promotional draws, e.g. those run every so often by brewers or petrol companies. Although the public will usually buy a pint of beer or some petrol to get a voucher it is never compulsory to do so. If it were then, unless the game involves skill, the scheme would be illegal.

Offences and penalties

Section 2 of the Lotteries and Amusements Act 1976 stipulates a wide range of activities connected with the organization or promotion of lotteries which will constitute offences. They include the printing, sale, advertising and distribution of lottery tickets or vouchers, possession of tickets for distribution and the use of, or allowing the use of, premises in connection with a lottery.

For a conviction in the Magistrates Court the maximum fine is £2000; at the Crown Court the offender is liable to an unlimited fine or a maximum of two years' imprisonment.

COMPETITIONS

As discussed above, if newspapers or other members of the media are to avoid lottery offences in connection with their promotional games they must either ensure genuinely free entry or turn the game into a competition by introducing an element of skill.

However, even if skill is required the scheme may still be legally unsafe. Under Section 14(1) of the Lotteries and Amusements Act 1976, certain types of competition are also illegal. It provides:

> . . . it shall be unlawful to conduct in or through any newspaper, or in connection with any trade or business or the sale of any article to the public:
>
> (a)   Any competition in which prizes are offered for forecasts of the result either:
>   (i)   of a future event; or
>   (ii)   of a past event the result of which is not yet ascertained, or not yet generally known.
> (b)   Any other competition in which success does not depend to a substantial degree on the exercise of skill.

Accordingly, any promotional game which requires the participant to select the winner of a forthcoming sporting event, e.g. a horse race or a football match, will contravene the section since it necessarily involves forecasting the result of a future event.

Similarly, a game which requires participants to judge what happened next from studying a photograph of a past event, e.g. picking the eventual winner by looking at a picture of the closing stages of a race, is likely to be unlawful under Section 14(1)(a) since it would amount to forecasting the result of a past event where that result is not generally known. If, on the other hand, the pictured event was so famous that the result would be generally known by those looking at the photograph, then the competition might easily contravene Section 14(1)(b) because success would not depend to a substantial degree on the exercise of skill.

The *News of the World*'s 'Spot the Ball' competition came close to falling foul of this section in 1973. The case went all the way to the House of Lords where it was eventually judged to be entirely lawful. Readers were shown a picture taken at a football match. The ball itself was erased from the photograph and those participating in the competition were required to mark with a cross the most likely position of the ball judging by the attitude and posture of the players shown. The winner was the entrant whose cross was closest to the spot chosen at a later date by a panel of experts. The court, describing the scheme as 'ingenious', held that since the spot selected by the experts was not necessarily the true position of the ball participants were not being required to forecast the result of a past event. Furthermore, the considered opinion of the panel did not constitute a 'future event' which would make the game illegal under Section 14(1)(a)(i). (*News of the World Ltd* v *Friend* (1973).)

The penalties for 'conducting' an unlawful competition under Section 14 are the same as those for running an illegal lottery under Section 1 of the Act.

16 PROFESSIONAL REGULATORY BODIES

There are, of course, occasions too numerous to mention when people have valid complaints about something which has been published or broadcast but have no recourse to law. Articles, for example, can be distressingly inaccurate but not in a way which gives the person involved any right of action in law. There are other occasions when the subject of a story does have a right to sue but either cannot afford it or prefers not to have the aggravation.

In such cases an alternative avenue of complaint is provided by the Press Complaints Commission in the case of newspapers and the Broadcasting Complaints Commission and other bodies in the case of television and radio.

THE PRESS: HISTORY OF SELF-REGULATION

For those who believe that media excess is a modern phenomenon a study of the newspaper industry's regulatory history is an enlightening experience. Outrage at the perceived misbehaviour of the Press has been with us for as long as newspapers themselves.

At least once every decade since the Second World War parliamentarians have threatened legislative controls and the industry has responded with tightened self-regulation and resolutions of good behaviour. The first of the post-war parade of professional regulatory bodies came into existence at around the time Queen Elizabeth II was crowned.

When it was established in 1953 the first self-regulatory body of the Press, it must be said, had all the appearances of an 'unwanted' baby. Those who brought it into the world, the proprietors and journalists of the newspaper industry, had spent the previous four years filibustering in the apparent hope that the self-regulatory body called for in 1949 by the first Royal Commission on the Press could be avoided.

The climate, however, changed drastically in 1953 when a Private Members' Bill was introduced into Parliament which would have had the effect of imposing outside control. Not for the last time the newspaper industry reacted swiftly when faced with the threat of statutory regulation. The result was the General Council of the Press.

Although it was enough to fend off Parliamentary interference the Council, in its early days, was a poor imitation of what the Royal Commission had seen as necessary, i.e. a voluntary body which would administer a 'code of conduct in accordance with the highest professional standards'. Lack of proper funding and the absence of any lay membership on the Council (along with a noticeable absence of enthusiasm from the press itself) made it fairly ineffective.

Reforms in the shape of an independent chairman, increased finances and a 20 per cent lay membership were squeezed out of the industry in 1962 after the second Royal Commission on the Press attacked the Council's poor record and once again raised the threatening spectre of a statutory body of control.

Although the performance of what, by then, was known as the Press Council improved drastically the last Royal Commission which reported in 1977 still found much to criticize. Once again funding and lay membership were increased. From 1977, the stature of the Council grew year by year, as indeed did the amount of work with which it dealt. Although it stopped short of laying down the comprehensive code of conduct which was suggested by the last Commission it issued Declarations of Principle on privacy, payments and financial journalism which defined the limits of acceptable behaviour in these important areas.

In the late-eighties, however, a clamour for legislative moves against the Press once again found a large level of support at the Palace of Westminster. Public and parliamentary disquiet had been fed by a stream of complaints about breach of privacy, harassment of individuals and their families, inaccurate reporting and intrusion. Some of the complaints were true, some were false, but their overall effect was to stir the politicians into real action.

In the 1988–89 Parliamentary Session two separate Private Members' Bills, one on privacy and the other concerning an enforceable right of reply, won considerable support and made it through the committee stages of the House of Commons.

Early in 1989, with the writing fairly clearly on the wall, the editors of all national newspapers met at the Newspaper Publishers Association in London and emerged with a written declaration that:

'We, having given due consideration to criticism of the Press by Parliament and public, accept the need to improve methods of self-regulation. Accordingly, we declare today our unanimous commitment to a common Code of Practice to safeguard the independance of the Press from threats of official control.'

Like Neville Chamberlain, the Editors quickly found that 'peace in our time' was not quite so easy. For the Government it was too little, too late.

A few months later, the Secretary of State for National Heritage set up a committee under David Calcutt QC to:

'. . . consider what measures (whether legislative or otherwise) are needed to give further protection to individual privacy from the activities of the Press and improve recourse for the individual citizen.'

The Report of the Calcutt Committee on Privacy and Related Matters was published in June 1990. Although it recommended against the introduction of a statutory right of privacy, it effectively placed the press on probation:

The press should be given one final chance to prove that voluntary self-regulation can be made to work.   (Paragraph 14.38)

The Government let it be known immediately that it accepted Calcutt's findings. Writing in *The Times* on 22 June 1990, the Home Secretary, David Waddington, stated that the newspaper industry had a twelve-month period 'to put its house in order or face tough statutory controls'.

Calcutt recommended that the existing Press Council should be disbanded and, in its place, a Press Complaints Commission should be set up. That Commission should:

- Concentrate on providing an effective means of redress for complaints against the press.
- Be given specific duties to consider complaints of unjust or unfair treatment by newspapers or periodicals and of infringement of privacy through published material or the behaviour of reporters.
- Publish, monitor and implement a comprehensive code of practice for the guidance of both the press and the public.
- Operate a hot line for complaints on a 24-hour basis.
- In certain circumstances, recommend the publication of an apology or a reply in favour of a successful complainant.
- Have an independent chairman and no more than twelve members, with smaller complaints committees.
- Have clear conciliation and adjudication procedures, with a fast-track procedure for the correction of significant factual errors.
- Should not operate a waiver of legal rights as a required prerequisite to having a complaint heard.

Finally, Calcutt recommended that:

> If the industry wishes to maintain a system of non-statutory self-regulation, it must demonstrate its commitment, in particular by providing the necessary money for setting up and maintaining the Press Complaints Commission.

The Industry took the warnings to heart. Within a few months of the Calcutt Report a Press Standards Board of Finance had been established. It eventually decreed that the Press Complaints Commission should have an annual budget of £1½ million, a fund which, of course, would be provided by the newspaper industry. In its last year of existence the Press Council's budget was £600,000.

In October, 1990, Lord McGregor of Durris, who in 1977 had chaired the Third Royal Commission on the Press, was appointed the first Chairman of the proposed Press Complaints Commission.

By mid-December a Code of Practice was issued and two days after Christmas the names of the Commission's sixteen members were announced. They included seven current editors of newspapers or magazines, the executive Vice-Chairman of *Times Newspapers*, a former Editor-in-Chief of the Press Association and a former Northern Ireland Secretary.

THE PRESS COMPLAINTS COMMISSION

Structure

The cornerstone of the newspaper industry's system of self-regulation is the Press Standards Board of Finance Ltd (Presbof). Incorporated in the immediate aftermath of Calcutt as the representative body of the entire Press, its consitutent members are the:

Newspapers Publishers Association
Newspaper Society
Periodical Publishers Association
Scottish Newspapers Publishers Association
Scottish Daily Newspaper Society

In other words, all of the trade associations for the newspaper and magazine industry.

The stated purposes of Presbof are to:

- Coordinate and promote self-regulation within the industry.
- Finance the Press Complaints Commission (PCC).
- Provide a ready means of liasion between the PCC and the industry.
- Monitor and review the Code of Practice through a Code Committee.

How your complaint is dealt with

The Commission acknowledge your letter and decide whether it is within their remit and presents a possible breach of the Code of Practice

A copy of your letter is sent to the editor of the publication suggesting that they resolve the matter with you direct

The Commission write to you if they decide not to deal with your complaint, explaining why

If the matter is not resolved at that stage, the Commission decide whether there has been a breach of the Code. They may ask you and/or the editor for more information or comment

The Commission would not normally consider the matter further if the complaint is resolved with the editor

The Commission reach a formal adjudication on the complaint

The commission write to you and the editor to say that they do not intend to take the matter further

Complaint upheld   Complaint not upheld

Copies of the adjudication are sent to you and the editor. The publication concerned is required to publish this ajudication in full whenever a complaint is upheld

Below Presbof there exists an Appointments Commission charged with finding and appointing suitable members of the PCC and a Code Committee (consisting almost entirely of editors), the function of which is to review and, if necessary, amend or extend the Code of Practice.

How complaints are dealt with

The flow-chart opposite illustrates the step-by-step passage of complaints. At the outset complainants are also told that the PCC will apply the following principles:

1 All complaints are judged against the Code of Practice. If there is no *prima facie* breach of the Code, the PCC tells the complainant that it can take the matter no further.
2 The objective of the PCC is to achieve a speedy resolution of the grievance. To that end, it will normally deal only with complaints which are lodged within one month of publication of the relevant story or, if the complainant first wrote to the editor, within one month of the editor's reply.
3 The PCC will not usually entertain complaints from third parties, i.e. anyone not directly involved in the published piece. In such circumstances, however, it frequently writes to those who are concerned in the story asking if they wish to co-operate in the complaint. If not, the matter goes no further. The PCC justifies this principle on the grounds of practicality in that if the subject of the story does not wish to give his or her side of things, the evidence is bound to be one-sided.
4 The PCC will not deal with a complaint if litigation in respect of the story is either in progress or about to commence. At the conclusion of the PCC procedure there is, however, nothing to prevent the complainant issuing proceedings.

CODE OF PRACTICE

All members of the Press have a duty to maintain the highest professional and ethical standards. In doing so, they should have regard to the provisions of this Code of Practice and to safeguarding the public's right to know.

Editors are responsible for the actions of journalists employed by their publications. They should also satisfy themselves as far as possible that material accepted from non-staff members was obtained in accordance with this Code.

While recognizing that this involves a substantial element of self-restraint by editors and journalists, it is designed to be acceptable in the context of a system of self-regulation. The Code applies in the spirit as well as in the letter.

It is the responsibility of editors to co-operate as swiftly as possible in PCC enquiries.

Any publication which is criticized by the PCC under one of the following clauses is duty bound to print the adjudication which follows in full and with due prominence.

1   Accuracy

(i) Newspapers and periodicals should take care not to publish inaccurate, misleading or distorted material.
(ii) Whenever it is recognized that a significant inaccuracy, misleading statement or distorted report has been published, it should be corrected promptly and with due prominence.
(iii) An apology should be published whenever appropriate.
(iv) A newspaper or periodical should always report fairly and accurately the outcome of an action for defamation to which it has been a party.

2   Opportunity to reply

A fair opportunity for reply to inaccuracies should be given to individuals or organizations when reasonably called for.

3   Comment, conjecture and fact

Newspapers, while free to be partisan, should distinguish clearly between comment, conjecture and fact.

4   Privacy

Intrusions and enquiries into an individual's private life without his or her consent, including the use of long-lens photography to take pictures of people on private property without their consent, are not generally acceptable and publication can only be justified when in the public interest.

Note: Private property is defined as any private residence, together with its garden and outbuildings, but excluding any adjacent fields or parkland. In addition, hotel bedrooms (but not other areas in a hotel) and those parts of a hospital or nursing home where patients are treated or accommodated.

5   **Listening devices**

Unless justified by public interest, journalists should not obtain or publish material obtained by using clandestine listening devices or by intercepting private telephone conversations.

6   **Hospitals**

(i)   Journalists or photographers making enquiries at hospitals or similar institutions should identify themselves to a responsible executive and obtain permission before entering non-public areas.

(ii)   The restrictions on intruding into privacy are particularly relevant to enquiries about individuals in hospital or similar institutions.

7   **Misrepresentations**

(i)   Journalists should not generally obtain or seek to obtain information or pictures through misrepresentation or subterfuge.

(ii)   Unless in the public interest, documents or photographs should be removed only with the express consent of the owner.

(iii) Subterfuge can be justified only in the public interest and only when material cannot be obtained by any other means.

8   **Harassment**

(i)   Journalists should neither obtain nor seek to obtain information or pictures through intimidation or harassment.

(ii)   Unless their enquiries are in the public interest, journalists should not photograph individuals on private property (as defined in the note to Clause 4) without their consent; should not persist in telephoning or questioning individuals after having been asked to desist; should not remain on their property after having been asked to leave and should not follow them.

(iii) It is the responsibility of editors to ensure that these requirements are carried out.

9   **Payment for articles**

Payment or offers of payment for stories, pictures or information should not be made directly or through agents to witnesses or potential witnesses in current criminal proceedings or to people engaged in crime or to their associates – which includes family, friends, neighbours and colleagues – except where the material concerned ought to be published in the public interest and the payment is necessary for this to be done.

10   *Intrusions into grief or shock*

In cases involving personal grief or shock, enquiries should be carried out and approaches made with sympathy and discretion.

11   *Innocent relatives and friends*

Unless it is contrary to the public's right to know, the press should generally avoid identifying relatives or friends of persons convicted or accused of crime.

12   *Interviewing or photographing children*

(i)   Journalists should not normally interview or photograph children under the age of 16 on subjects involving the personal welfare of the child in the absence of or without the consent of a parent or other adult who is responsible for the children.

(ii)   Children should not be approached or photographed while at school without the permission of the school authorities.

13   *Children in sex cases*

1   The press should not, even where the law does not prohibit it, identify children under the age of 16 who are involved in cases concerning sexual offences, whether as victims, or as witnesses or defendants.

2   In any press report of a case involving a sexual offence against a child:

(i)   The adult should be identified.

(ii)   The term 'incest' where applicable should not be used.

(iii) The offence should be described as 'serious offences against young children' or similar appropriate wording.

(iv)   The child should not be identified.

(v)   Care should be taken that nothing in the report implies the relationship between the accused and the child.

14   *Victims of crime*

The press should not identify victims of sexual assault or publish material likely to contribute to such identification unless, by law, they are free to do so.

15 Discrimination

(i) The press should avoid prejudicial or pejorative reference to a person's race, colour, religion, sex or sexual orientation or to any physical or mental illness or handicap.

(ii) It should avoid publishing details of a person's race, colour, religion, sex or sexual orientation, unless these are directly relevant to the story.

16 Financial journalism

(i) Even where the law does not prohibit it, journalists should not use for their own profit financial information they receive in advance of its general publication, nor should they pass such information to others.

(ii) They should not write about shares or securities in whose performance they know that they or their close families have a significant financial interest, without disclosing the interest to the editor or financial editor.

(iii) They should not buy or sell, either directly or through nominees or agents, shares or securities about which they have written recently or about which they intend to write in the near future.

17 Confidential sources

Journalists have a moral obligation to protect confidential sources of information.

18 The public interest

Clauses 4, 5, 7, 8 and 9 create exceptions which may be covered by invoking the public interest. For the purposes of this code that is most easily defined as:

(i) Detecting or exposing crime or a serious misdemeanour.

(ii) Protecting public health and safety.

(iii) Preventing the public from being misled by some statement or action of an individual or organization.

In any cases raising issues beyond these three definitions the Press Complaints Commission will require a full explanation by the editor of the publication involved, seeking to demonstrate how the public interest was served.

BROADCASTING

Television and radio in the 1990s is one of the most sophisticated industries known to the world. The second-perfect organization of its technology and services defies belief to those (most of us) who are not multimedia-literate.

Unfortunately, in this country at least, the system by which broadcasting is regulated has been left far behind the technology, It is unwieldy and far from efficient. Apart from the Broadcasting Complaints Commission, there is the Broadcasting Standards Council, the Independent Television Commission and the Radio Authority. All have authority to handle complaints.

THE BROADCASTING COMPLAINTS COMMISSION

Broadcasting companies in Britain managed for many years to escape the widespread public distrust with which the press have historically been associated. Although they have never been above criticism – for example Winston Churchill complained about political bias at the BBC as long ago as 1953 – somehow both the BBC and independent television and radio were always regarded as being above the more criticized practices of the popular newspapers.

It is perhaps for that reason that the broadcasting industry had no equivalent of the Press Complaints Commission until 1981. Up to that time the BBC, the IBA (the governing body of independent television) and the Radio Authority each ran their own complaints tribunal, the adjudications of which were usually printed in one or other of the magazines produced by these organizations, i.e. the *TV Times* or *The Listener*.

However, in 1977 the Annan Committee on the Future of Broadcasting recommended the establishment of a statutory body which would sit in public in order to investigate and decide upon complaints from the public. The result in 1981 was the establishment of the Broadcasting Complaints Commission (the BCC).

Function

When the relevant legislation was passing through Parliament a chorus of protest was heard from the broadcasting industry. The proposed Complaints Commission was described variously as a 'potential monster' (Colin Shaw, Deputy Director of the IBA), a 'pain in the neck' (Alasdair Milne, Managing Director of BBC television) and a 'threat to editorial enterprise' (Sir Hugh Greene, former Director General of the BBC).

Despite the much-publicized fears of eminent broadcasters, the BCC, in the powers bestowed upon it by Parliament and in the way it chooses to exercise them, has not had a major impact upon the industry.

Established by the Broadcasting Act, 1981, and currently governed by Part V of the Broadcasting Act, 1990, its function is to investigate and adjudicate upon complaints of:

- Unjust and unfair treatment in programmes – in radio or television programmes.
- Unwarranted infringement of privacy in programmes or in connection with their preparation.

The Commission may only consider complaints about programmes which have actually been broadcast and, significantly, is not empowered to adjudicate upon complaints based solely upon:

- The deception of sex or violence.
- Bad language or bad taste.
- Programme scheduling.
- Background music.

The jurisdiction of the Commission extends to BBC-TV, BBC Radio, BBC World Service, ITV, Channel 4, Independent Radio and all licensed cable and satellite programme services. In its first year 114 complaints were received by the BCC of which ninety-one were rejected because they concerned matters outside its jurisdiction.

The number of complaints more than doubled in 1982–3 to 234, though only forty-six of them were found to be within the Commission's jurisdiction. The rest were mainly concerned with matters of taste, content, programme balance, scheduling or standards. By 1994 the figure had risen to 1049 of which 893 were outside the remit.

Procedure

The BCC will deal only with complainants who either participated in the programme or who have a direct interest in it. This includes the relatives of 'victims' who are infants or who have died within the five years preceding the broadcast. It will not entertain a complaint if legal proceedings concerning the same matter are either in progress or in prospect. It will also not entertain any complaint which appears to be 'frivolous'.

When a written complaint is received the BCC will forward it to either the BBC or the IBA and require a reply in writing which answers the points raised, together with copies of whatever correspondence has already been exchanged on the matter. It has a right to view the programme which gave offence and may then decide the complaint either on the basis of the written submissions or after conducting an oral hearing.

Powers

Under the Broadcasting Act 1990, the BCC has legal power to direct that an offending television or radio company should broadcast and/or publish the finding and may specify how and when it should do so. Usually this involves the publication of the adjudication in either the *Radio Times*, in the case of the BBC, or the *TV Times* for complaints against independent television or radio.

A summary of the Commission's adjudication is also ordered to be broadcast on the same channel and at a similar time to the programme which was the subject of the complaint.

THE BROADCASTING STANDARDS COUNCIL (BSC)

The BSC considers complaints about the portrayal of violence and of sexual conduct and about matters of taste and decency. It has the same wide jurisdiction as the BCC. Complaints should normally be submitted within two months of the relevant programme being broadcast. Again, like the BCC, the Broadcasting Standards Council has power to direct that its adjudications should be published in the *Radio* or *TV Times* and broadcast in summary form on the relevant channel.

THE INDEPENDENT TELEVISION COMMISSION (ITC)

The ITC was established by the Broadcasting Act, 1990, to govern the licensing and regulating of independent television and teletext and licensed cable and satellite services in the United Kingdom. Among its extensive statutory powers, it has the authority to lay down and enforce Codes of Practice in order to maintain what it considers to be proper standards.

From the public's point of view, the most significant of the existing codes is the ITC Programme Code which covers matters such as taste, decency, the portrayal of violence, privacy, impartiality, charitable appeals and religious programmes.

There are also ITC Codes covering Advertising Standards and Practice (to prevent ads which are misleading, offensive or likely to encourage dangerous or anti-social attitudes or behaviour) and Programme Sponsorship (to protect editorial independence and prevent sponsor credits from intruding unacceptably on programmes).

The ITC's powers are fairly wide. Apart from directing that an apology or correction should be broadcast by an offending channel, it can also order the company involved not to repeat the programme. In more serious cases the company can be given a formal warning that it is in breach of its licence, can be fined (often large amounts), can have its licence shortened or, in extreme circumstances, even revoked altogether.

The ITC, of course, has no jurisdiction over the BBC.

OTHER BODIES

Apart from the BCC, BSC and ITC, complainants can also address their grievances to the Radio Authority, for independent radio, or to BBC Viewer and Listener Correspondence, for BBC TV and radio.

17 ADVERTISING

Today there are very few people, particularly among those working in the media, who underestimate the power of advertising. Since commercial television was introduced in the 1950s the advertising industry has grown massively and large companies are now happy to spend millions of pounds each year on publicizing their products. Since a large part of these advertising budgets is devoted to buying space on television and in newspapers the media are among the many beneficiaries of the boom.

In 1961 the advertising industry itself recognized that there was a need for a unified system of control over the content and presentation of advertisements. For this reason it devised and published the first Code of Advertising Practice and established the Advertising Standards Authority to monitor it.

The Code has been redrawn and expanded over the years to take in the changing trends and needs in advertising. It is currently in its seventh edition.

Apart from a chairman and director general, the Advertising Standards Authority has nine members and runs a permanent secretariat and various specialist sub-committees. The ASA frequently receives more than 500 complaints about advertisements in a month.

THE CODE OF ADVERTISING PRACTICE

Aims and functions

In the words of the Code itself:

The British Code of Advertising Practice is the body of rules by which, the British advertising business has agreed, the overwhelming majority of the advertisements it produces should be regulated.

The only major areas of advertising not directly subject to the Code are television and radio commercials. However, the IBA which controls independent TV and radio enforces a similar set of rules.

Essentially the Code is a set of principles and guidelines on the content of advertisements. It claims a twofold function: first, as a guide to 'those concerned with commissioning, creating and publishing advertisements', and second, as the rulebook against which the Advertising Standards Authority will judge complaints.

In respect of the first of the above functions the ASA is happy to give advice about the content of an advertisement prior to its publication to ensure compliance with the Code.

Since the Code has no legal authority the fulfilment of its second function, i.e. the effective handling of complaints, relies upon what it calls 'the self-regulatory system'. It explains:

> The system is not simply one of self-discipline and it does not depend upon the individual conscience as its only sanction. Self-regulation goes beyond the regulation of the individual by himself and connotes the regulation of a whole profession by its practitioners acting together.

What this means in practice is that where the ASA finds that a breach of the Code has occurred and requires that an advertiser desists from a certain activity (usually the running of a particular advertisement) it can effectively enforce it through the other members of the industry. Thus, if an advertiser refuses to give the ASA an undertaking not to re-run a certain advertisement the ASA will simply ask advertising agencies and media companies not to handle the offensive material.

The rules of the Code

1 '*All advertisements should be legal, decent, honest and truthful*':   Under this, the first principle of the Code, the requirements are as follows:

   - Legal – this is self-explanatory; advertisements must comply with the law.
   - Decent – although the ASA claims not to be an arbiter on matters of pure taste, it does require that advertisements should contain nothing which because of 'failure to respect the standards of decency and propriety that are generally accepted . . . is likely to cause either grave or widespread offence'.
   - Honest – advertisers should not try to take unfair advantage of consumers, e.g. 'by exploiting their credulity or their lack of experience or knowledge'.
   - Truthful – 'no advertisement, whether by inaccuracy, ambiguity,

exaggeration or otherwise, should mislead consumers about any matter likely to influence their attitude to the advertised product.'

The Code gives detailed guidance on areas where advertisers need to exercise particular care over truthful presentation. Among others it singles out political advertisements, quotation of prices, use of the words 'free', 'up to' (as in 'up to *x* miles per gallon') and 'from' (as in 'from £*x*'), use of testimonials or indications of approval from third parties and the recognizability of advertisements for what they are.

2 *'All advertisements should be prepared with a sense of responsibility to the consumer and to society'*:   Under this rule the ASA requires advertisers not to play on fear without good reason and not to incite or condone violence or anti-social behaviour. It also sets out principles designed to protect consumers against exploitation or infringement of their privacy. Thus advertisers should not portray or refer to individuals without their permission. They should also avoid showing or advocating dangerous behaviour, e.g. excessive drinking or smoking, and take special care with advertisements directed towards children.

3 *'All advertisements should conform to the principles of fair competition generally accepted in business'*:   The ASA makes various points about the fairness of comparisons between products, about denigrating the products of rivals, about the exploitation of goodwill belonging to others and about imitating other people's advertisements.

4 *Rules applying to particular categories of advertisement*:   This section of the Code lays down rules for particular areas of advertising where special care is called for in the interests of the consumer. The Code singles out:

- Advertisements containing health claims, especially those made for medicinal and related products.
- Hair and scalp products.
- Advertising claims for vitamins and minerals.
- Slimming.
- Cosmetics.
- Mail order and direct-response advertising.
- Advertising financial services and products.
- Advertisements containing employment and business opportunities.
- Advertising limited editions.
- Advertisements aimed at children.
- Betting tipsters.

The Code also sets out, as an appendix, a separate 'Cigarette Code' which is administered by the ASA and which contains the body of principles accepted by the tobacco and advertising industries as governing the advertising of cigarettes and tobacco products.

The complaints procedure

The procedure adopted by the ASA for handling complaints about breaches of the Code is very similar to that used by the Press Complaints Commission.

Upon receipt of a complaint the ASA secretariat will initially evaluate it to ensure that the point raised comes within the remit of the Code and is neither frivolous nor obviously misconceived.

Where it considers there are proper grounds for investigation it submits the complaint to the advertiser and asks for comments. If the matter seems particularly grave the ASA will ask for the relevant advertisement to be stopped until the investigation is concluded.

The onus is now upon the advertiser to reply in writing as soon as possible and to satisfy the ASA that no breach of the Code has occurred. Under the rules, particular emphasis is placed on preserving and supplying all evidential matter and documentary evidence in support of the advertisement.

When all available evidence and comments of the parties are gathered in, the secretariat, after due consideration, makes a recommendation to the ASA Council.

An advertiser found by the Council to be in breach of the Code will be asked to undertake not to repeat the breach and to amend or withdraw the offending advertisement. In the event of that request being refused, media organizations which subscribe to the ASA will be instructed not to handle the advertisement.

Adjudications of the ASA are published in the form of case reports each month.

18 THE RIGHT TO PRIVACY

In all the debates which have raged over this subject during the last forty years, and there have been plenty, nobody has sought to deny the existence of a general right to privacy.

The issue has been whether Parliament should legislate in order to make privacy enforceable through the courts.

That question always seems to focus upon the activities of the press. Not surprisingly it produces strong emotional argument both ways. Freedom of the press has always been the cornerstone of freedom of speech. On the other hand, the media (in the past mostly tabloid newspapers) are not noted for their subtlety when exercising their freedom to speak about private lives.

During the Parliamentary debate of John Browne MP's Private Member's Bill on Protection of Privacy in January 1989, the Government's spokesman, Timothy Renton, put both sides of the argument:

> The truth is that the Government starts from the premise that you cannot have a free society without a free press.

For that reason, he said, legislative curbs on newspapers should only be imposed 'after careful thought and when some overriding national interest is involved.'

The other side of the coin, however, was that:

> There is something very objectionable indeed in seeing the privacy of individuals invaded and lives, reputations and families destroyed by newspapers simply in pursuit of higher circulation figures. At times it seems the press has degenerated into unpleasant, unforgiveable licence.

This chapter seeks to explain the background to the public debate which led to the establishment of the Government Committee on Privacy and Related Matters chaired by David Calcutt QC. It also sets out the essential propositions in any fair discussion of whether there should be a Privacy Law. It deals with Calcutt's proposals, what his Committee said about a possible tort of privacy, its recommendations for new offences related to physical intrusion and its blueprint for tighter self-regulation by the press. Finally, it traces developments in the privacy debate since the Calcutt Committee's report was published in 1990.

BACKGROUND

In the last forty years there have been five separate Bills before Parliament aimed at introducing a statutory tort of privacy: 1961–Lord Mancroft; 1967–Alexander Lyon; 1969 – Brian Walden; 1987 – William Cash; 1989 – John Browne.

All were unsuccessful. Quite apart from whether a majority of the House supported the principles, there were found to be insurmountable problems in adequately defining either the civil offence itself or the acceptable defences.

During the same period there have been various Committees and Royal Commissions which have considered the same question, for example the Younger Committee on Privacy in 1972, the McGregor Commission on the Press in 1977 and more recently, of course, the Calcutt Committee which reported in 1990.

All have recommended against the introduction of a statutory law of privacy. As with the Parliamentary Bills, satisfactory definition was a major stumbling block. The prevailing view, however, has been that, even if the definition problems could be overcome, such a law would be undesirable.

The fact that the issue has been studied, considered and argued so often, so publicly and at such high levels – always with the same result – might in itself be thought to be conclusive.

The basic propositions throughout the various debates have been as follows.

BASIC PROPOSITIONS

Any proposed new law, especially one which would have the effect of curtailing freedom of speech and freedom of information, ought to satisfy two basic criteria before it is allowed to pass on to the statute books:

1 Can the proposed law work efficiently, i.e., with certainty and consistency? (This is a question of definition and scope.)
2 Is there an overriding social need for legislative control?

In stating the Government's opposition to the Browne Bill in 1989 Timothy Renton declared that:

. . . It was one thing to feel a sense of outrage and distaste at such things, and quite another to devise a sensible, satisfactory way of putting matters right. . . . Questions of privacy will often involve a more complicated and subjective judgment than would be required in other contexts. . . . We have already a good deal of experience of the uncertainties which arise, for example, in obscenity cases where the courts have to make judgments on controversial matters where statutory definitions are unclear or unsatisfactory and there is no consensus on the difficult social or moral issues that arise.

1 Definition and scope

The framing of a statutory right of privacy would necessitate a clear definition of two concepts, i.e.:

● Privacy itself: what it encompasses.
● The public interest defence: in what circumstances would the public interest in disclosure override the individual's right of privacy.

In considering these concepts, Calcutt noted that both the Younger Committee in 1972 and the Royal Commission under Lord McGregor in 1977 had found that they were unable to produce a satisfactory legal definition of privacy. The former said that, of possible definitions, 'either they go very wide, equating the right of privacy with the right to be let alone, or they boil down to a catalogue of assorted values to which the adjective "private" or "personal" can reasonably, but not exclusively be attached'.

Calcutt also reported that similar reservations have frequently been expressed about the formulation of private interest as a defence:

As a legal technician I would be unhappy dealing with the law of privacy . . . It seems to me that the legal difficulties of defining what is privacy and what are the proper defences are too elaborate. The courts, I would have to say, are quite good at some things, but they are not famed for their delicacy of touch, and when you have matters which are a very complicated balancing of imponderables, where the essence of the matter is flexibility, not certainty, I believe the courts may not be the best body to administer it.

Vice-Chancellor, Sir Nicolas Browne-Wilkinson (1988)

Surprisingly, in view of the above, the Calcutt Committee concluded that the difficulties over definition did not necessarily rule out the formulation of a limited tort directed towards the publication of personal information towards the world at large. It suggested that *personal information* could be defined:

. . . In terms of an individual's private life, that is to say, those aspects of life which reasonable members of society would expect as being such that an individual is ordinarily entitled to keep them to himself, whether or not they relate to his mind or body, to his home, to his family, to other personal relationships, or to his correspondence or documents.

The Committee specifically excluded from the suggested definition any material concerning corporate entities, individuals in relation to their business or employment and information which was available for public inspection. It also set out what it considered might be an acceptable form of public interest defence. Defendants would not be made liable for the publication of personal information if they had reasonable grounds for believing that:

(a) Publication of the personal information would contribute to the prevention, detection or exposure of any crime or other seriously anti-social conduct.
(b) It would be necessary for the protection of public health or safety.
(c) There would, but for the publication, be a real risk that the public, or some section of the public, would be materially misled by a statement previously made public by or on behalf of any individual whose privacy would otherwise be infringed (whether the plaintiff or otherwise).

In the event, the Calcutt Committee recommended *against* the introduction of a statutory tort of infringement of privacy though not, however, because definition would be an insurmountable problem.

2 Overriding social need

Like the earlier commissions of inquiry the Calcutt Committee's consideration of whether a statutory right of privacy was necessary focused upon two questions, is:

- How large is the problem?
- How adequate is the existing legal protection?

In relation to the first question, Calcutt's report noted that the Younger Committee of 1972 recommended, by a majority, against a statutory right of privacy on the grounds that there was no compelling evidence of a substantial wrong to be tackled. Instead of legislation Younger proposed improvements to the existing system of self-regulation by the Press Council. A similar approach was adopted five years later by the McGregor Commission on the Press.

Calcutt stated (paragraph 4.8) that his committee 'found no reliable evidence to show whether unwarranted intrusion into individual privacy has or has not risen over the last twenty years'.

On the second question concerning the extent of existing legal protection, Calcutt explored the range of remedies available to the individual against a prying or intrusive press. There are laws offering protection in the following areas:

- *Untruths*: the libel law and those relating to malicious falsehood are available against many forms of published untruths, especially those of a personal or damaging nature.
- *Confidential information*: the law of confidence offers some protection against abuse or unauthorized use of confidential information whether of a personal or business nature. This area of the law has seen its parameters extended in recent years and can be very effective, particularly at restraining a publication.
- *Private property*: the law of trespass, though not very effective against the occasional incursion, is there to enforce the individual's right to decide who remains on his property.
- *Private correspondence*: interference with letters and communications is afforded wide protection through the criminal law and the laws of copyright and confidence.
- *Family matters*: under the courts' inherent powers relating to wardship and the guardianship over minors judges are usually willing to protect children and their families against publicity and press intrusion. Blanket injunctions against all sections of the media can be obtained very quickly. Reporting of family cases, including divorce matters, is also severely restricted.
- *Interception, bugging, etc*: the Wireless and Telegraphy Acts and the Interception of Communications Act 1985, apply criminal sanctions against those who plant listening bugs or who intercept postal or telephone communications.

The conclusion reached by the Calcutt Committee in relation to social need for legislation was, rather like its finding on the question of definition and scope, somewhat surprising. On both issues, after acknowledging and seemingly bowing to the persuasive force of the evidence against statutory interference, it decided that a law of privacy was both practicable and justifiable:

> We are satisfied that the absence of sufficient protection for the individual against intrusion by the press satisfies the criterion of 'pressing social need'. This need is especially pressing in the case of individuals who are vulnerable to exploitation because, for example, of age, immaturity, infirmity, grief or the need to undergo medical treatment
>
> (Paragraph 12.6)

The committee went on to express the view that a well-drafted tort of privacy would not unduly inhibit either freedom of speech or investigative journalism.

CALCUTT'S RECOMMENDATIONS

1 A law of privacy?

Despite reaching the above conclusions, the Calcutt Committee recommended against legislation to create an enforceable general right of privacy. It gave notice, however, that the press must clean up its own house *or else*.

> We have concluded that an overwhelming case for introducing a statutory tort of infringement of privacy has not so far been made out and that the better option lies with the measures set out elsewhere in this report. We therefore *recommend* that such a tort should not presently be introduced. . . . We have come to our conclusion from a variety of standpoints and for different reasons. No single argument has prevailed for us all. Our grounds for deciding against the proposed tort include arguments of principle, practical concerns and the availability of other options for tackling the problems which we have identified. We make our recommendation on the assumption that the improved scheme for self-regulation recommended in Chapter 15 [of the report] will be made to work. Should this fail, the case for a statutory tort of infringement of privacy might have to be reconsidered
>
> (Paragraph 12.5)

2 Self-regulation

The 'improved scheme for self-regulation' proposed by Calcutt was the Press Complaints Commission which came into existence on 1 January 1991. Its structure and Code of Practice are dealt with in Chapter 16 of this book.

3 New laws of criminal trespass

While Calcutt's committee was not prepared to recommend a general law of privacy to protect against the publication of intrusive stories, it did suggest that the law of *trespass* should be extended by statute to outlaw what it saw as abuses in the way such stories are sometimes gathered. Three new criminal offences were proposed. They were:

(a) Entering private property, without the consent of the lawful occupant, with intent to obtain personal information with a view to its publication.
(b) Placing a surveillance device on private property, without the consent of the lawful occupant, with intent to obtain personal information with a view to its publication.
(c) Taking a photograph, or recording the voice of an individual who is on private property, without his consent, with a view to its publication with intent that the individual shall be identifiable.

As with the limited law of privacy which Calcutt favoured but did not recommend (see above) a defence of public interest should, the report said, be available if the act was done:

- For the purpose of preventing, detecting or exposing crime or seriously anti-social conduct.
- For the protection of public health or safety.
- Under any lawful authority.

At the time of writing, these proposals for new legislation have not been implemented.

POST-CALCUTT DEVELOPMENTS

Some two years after the publication of his committee's report, David Calcutt was asked by the Department of National Heritage to review the behaviour of the press in relation to privacy and self-regulation during the intervening period. On this occasion he worked alone; the other six members of his original committee were not consulted. After several months of evidence-gathering his findings were published in January 1993.

Calcutt noted that, although the industry had been quick to establish the Press Complaints Committee, it had not implemented a number of his committee's recommendations in relation to the constitution of the PCC and the content of the Code of Practice. He found that the PCC was 'not the truly independent body it should be' and recommended its abolition and the introduction in its place of a statutory regime. The 'Press Complaints Tribunal' should, he proposed, be established by Parliament with formidable powers to order fines, compensation and costs.

Among his other recommendations was '. . .that the Government should now give further consideration to the introduction of a new tort of infringement of privacy.'

'Calcutt 2', as it became known in the industry, was widely critized for being less than fair to the genuine efforts towards improved behaviour made by the press and for the harshness of its proposals. Judging by the tiny number of instances cited in the *Review Report* (three in all, two of which involved the *Sunday Sport*) where ordinary citizens, as opposed to Royals or politicians, suffered intrusion of privacy, there were grounds for saying that Calcutt's findings were based on instinct rather than evidence.

In the wake of Calcutt 2, the PCC's constitution was altered to ensure a non-industry (i.e., independent) majority.

Later in 1993 a Select Committee of the National Heritage Committee went even further than Calcutt 2 by issuing forty-three proposals including not only a statutory Press Commission and a Protection of Privacy Bill but also a statutory Press Ombudsman and legal aid for both privacy and defamation claims. The Select Committee's report quickly sank without much trace.

Finally, in 1993 also, the Lord Chancellor's Department published a consultation paper called *Infringement of Privacy* which proposed the introduction of legislation to create a civil right to privacy. The Paper stated that privacy should cover '. . .a person's health, personal communications and family and personal relationships'. An individual would be entitled to compensation if an intrusion led to 'substantial distress'. Possible defences would include '. . .consent, lawful authority, absolute and qualified privilege and a public interest defence'.

Despite these recent developments, there is a widespread feeling among those who have been monitoring the privacy debate that neither the need nor the Government desire for legislation in this field is any greater than it was when the first Private Member's Bill (Lord Mancroft's) was rejected in 1961.

APPENDIX 1 GLOSSARY OF LEGAL TERMS

Actus reus The physical act which (usually in conjunction with the required mental element) constitutes a crime.

Antecedents A person's past history. Usually used in the context of a defendant who has pleaded or been found guilty in a criminal court. His or her antecedents, i.e. history, personal circumstances and any previous convictions, are read to the court prior to sentence being passed.

Arraignment In criminal procedure, the formal process of putting the charge to the accused in court and calling for his plea.

Arrest Detaining someone or depriving him of his or her liberty; an arrest can be achieved by words alone, e.g. 'you are under arrest'.

Bail The sum put up by the accused or another person to ensure the accused's appearance at his trial.

Bankruptcy When a person is adjudged insolvent by a court, his or her remaining property being administered for the benefit of his creditors.

Binding-over Placing a person under a legal obligation to the court, usually to be of good behaviour or to keep the peace.

Care order An order of the court placing a child or young person under the control and guardianship of the local authority.

Case stated A means of appealing a court's verdict, usually on a point of law. An appeal by way of case stated involves setting out in writing a summary of what happened at the first trial and how it is alleged the court erred in its decision.

Cause of action A legal right which may be enforced through the courts.

Common law The body of law derived from judicial precedents or custom as opposed to statute.

Contempt of court Wilful disregard of the authority of the court or interference with its processes.

Contract A legally enforceable agreement, i.e. an exchange of promises supported by consideration given by each side. It may be oral or in writing.

Copyright The exclusive right to produce copies and to control an original literary, musical or artistic work.

Corroboration Independent facts or testimony which support an existing piece of evidence.

Cross-examination The second phase of a witness's examination in court, i.e. the answers given to questions asked by the other side's counsel. Leading questions may be asked during cross-examination.

Damages The monetary sum ordered by the court to be paid by the defendant to the successful plaintiff in civil proceedings. It usually represents compensation for loss but may, if exemplary damages are claimed, be a punishment.

Decree absolute The final and irrevocable order of divorce which leaves the parties free to remarry. Unless cause is shown why it should not, it will follow automatically some weeks after a decree nisi.

Decree nisi The first stage of a formal divorce. A provisional decree of divorce which will later (usually after about six weeks) be made absolute unless cause is shown why it should not.

Discovery The process in civil actions of formally exchanging lists of relevant documents in the possession of each party and allowing them to be inspected.

Evidence in chief The first phase of a witness's examination in court, i.e. the answers given to the initial set of questions asked by counsel who calls him or her into the witness box. Leading questions may not be asked during examination in chief.

Ex parte application Application to the court where one side only is present – frequently encountered where emergency injunctions are sought.

Hearsay evidence Matters which were not seen or heard directly by the person giving evidence, e.g. 'X told me that he saw Y take drugs' as opposed to 'I, myself, saw Y take drugs'.

In camera A legal hearing or trial from which the public is excluded and which may not be reported.

Information A charge or complaint made before a Justice of the Peace, usually on oath, to institute criminal proceedings.

Injunction An order of the court instructing a person to do or (more usually) refrain from doing a certain act.

Interdict The Scottish equivalent of an injunction.

Inter partes application Where both sides are heard (as opposed to an ex parte application).

Justification Truth as a defence to a libel action.

Juvenile A person under the age of seventeen appearing on a charge.

Mens rea The mental element in a crime. A guilty mind.

Obiter dictum The opinion of a judge not forming part of his decision.

Onus (or burden) of proof The obligation of establishing, through evidence, a matter of fact (or a state of mind) to the satisfaction of the court.

Patent   The legally registered and enforceable grant to an inventor of the sole right to make, use or sell his invention for a certain period.

Precedents   Judicial decisions that act as authorities for deciding later cases.

Pre-trial review   In the County Court the administrative process of going before the registrar at the close of written pleadings for directions on outstanding preliminary matters and the future course of the action. In the High Court this process is called the summons for directions.

Ratio decidendi   The legal reasoning behind a judge's decision.

Recognisance   The monetary bond entered into before the court by which a person binds himself to do a certain thing – usually to turn up for his trial.

Re-examination   The final phase of a witness's examination in court, i.e. the re-questioning by the counsel who called him or her into the witness box. Re-examination may only deal with matters which arose during cross-examination. Leading questions may not be asked.

Remission of sentence   The part of a sentence of imprisonment (usually one-third) which a prisoner is automatically released from serving unless he or she is of bad behaviour.

Setting down   In civil cases the process of informing the court office that the written pleadings are complete and the action is ready for trial. The case is put on the court's list of forthcoming actions and waits its turn to be heard.

Summing up   The judge's address to the jury at the end of a case. He sums up the evidence and the arguments of both the prosecution and defence. After the summing up the jury is sent out to consider its verdict.

Summons for directions   The High Court equivalent of the pre-trial review in the County Court. When the written pleadings are complete the parties go before a High Court Master for directions on the future course of the action and on any outstanding preliminary matters.

Surety   A person who assumes legal responsibility for the fulfilment of another's obligation. A person who puts up bail for another.

Tort   A civil wrong or injury arising from an act or failure to act for which an action for damages (other than arising from a breach of contract) may be brought.

Tortfeasor   One who commits a civil wrong or injury for which damages may be claimed at law.

Ultra vires   Beyond the legal power of authority of a person, corporation, agent, etc.

Ward of court   A minor or person legally incapable of handling his or her own affairs who is placed under the control and protection of the court.

Warrant   An authorization granted by a magistrate allowing the police to arrest a person, or search or seize property.

APPENDIX 2 THE LAW
IN SCOTLAND

Scotland has a legal system which is different and separate from that which operates in England and Wales. Its continued independence was guaranteed by the Treaty of Union, 1707, by which statute the Parliaments of each country were merged.

While it is not possible in the space available here to do more than refer briefly to the notable points of difference, those who wish to study the Scottish Law as it affects the media should read *Scots Law for Journalists* by Eric Clive and George Watt.

CRIMINAL COURTS

The three principal tiers of criminal courts in Scotland are the District Court, the Sheriff's Court and the High Court of Judiciary.

The District Courts are the equivalent of the Magistrates Courts in England and Wales. There is one for each local government district and they are presided over principally by lay justices of the peace.

The Sheriffdoms of Scotland are similar to the Circuits which exist south of the border. There are six of them, each presided over by a Sheriff Principal, and split into districts. Each district has, in turn, its own sheriff and court. He is a lawyer of some experience and has jurisdiction over all but the most serious criminal matters. He may deal with cases summarily or with a jury. In Scotland juries consist of fifteen people.

The High Court of Justiciary hears the most serious criminal cases, e.g. treason and murder. It is based in Parliament House, Edinburgh, but also goes on circuit. Sitting as a court of at least three judges this court also hears appeals.

CIVIL COURTS

As in England and Wales, there is a two-tier system of civil courts in Scotland. The primary court of first instance for most civil claims is the Sheriff's Court. The superior court which deals with appeals and some of the few matters over which the Sheriff has no jurisdiction is the Court of Session. Unlike in the criminal legal system the ultimate appeal goes to the House of Lords in London.

CHILDREN

In place of the youth courts which deal with children and young persons South of the border, the Scottish legal system has what are called Children's Hearings. They deal with the same set of problems handled by youth courts, i.e. alleged crimes, lack of parental care and control, danger to moral welfare, etc. Their normal jurisdiction extends to young persons up to the age of sixteen years.

If the child and the parents do not dispute the charge or complaints the Children's Hearing will adjudicate upon the matter. If the substantive matters are contested, however, the case must be referred to the Sheriff for a full hearing and verdict upon the evidence.

Whether a case is dealt with by the Children's Hearing or the Sheriff, the media are prohibited from publishing anything likely to identify children (of up to sixteen years) appearing at the proceedings as defendants or as witnesses/victims. This includes name, address and school. Where the person under sixteen appears solely as a witness as opposed to a witness/victim or an accused the ban on identification applies only if the court directs.

RAPE

The restrictions on identifying victims in rape cases which apply in England are no part of the law in Scotland. However, it is customary for Scottish courts to exclude the public while victims give their evidence and the media, as a rule, refrain from publishing their identities. It should be stressed that this restraint is a matter of convention rather than law.

CONTEMPT OF COURT

Although in the past Scottish courts have been quicker to reach findings of contempt and harsher in their punishment than their English counterparts, there is essentially no difference between the laws of contempt in either jurisdiction. The Contempt of Court Act 1981, which introduced the strict liability rule applies equally in England and Scotland.

APPENDIX 3 TABLE OF STATUTES

APPENDIX 4   TABLE OF CASES

INDEX